REEF LIFE

AN UNDERWATER MEMOIR

CALLUM ROBERTS

with photographs by

ALEX MUSTARD

PEGASUS BOOKS

NEW YORK LONDON

Pegasus Books, Ltd.
148 West 37th Street, 13th Floor
New York, NY 10018

Text copyright © 2019 Callum Roberts
Photographs copyright © Alex Mustard, Callum Roberts (see credits)

Typeset in Sina to a design by Henry Iles.

First Pegasus Books hardcover edition March 2020

ISBN: 978-1-64313-329-4

10 9 8 7 6 5 4 3 2 1

Printed in the United States of America
Distributed by W. W. Norton & Company.

REEF LIFE

For Felicity 'Flic' Wishart (1965–2015), who campaigned tirelessly for coral reef protection so that wildlife could thrive and future generations might still revel in their wonder.

And with deep gratitude to Alex Mustard MBE for his wonderful photos, which bring coral reefs to life within these pages.

Contents

PREFACE 9

CHAPTER ONE 17
Red Sea explorer

CHAPTER TWO 49
Voyage to the end of the world: Saudi Arabia, 1983

CHAPTER THREE 71
Looking back

CHAPTER FOUR... 77
Seaweed and lava

CHAPTER FIVE... 97
Country under construction

CHAPTER SIX... 109
Reflections

CHAPTER SEVEN 125
Science diving for Muslim ladies

CHAPTER EIGHT 149
Moving a research centre

CHAPTER NINE.. 173
Sharm-el-Sheikh revisited

Preface

LEAPING INTO THE SEA, we plunge mid-stream into a fast current. Despite brilliant sunshine above, underneath the water is evening blue, darkening to twilight beyond the play of sunbeams. We dive immediately in the direction we expect the coral reef to be; even a momentary pause risks hopeless disorientation in this formless space. I fly downward into what seems like eternity, wondering as the water deepens whether there is anything there. But the blue soon becomes shadowed and outlines of fish appear, then a beetling cliff, its face pocked with caves, sea fans and flourishes of coral.

From our eagle's-eye view, this reef is an elongated hill, its rounded summit peaking fifteen metres below the surface. We level off beside the cliff twenty-five metres down, battling the current towards a promontory at the northern edge, keeping tight in to ride the boundary layer where corals slow the flow. The corals here are fantastically varied, with pillows, branching shrubs, filigreed tables, towering trunks like oak limbs, or delicate lace frills. Around them a commotion of fish renders the current visible as they stream past or hold position, tails beating like flags in a gale. Nearing the point, I am kicking furiously but can only edge forwards. Finding ourselves at last at the foot of the escarpment, faces full into the blow, we drop our reef hooks and ride the stream at anchor, fixed to the bottom by a thrumming umbilical of parachute cord.

Here in the eye of the current, fish mass in shoals, milling, swooping and turning, sheering away and streaming back, like winter wader flocks above an estuary. The water is thick with fusiliers nodding plankton from the rich draft pouring from the open sea. They are similar in size to herring and share their sleek lines, but instead of cool monotones, fusiliers are coloured with bold strokes of tropical blue, canary yellow and orange, like nursery school paintings. Greater fish glide past further off, casting predatory looks over the shoals. Half a dozen giant trevallies at least a metre long scud past with chopping tail beats. Their steep heads and scowling mouths lend them dangerous purposefulness. The bodies are deep and muscular, the flanks silver-plated, and from shoulders to tail the arc of their backs is the blue of tempered steel. Further down, a tunny patrols the footing of the reef, streamlined like a torpedo, throwing flashes of sunshine from its metallic belly. It's watching for a fish off its guard, perhaps one that has strayed too far from the safety of the coral following a crumb trail of incoming plankton.

Then in the misted emptiness beyond the reef, a white crescent moves centre stage attached to a bigger shadow: a grey reef shark. The crescent edges the curve of a dorsal fin, the body is ghostly, half real, half imagined. As my eyes adjust, other crescent moons cut and weave through the dark water, rounded backs and angular fins briefly visible as they catch sunbeams. It's hard to tell how many there are. The current shakes the mask on my face and swings me side to side on my reef hook anchor. But the sharks ride the current slowly, purposeful and effortless, bending it to their will with movements too subtle to see. Hanging at the edge of visibility, the big fish seem to taunt, tempting us to follow them away from the reef. But we are rooted here by the press of water. The source of their freedom holds us. The currents they command will sweep us away the moment we unhitch, which we do now, our tanks already half empty.

Free to drift, the reef rushes past, rewinding the first part of the dive and then sweeping us into new terrain. Looking up the dark cliff face, I see silhouetted sea fans spread like netted fingers and branching corals that look like winter trees. But the leaves of these trees are still there, unattached and swirling about the branch tips. At least that is how the thousands of tiny fish appear from below, dark ovals against the light. As we approach the downstream tail of the reef, the slope shallows and the bottom is bathed in light. Blood-red encrusting sponges splash the seabed, wrapping coral stems like canker. Tiny fish shimmer above dense beds of branching coral, noses to the current, tails beating feverishly to hold their positions. Their bodies form ever-changing clouds of jewel green, olive, and the orange of autumn leaves. Driven by the current, we swing up slope to shelter in the lee of giant coral hummocks that look like the remains of a rockfall.

A mantis shrimp peers from beneath the edge of an upturned clamshell. Its carapace is mottled green, edged with a thin red line like the piping on an iced cake. Its eyes are frosted glass balls on blue stalks, marked with a horizontal line like the slot of a helmet visor. Their science fiction appearance accords with an almost supernatural power, the ability to see polarised light. The shrimps can peer further and more clearly in the particle-laden water just above the seabed.

The upper surfaces of the coral blocks are a continuous carpet of green tentacles that shivers in the current like wind through summer hay. The current lifts the edges of these anemones to show purple and carmine underskirts. Above the tentacle sward, the water is thick with fish, their bodies bobbing and dipping in a fluid dance. Black damselfish snowflaked with titanium spots mingle with fish whose mocha bodies, scored with three white bars, are outlined by a poster-yellow fringe of rounded fins. Their faces are blunt, with big dark eyes above thick-lipped glowering mouths. But above all there are hundreds of orange anemonefish flocking above the tentacles, their faces outlined behind the eye with a single white bar, their underbellies black streaked, their tails sunshine yellow. The water is filled with the crackling chatter of grunted conversation as fish see off rivals and keep allies close.

There are fishes of all sizes here, golden as pennies, spotted like dominoes or showy chrysanthemum flowers. The smallest dive among the tentacles at my approach, turning to peer back like children hiding behind curtains. The big fish launch bold sallies and warn me off with shouted staccato grunts. There is a buzzing energy that feels like an angry mob, but in fact there is a well-honed hierarchy, albeit one constantly tested. The largest fish are matriarch females that do all the breeding, laying their eggs under the skirted edges of the anemones. Normally, there would be just one such female in a group, but the anemones are so densely packed that dozens share the space, each with her own attendant males. When a matriarch dies, the largest of her males changes sex to replace her. From the abundance of miniature fish here, it looks like a crèche, but probably none are the offspring of resident fish. They arrived as larvae that had drifted from far away, hatched from the eggs of others.

I could watch this anemone city forever. But with our air now low, we must leave the eddied turbulence of this bluff. Catching the current, we rise like balloons let go on a blustery day. A group of pale fish, dark-barred like jail windows, rise with us. As I look back, the reef shrinks with distance and fades to dark blue; the fish drop away in twos and threes until none remain.

For a coral reef lover and marine scientist like me, heaven is a dive like this, made in 2014 with my wife and two daughters in the Maldives. This country lies amid the watery immensity of the Indian Ocean. It is a nation built on coral and made by coral. Every one of its reefs and islands is a masterwork of nature, pieced together over thousands of years. In a primordial alchemy stretching back half a billion years, corals conjure rock from water and create teeming oceanic oases for life. Tropical coral reefs are the richest of all marine ecosystems. They cover just a tenth of one per cent of the global ocean but support at least a quarter of all the species that live in the sea.

When the photographer David Liittschwager placed a one-cubic-foot frame on a coral reef in Tahiti, for a museum exhibition in the

US, he recorded 366 species inside or passing through it. This was more than twice the number of species he recorded from any other habitat on Earth, including tropical rainforests. Some species were as small as, well, the word 'as' on this page. An increase in diversity with decreasing body size is just one of the many remarkable things about coral reefs. As rich and flamboyant as they appear, much of their diversity is too small or cryptic to see. Beyond the many layered gardens of coral and the fish torrents, there is a hidden world we have barely explored.

A few years ago, an international team of researchers undertook a sampling blitz on the reefs of New Caledonia, an island in the southwest Pacific. Although thought to be relatively well explored, in 400 person-days of search they uncovered more than 3,700 species of molluscs, several times the number known from any comparable area of reef anywhere in the world. One fifth of the species were represented by a single animal and nearly 30 per cent by enigmatic, empty shells; one in three was found at only a single location. Herein is another wonder of the coral reef. How do such rare species persist? When it comes to reproduction, people are surrounded by countless possible mates (although as any singleton will readily attest, not many are suitable). But imagine that in a city the size of Seattle, or Singapore, or Sydney, there were only three or four other creatures like you, with whom you might forge a relationship. How would you find them? With no handy app to put you in touch, you could search for a lifetime and never come across anyone like yourself. But in one of life's miracles, enough reef creatures do find each other for their species to carry on.

Some of the most exquisite creatures on reefs are no bigger than gemstones, just as hard to find, and in lustre and brilliance equal to the finest jewels. My favourites are the porcelain and guard crabs that live between the branches of corals or in the pleated skirts and tentacle forests of sea anemones. They have flattened bodies, pugilistic claws and outrageous colour schemes. One has a ruby-spotted cream carapace with olivine eyes, another pale garnet splashed on lapis lazuli, and a third striped-stocking legs, a Christmas-jumper body and claws embellished with living sea anemones. The crabs that live among coral branches pay rent for their accommodation, launching nipping defences against coral predators like snails and crown-of-thorns starfish. But you could stare at a patch of reef all day and not glimpse one of these animals, even if you know where to look.

When I began my career as a marine biologist, we knew little about this hidden world. These secrets have been revealed gradually over the thirty-five-year span of my career, by the thousands of scientists, naturalists and photographers who have looked and wondered and questioned. But as we have come to know coral reefs with ever greater intimacy, we have learned that this world is fragile and increasingly endangered, by us. We are changing the Earth in ways that are deeply destructive to coral reefs and the countless creatures that inhabit them. Today's corals face a peril unlike any they have experienced in the hundreds of millions of years that reefs have existed.

Coral reefs are such finely tuned ecosystems that a slight upshift in temperature can cause the death of almost all the coral. We have, in the last four decades, experienced three catastrophic pulses of global warming that have devastated reefs around the world. Scientists predict that without urgent action to reduce greenhouse gas emissions, such events will increase in frequency and severity. By the end of this century, coral reefs could disappear, taking with them all the richness and wonder forged over hundreds of millions of years.

We live in extraordinary times; strange and unexpected happenings have become commonplace and the unthinkable must be contemplated. When I began my career in the early 1980s, nobody foresaw that in a few tumultuous decades such a monumental upheaval would overtake our planet. Nor did we expect that coral reefs would become sentinels of humanity's reshaping of the world. They offer an early warning that we are on a destructive path that threatens the very fabric of life on Earth. Left unheeded that warning foretells dark days to come.

This then is the story of coral reefs and my love affair with them. My coral reef odyssey has taken me from the wild shores of Arabia to some of the remotest places on Earth. It began in the 1980s when I was a fresh-faced twenty-year-old, anxious to make a mark. Over the years, I've had many adventures and through my own and other's research, I have learned just how remarkable coral reefs are and how vulnerable their beauty is. Coral reefs are one of nature's grandest creations and, in the existential threat they now face, they have become one of the most important ecosystems on Earth. For if we listen to their warning today, and find the will and the means to save them, we might also save countless other species with which we share the planet. That would spare numberless human generations to come from misery and hardship.

CHAPTER ONE

Red Sea explorer

Saudi Arabia, 1982

THERE ARE MOMENTS IN LIFE when everything changes. At my back is searing desert and before me a sea of startling blue. The water lapping my ankles is hotter than I ever thought the sea could be. For months, I have devoured everything I can find about coral reefs, but nothing prepares me for the real thing. I struggle forwards across the shallow lagoon, scraping belly and knees (the books didn't say coral was *this* sharp), and then stand to wade through the line of white breakers that conceals the reef crest. Beyond, the open sea darkens to indigo where the reef plummets into the depths. This is where the richest life will be. Teeth clenched around a snorkel, I plunge forward as a mass of fish flies apart in alarm, like exploding fireworks. I recoil as a foot-long surgeonfish with electric stripes charges and veers away at the last, its scalpel spines erect. A sharp pinch at my elbow makes me spin around only to find an indignant damselfish, no bigger than a hand, into whose territory I have blundered. Half terrified, half mesmerised, I inch seawards as life heaves about me, such a contrast to the parched desert shore.

Shock blossoms into wonder. Fish throng a labyrinth of coral: fat fish, slender, spiny, smooth, bulbous-eyed, serious, striped, barred, spotted, dotted, ringed, plain, lemon peel, orange, aquamarine, black; a mind-bending confusion coming and going. The reef sheers away at its edge like a precipice, making my stomach lurch as I swim over it, even though I can't fall. Shafts of light play on the seabed far beneath like spotlights on a stage, picking out coral outcrops and the chromium flashes of barracuda. By the time I drag myself from the sea two hours later, I have discovered my vocation.

I understand at last what Jacques Cousteau felt after his first look at the Mediterranean through a diving mask. I have a tattered copy of his book, *The Silent World*, bought years before, in which he wrote: 'Sometimes we are lucky enough to know that our lives have been changed, to discard the old, embrace the new, and run headlong down an immutable course. It happened to me at Le Mourillon on that summer's day, when my eyes were opened on the sea.' You can wait a lifetime for a moment like this, which is exactly how it felt.

Cousteau inspired me to learn to dive. Every Sunday evening his wondrous underwater visions drove the winter chill from the Scottish living room of my childhood. From an early age I longed to be an explorer. I don't remember exactly what prompted this yearning, but I grew up steeped in the wild beauty of the Scottish Highlands. Pitlochry is a small town on the shore of a peat-dark loch amid a plaid landscape of forested hills, mountain and moor. My bohemian parents eked a living there as artist-craftsmen and worked long days through the summer tourist season. Since my two brothers and two sisters didn't share my enthusiasm for the outdoors, I sought adventure alone.

With the passing years, the idea of exploration grew. As a ten-year-old, I was asked to collect items door-to-door for a Boys' Brigade jumble sale. Not far from my house there was a driveway that had long fascinated me. It led between high walls overhung with trees and rhododendron, forming a shadowed tunnel that bent left. Everything beyond was a mystery. The drive hadn't been used by a vehicle for years so thick grass grew between mossy ruts. The track smelt of wet earth and honeysuckle and seemed to go on and on, twisting back on itself more than once. I almost lost my nerve, but then it opened to a lawn that fronted a large Victorian house with an imposing wooden door edged by stained-glass windows. I knocked. For a long time there was silence and I was on the point of flight when footsteps sounded in the hall beyond. After a rattling of keys, the door creaked open to reveal a thin and heavily wrinkled man with an unkempt grey beard. He did not look pleased. Behind him half a game park of African wildlife stared from the walls: an enormous buffalo, a kudu with spiralling horns, several smaller antelopes and a fierce yellow-tusked warthog. I blurted my errand, fixed by their sightless gaze, only to be dismissed with a gruff 'no' and the hollow boom of the closing door. Now I fled but taking with me a vision better than any jumble, terrifying, exotic and alluring.

At another jumble sale I found a set of musty books called *Peoples of All Nations*. Published in 1920, their foxed pages were crammed with photographs and illustrations of fierce tribesmen, graceful dancers, men with straw hats, women in flowered dresses, temples, pagodas, pyramids, camels and yaks. Here was the entire world in seven volumes for a crumpled ten-shilling note. Through rain-soaked days I slaked my curiosity in these books and the urge to explore took root and grew. I climbed mountains, roamed forests, built shelters, swam bone-chilling lochs and canoed torrents. My bedroom filled with wild cat skulls, desiccated weasels, butterflies, birds' eggs (although never from nests still in use), minerals and fossils. For another ten shillings, a friend sold me the skull of a leopard, shot by his uncle in Burma. Watching over my bedroom, it became a touchstone for travel and discovery. What paths had this great beast once trodden, what scenes those hollowed sockets beheld?

Then in the mid-1970s, my parents' business sank in a deep recession triggered by the OPEC oil crisis. The outside world, so far away, forced us to move to the coastal fishing town of Wick at the north-eastern tip of Scotland. If Pitlochry had felt isolated, Wick was desolate, its hinterland low and treeless. There was a good reason why property was cheap enough here even for those close to bankruptcy. But this unfamiliar landscape was filled with new opportunity as I swopped hillsides for sea cliffs and learned to snorkel. But I never went abroad. There were no budget airlines in the 1970s and we were too poor for such extravagance. I looked on in quiet envy and frustration as friends travelled to Europe with school and family. Instead I lost myself in yet more books of adventure, real and imagined, and took long hikes. Finding some quiet inlet, deep carved into the Scottish sea cliffs, I would daydream.

Lying on a tilted slab of ancient lake bed, its 370-million-year-old ripples as clear as if made yesterday, I watched the seabirds come and go. Whiffs of seaweed and the sharp tang of guano mingled in the summer heat. Kittiwakes packed ledges, their young erupting in the clamour of crying babies to the mewl of a returning adult. Fulmars nested higher up on grassy hummocks purpled with nodding thrift, wheeling in on stiff-bladed wings like miniature albatrosses, muttering throaty churrs. Black and white guillemots barrelled past, quick-fire wings beating like clockwork toys as they headed to sea. The water was so clear that on a still morning it wore what I imagined to be the azure of the Mediterranean or Caribbean. Where the cliffs slid into the sea they gained a shaggy coat of anemone and weed and I imagined myself diving in to follow an unbroken route to those distant seas. But this was Scotland's far north, where the sun rarely shone for more than a day or two before fog rolled in, transforming the scene in minutes from Mediterranean glow to Icelandic chill.

Time passes and reality meddles with ambition. There aren't many jobs in exploration, I am told, so I settle on biology instead. What better than to explore the make-up of the natural world, which holds the promise of travel too? In 1980 I leave Scotland for the University of York where I quickly learn to scuba dive and, drawn by the exotic, immerse myself in tropical biology. It is diving that gives me my break. As a twenty-year-old student, I can't believe my luck to be asked to join a team whose plan is to survey and map marine habitats along the length of Saudi Arabia's mostly empty Red Sea coast.

Arabia. Just thinking of the word conjures visions of rugged beauty and adventure, a heady mix from *Tales from the Thousand and One Nights*, T. E. Lawrence and Jacques Cousteau's Red Sea expeditions. My reading tells me that the Red Sea is a two-and-a-half-thousand-kilometre rip in the Earth's crust, running from Israel and Egypt in the north down to Yemen and Djibouti. This rent opened as Africa pulled away from Asia around 30 million years ago. It is edged with vibrant coral reefs built, I discover, by the collective action of countless billions of colonial animals. One of the wonders of coral reefs is that they are visible from space, but to see clearly the animals that build them you need a magnifying glass. Rupert Ormond, the marine biology lecturer who has invited me to join his expedition, lets me loose on his coral collection one afternoon ahead of the trip.

I cautiously open a drawer, finding inside neat rows of skeletal branching corals. Most are a pure, uniform white, like bleached bones in a desert, but some are stained with tints of rust or verdigris. Gingerly, I pick up a piece the size of a cauliflower. The branches are sharply angular and, peering closely, I can see that they are covered in cups a millimetre or two in diameter. In life, each cup would hold a single polyp, in appearance much like a sea anemone, near relatives on the evolutionary tree. Like anemones, a polyp has a ring of tentacles around a mouth that opens to a cavity enclosed within the skeleton. These are simple creatures. They have no circulation, digestive or nervous systems; they absorb and excrete oxygen, food, and waste products directly through their delicate tissues. What distinguishes corals from anemones is their ability to build skeletons, like the one in my hand, and the fact that they live cooperatively with hundreds or thousands of others. Together they construct colonies by secreting calcium carbonate, the basic ingredient of chalk and cement, which they extract from seawater.

I tap the colony lightly with a fingernail. It makes a brittle sound like the flat, monotone twang of a Jew's harp.

The next drawer is filled with what look like rounded stones patterned with angular honeycomb cells, or spaghetti rings. Each cell or ring corresponds to the cup where a single polyp lived. I pick one up. It feels like a rock, much heavier than the branching coral. Seen under a magnifying glass the cups appear like flowers. A circle of thin plates radiate from the centre of each like the petals of a bloom, or the spokes of a wheel. Some plates are tall and serrated, giving the inside of the cup, or corallite as it's called, the look of a crown. There must be fifty corals in this drawer, each one a variation on honeycomb or spaghetti-hoop themes. In some the corallites are the size of a penny, in others no more than pinpricks.

Another drawer is filled with petrified brain corals. Instead of separate cups, their corallites merge in sinuous valleys like the folds of a human brain. Several have thin angular valleys and ridges that zigzag like Elizabethan mazes.

Today's corals were not the first. Creatures developed the means to extract carbonate from seawater over half a billion years ago, but modern corals do it better than any that came before. They have built geological edifices that from space look like the marbled turquoise stones of Navajo necklaces hung from continents or strung across oceans. They originated in the aftermath of a planetary disaster that, 252 million years ago at the end of the Permian, erased 95 per cent of marine species. We're still not certain of its cause, but this mass extinction wiped life's slate clean, heralding an era of fresh evolutionary experimentation.

Sometime in the next fifty million years, a new kind of coral forged a union with a new kind of microbe. That microbe, zooxanthellae, could photosynthesise, using sunlight to produce food from basic ingredients, mainly water and carbon dioxide. It was a winning partnership. Zooxanthellae gifted coral animals the ability to live like plants, offering up food and oxygen (a by-product of photosynthesis) in exchange for protection and carbon dioxide (a waste product of coral respiration). The result was a creature that could slap down carbonate skeleton much faster than it was eroded or dissolved, setting the scene for a new age of reef construction. Over the long course of geological history those reefs became home to a bewildering variety of species, a multi-hued blizzard of life that makes diving a coral reef feel like tripping without drugs. But in the 1980s this richness poses a puzzle for the new science of ecology, which captures my imagination. How can so many different species live together and why are they so abundant? I hope to find answers in the Red Sea.

In 1982, when as a twenty-year-old I step off the plane in Jeddah, it is the height of summer and the forty-degree heat hits me like the gust from an oven. For a moment, I think the engines are still running, but rather than exhaust fumes the blast bears a smell I will soon associate with Arabia, the septic whiff of open drains. On our way into Jeddah cars dodge and swerve around our expedition Land Rover at reckless speed, overtaking from either side in contempt of law and reason. The city's skyline is a jumbled mix of ancient and modern, minarets and tower blocks wobbling uncertainly behind a baking veil of umber dust.

Our base is a ground-floor flat in a nondescript concrete block in the spreading suburbs of Jeddah, surrounded by street after street of near-identical buildings. There I meet my four companions for the next two months. Rupert Ormond I already know a little from his lectures on animal behaviour and from meetings before the expedition. Now in his mid-thirties, as a student at Cambridge University in the early 1970s, Rupert led several expeditions to Sudan. There he lived far out to sea for months at a time, perched on a ramshackle platform built from scaffolding, with nothing in sight but water, coral and fish. I admire him immensely for such chutzpah. His sandy hair rolls over his head in low waves like beach ripples. His eyes are vivid blue and his looks alternate from penetrating intensity to distant contemplation. Square-jawed and handsome, there is something of the Arab about his face, especially as I will discover over the coming weeks, with his oft-worn head towel (not the familiar red-and-white-checked Arabian gutra, just a towel). But from the chest down he reminds me of Buddha.

Rupert's field manager is a whip-thin bundle of nervous energy named Rich Pitts. I find him in the kitchen making dinner. Rich has been here a month already, struggling to get the permits we need to camp and study on the coast. I watch as he stirs the pot. I guess he is about thirty, but it is hard to tell from his deeply lined face. Rupert has been contracted to undertake this coastal survey by the Saudi Arabian Meteorology and Environmental Protection Administration, Rich explains. We will inventory Arabia's marine biological riches for the first time. But this organisation cannot issue the permits. Rich has spent the last few weeks shuttling from one coastguard office to another, getting letters drafted and stamped, only to find that some new letter must be obtained from someone more senior, who is usually not available. When we later set off to our first seashore camp, he carries a thick folder of letters and passes covered in rubber stamps, elaborate signatures and a raft of postage stamps (which somehow validate everything). Their exact contents are a mystery, since none of us read Arabic. Confused by the office merry-go-round, Rich takes them all, hoping to have something for every eventuality.

Alec, the third member of our party, I almost meet when he comes in to see how dinner is getting on. He studied with Rupert at York and has just gained a PhD in fish behaviour. He looks rather like Jeremy Irons, a similarity strengthened by a stern public-school bearing which reminds me of Irons's portrayal of Charles Ryder in the recent television series of *Brideshead Revisited*. Seeing that food is still some way off, he departs without introducing himself, leaving me with my hand half raised and unshaken.

Over dinner, which we eat on the floor Arabian-style, I am introduced to the fourth team member, Mick. He tells me that he studied with Rupert at Cambridge and accompanied him on his Sudan expeditions. With his black wavy hair, dark-rimmed glasses and stubbled chin, he looks like a 1960s student radical. The conversation soon comes round to music and he is disgusted I like heavy metal and prog-rock. We find more agreement on turtles, about which he is passionate. After dinner he presses a Neil Young tape into my hand. So, four people with whom I am to work: Rupert is the mastermind, Rich is the fixer, Alec the brains, and Mick the turtle man. Where do I fit in? Brains; not yet. Brawn; probably. Acolyte; certainly.

I am woken at dawn by a crackling, amplified cacophony of muezzins calling the faithful to prayer from a clutch of nearby mosques. Desperate for my first sight of a coral reef, I can't get back to sleep so give up trying. Rich puts me to work washing the Land Rover while he and Rupert catch up with logistics. Even this early the sun is ferocious and I am soaked with sweat before starting. High walls surround the apartment buildings, to safeguard the dignity of their occupants, I assume. But apart from the drone of air conditioners, there are no sounds from within.

At last we get underway.

'Do you notice anything unusual about this road?' Rupert asks, after we have been driving along the coast for ten minutes.

The road follows the coast, winding in and out, here enclosing a maritime lagoon, there approaching pounding surf. Towering fountains jet from the middle of some lagoons, while others have little islands. The road is a raised causeway with sea to either side. It doesn't just follow the coast, it has been plonked directly on top of the coral reef, burying everything below it and stifling the flow of life-giving water to the ponded lagoons. My eyebrows rise and Rupert gives a solemn nod.

The coral reefs that fringe the Red Sea coast have a shallow platform, or lagoon, which forms as the corals grow, creeping seaward over thousands of years in a constant battle between growth and destruction. Depending on how good the conditions are for growth, this platform ranges from a few metres wide to well over a kilometre, and in depth from centimetres to several metres. The platform here is a little over one hundred metres from shore to the reef crest, a slightly higher ridge that separates the lagoon from open sea. In a flash of genius, the architects of the Corniche Road dispensed with the need for artificial lagoons and water features, hijacking nature instead. Titans of urban planning they may be, but these people (an American company, I discover later) knew nothing of the beauty, wonderment or delicacy of coral. With a resigned look born of long experience in Arabia, Rupert adds, 'Building the road on this reef is like cutting a highway through ancient woodland. It's done a lot of damage, but we're going to a section that is still in good shape.'

For that life-changing introduction, we enter the sea where the road sits far back from the reef edge. The shallow lagoon with its hot water and tide-scalloped rocks is already richer than any Scottish sea. But when we crest the ridge between lagoon and open water, plunging into the sea beyond, there is a heart-stopping confrontation of imagination with reality. The biological richness and complexity of the tropics, until now an idea half formed from books, explodes into being. Beyond the crest, the reef inclines gradually towards the open sea, ending abruptly about twenty metres ahead in a cliff edge. Its surface is pillowed with mounds and shrubby clumps in a colour burst unlike any I've seen in nature. Salmon, purple, cream, amber, mauve and sky-blue ripple and blend in patterns reminiscent of 1960s art posters. Colonies shoulder each other or thrust upwards in fungal riot. Thick-fingered corals reach for the surface like spread hands, while others with slender, more pointed branches form low thickets from which smooth and rounded corals rise like painted boulders mid-stream. Toward the edge the corals are more luxuriant, clambering one on top of another as they approach the plummet. Their branches froth with fish like flung spray at the edge of a waterfall. Below, in their petrified immobility, corals tumble and cascade downslope, their colours fading into the gathering blue.

This feels like falling headlong in love, and I leave the water shaking, struggling for breath. Later, driving back, Rupert asks 'So what do you think?' My head is full of superlatives, all inadequate. Rupert looks at me quizzically and, seeing my struggle, smiles. After a long pause I find a fitting expression. 'Out of this world!'

It is several days before Rupert takes me for my first dive. I'm nervous. My previous dives felt like near-death experiences from hypothermia, since I wore a home-made and fearsomely inadequate wetsuit. A wetsuit must hug every curve and angle of your body, placing a layer of air bubbles trapped within the neoprene rubber between you and cold water. The water inside should be no more than a damp layer. My wetsuit had been delivered, as the least expensive were, as a bag of cut-outs, a roll of rubber tape for the seams and a tin of glue. Amid much cursing and stuck fingers, over several evenings a wetsuit took shape from the parts. But to my regret and future discomfort, it was not exactly my shape, leaving large gaps for the icy North Sea to flush through. The water here is blissfully warm though, so I pull my tank on this afternoon over nothing more than a T-shirt.

We pause at the reef crest, sweaty and uncomfortable after a laborious wade in knee-deep water with cumbersome tanks and lead-weighted belts. A swell has built up since morning and the ragged crest is hidden beneath dazzling foam. The breakers are chest high and their roar drowns any attempt at conversation. Rupert strides out quickly in a gap between swells and dives under the smooth face of the next wave. His head pops up moments later in blue water beyond the break, shouting for me to follow. But I mistime my entry and am thrown on my back, scrambling through breakers and coral, spluttering saltwater and with a deep scratch on my shin that begins leaking a red trail. Feeling my leg, I discover a slug-slime of coral mucus around the cut. My first thought is of sharks and how I am sure to attract a ravening bevy within minutes, but Rupert is signalling to descend so I suppress my misgivings and follow.

The cooler water here brings instant relief from the withering sun. Pursuing Rupert's bubble trail, I soar bird-like down the cliff face, throwing my arms wide. A coral pinnacle rises from the seabed like a castle turret and I fly towards it, banking in slow motion as I pass. We descend. By a quirk of optics, warm colours fade from the spectrum as the deepening water filters longer wavelengths. At five metres down, there are no reds left, by seven no orange and by ten, no yellow. Poster colours cool to sombre shades and stony corals are joined by feathery banks of soft coral, their grey tentacles rippling in the current. The blood trail from my leg is now an alarming green. I do a quick spin to check for sharks, but none are visible.

Rupert is well ahead now, intent on his fish count, scribbling on his board. We both carry a pencil and plastic board to write on, roughened with fine sandpaper. I stop to scribble a description. This fish is a little bigger than my hand and shaped like a diamond. Two tiny yellow-ringed eyes sit at the top of a steep forehead. One of them watches me warily, while the other searches the interstices of the reef for prey. Its smooth face is the colour of mallow flowers touched with moss green. The flanks are scored diagonally with blazing orange stripes, some of which break into morse code dots and dashes. A red 'V' brackets a tiny mouth within which tartar-stained peg teeth are just visible. It's a triggerfish, although at the moment the eponymous trigger is slotted away on its back. I hurry to catch up with Rupert, parting shoals of fish like one of the deep-bodied jacks that hunt in packs along the reef edge. An enormous moray eel gapes in silent hiss from a hole in the coral, its razor teeth glinting in the darkness of its maw. Morays spend most of their time peeping from holes like this, but while snorkelling I have seen one exit its cave and disappear into another, its chocolate body thick as a man's thigh and longer than I am tall.

My task is to learn the fish but I'm in difficulty. The bewildering churn and rush of bodies is like a feeding frenzy of birds in a park, but instead of a few ducks, geese and pigeons, there must be thirty or forty different kinds, from the size of a coin to man-size giants. They look different in life to the pictures in my books, their colours more vivid, the patterns subtler, and the contrasts among species less certain. There seems to be an unending supply of small striped parrotfish and chocolate surgeonfish and I soon wonder if I will ever master them. It is hard enough to concentrate, but I can't shake off a nagging feeling of being followed. My leg is still leaking a green scent trail and I imagine that by now it has excited predatory interest across half a kilometre of reef. I wouldn't willingly step out of a vehicle for a stroll in the Serengeti, so why am I here, out of my element amid predators who are very much at home? I do another quick spin and this time there is indeed a huge fish coming straight at me, tightening my stomach with an adrenalin rush. It must be a half metre deep and one and a half long. But this is no shark. Its scales are dark emerald and the face has a steep forehead topped by a grotesque fleshy knob, a pair of broad rubbery lips, and cheeks covered with a squiggled maze of luminous blue. Black lines, much like the kohl worn by Egyptian pharaohs, highlight small but kindly eyes. I already know its name from my book, the Humphead wrasse, but this is the first I have seen. Its face is scarred and its lips speckled with the black spots left by the broken tips of sea urchin spines, leading me to wonder if their lips tingle eating urchins as ours do from hot chilli sauce.

All too soon, Rupert finishes his count and, with our air low, signals to ascend. My board is jammed with notes and sketches to follow up later with the guidebooks. Still no sharks, which, although reassuring given my bleeding leg, is also slightly disappointing. In fact, I haven't seen any sharks on Jeddah's reefs, not at all what I had expected from the 1950s tales of Jacques Cousteau and the Austrian explorer Hans Hass, another boyhood hero. As we rise toward the surface, the curling faces of waves steepen, glossy and vivid blue as the sky beyond, before exploding into a white cumulus, like the airburst of a bomb, spinning off bubble vortices.

Most evenings I seek out Rupert and Mick and we talk until late about fish and coral. Alec keeps his own counsel, mostly, and I have a sense that he sees me more as nuisance than asset. As a fish biologist himself, I wonder whether Alec might feel I am redundant here and, as an inexperienced undergraduate, my data suspect in its reliability. The learning curve is certainly steep. Rupert has just published a book called *Red Sea Coral Reefs*, which to me means he must be an expert on everything. But through these conversations, it becomes clear that there is far more we don't know about reefs than we know. What sustains their magnificent diversity, equivalent to the richest rainforests on land? After all, they support far more species and are much more prolific than the rugged coasts and cold waters I know from Scotland. And the Red Sea doesn't even have the most diverse reefs in the world. Those are in South East Asia with more than double the number of species found here. There are lots of ideas flying around, one of which Rupert is especially keen on and wants me to study: is it possible that reefs support so many species because animals and plants divide up the resources more finely than in colder waters? Over the coming weeks, I am to count fish inhabiting the characteristic physical zones of the reef – from the shallows into deep water – plotting how their abundance and species composition shifts from one zone to another. Do similar species, as Rupert suspects, inhabit different places, so reducing competition and allowing peaceful coexistence?

As days pass into weeks, my notebook fills with sketched fish, diagrams of reef structure and table upon table of numbers. I get my first taste of expedition life at Ras Hatiba, a headland north of Jeddah which encloses a patchwork of reefs, channels and dark seagrass meadows within a rim of olive mangrove. Aquamarine tongues of sea lick dazzling sand bars dotted with the silhouettes of resting birds that shimmer uncertainly in the distance. Before we can work, we must check in with the local coastguards. Despite an emptiness bordering on desolation, there is a coastguard station every five kilometres, suggesting an obsessive concern for national security. This post is no more than a two-room concrete block with a flat roof. The two coastguards present are asleep when we arrive. Hastily struggling into their uniforms, they look us over in bleary confusion, as if unsure whether awake or dreaming.

When Rupert introduces us in hesitant Arabic, the coastguards' natural hospitality overtakes surprise. Ten bags of Lipton tea and a heap of dried mint are soon bubbling in a blackened and battered kettle. The tea is poured into small glasses half-filled with sugar. The glass burns my lips but the drink is surprisingly refreshing given the thick heat inside the building. The coastguard leafs through our permits and letters of introduction, peering at them in a cockeyed manner that leaves me wondering how well he can read. To Rich's immense relief, he signals his satisfaction and we are free to work.

I feel fitter than ever after a week in the field but my ears are aching and I have had trouble equalising the pressure on dives. When I squeeze my nose and blow gently, instead of a brief hiss of air into the middle ear, there is a crackling gurgle. The Red Sea is notorious for ear infections, Rupert tells me, and recommends washing out my ears with fresh water every day, followed by a squizzle with an earbud for good measure. We return to Jeddah from the camp a week later, brine-dipped and dark brown, all bar Rich whose fair skin has passed through several disturbing shades of red before his freckles coalesce into a rudimentary defence.

Yanbu Al Bahr – Yanbu-on-Sea – is not, as its name might suggest, a resort. South of the old town, 340 kilometres north of Jeddah, an industrial complex clutters the skyline with jumbled pipes, vats, cables and smoking chimneys. The air has a sweet, hydrocarbon tang that cloys in the throat. To the north, squat apartment blocks radiate from a crumbling fragment of old Arabia. Derelict buildings sag inwards, their cracked facing exposing muddled masonry.

Intricately carved shutters once preserved the modesty of Yanbu's rich and powerful, but now dangle half off their hinges, caked with a century of dirt.

Beyond the city limits, dust devils spin above the plain in the torrid wind. An empty box bounds like tumbleweed across the road ahead. We cut off the highway onto a rutted track ten minutes north of town, raising a dense dirt plume in our wake. In the distance the solitary chimney of a vast cement factory belches grime above the horizon, which the wind has smeared into a tawny streak. We set up camp on a promontory at one end of a narrow beach just south of the factory, finishing as the red sun melts into darkening sea.

That night, having found fresh signs of turtle nesting while setting up camp, we do a shoreline reconnaissance. Hardly two hundred metres along the beach my torch picks out the smooth arc of a carapace in the water. 'Turtle!' Mick whispers excitedly, 'Wrap the light in your T-shirt to dim the beam,' and then gestures for me to follow. The tide is low and the water only ankle-deep on top of the reef. Straining all four flippers, the turtle drags itself a short distance, its shell rasping coral rock with the hollow scratch of a wardrobe pulled across a stone floor. With a loud gasp of exertion, it rests its chin on the bottom, water lapping its eyes. After a short pause, another heave inches it forward, then another.

Watching this green turtle huff and heave its way off the reef platform and then up the beach, sand crusting mucous tears dripping from its eyes, I can't help feel that evolution could have dealt it a kinder hand. Well adapted to life at sea, turtles must quit the water to nest in a leftover legacy of terrestrial origins. At sea, turtles don't appear to exert themselves much. Cradled by buoyant water and protected by a shell that only the most determined predators can overcome, they amble through life, unhurried, methodical, purposeful. At least that is my impression. Overweight and underfit, gravity renders this short crawl inland a feat of endurance.

After an hour of struggle, she halts at the top of the beach in a scoop of sand ploughed by her shell. For ten minutes she lies motionless, head down, deep rasping breaths raising sand fountains in front of her nostrils. Finally, she digs. At first, with sweeping strokes of her front flippers, she excavates a pit. Then, cupping a hind flipper like a baseball glove, she grasps a plug of damp sand and begins the egg chamber. When the hole is deep enough to hold a football, the soft sough of scooped sand is interrupted by toenails clattering on rock. Several more scoops expose a slab of beachrock. Another long pause, and with a sigh that sounds almost mournful, she begins to turn back to sea. 'The sand here is too shallow to finish the nest,' Mick whispers from the shadows. 'She'll have to come back tomorrow night and try again.' I can hardly bear it: to leave without laying eggs after such agony.

It is past midnight by the time she reaches the water and we slip away to our camp beds. The night is sultry and the day's lingering warmth caresses like soft down. Sleep comes quickly in the open, under a brilliant canopy of stars.

I wake early, almost chilly, my bed sheet soaked in dew and caked with orange dust. During the night, the wind turned and the thick pall from the cement factory now hangs directly above us. There is no better encouragement to get in the sea.

At the place where our turtle tried to nest, two lines of neat waves pressed into the sand by flippers pass from the water's edge up the beach. Further on two other turtles lie exhausted on the shallow reef platform, stuck fast by low tide. Water rims their carapaces with dark green, while their backs are dry and grey. An unexpected movement on the beach catches my eye. A bottle crate is wedged upside down, half buried in sand, and something is moving underneath.

I approach cautiously, wondering whether it might be a snake, but instead the crate seethes with hatchling turtles struggling for freedom. The scaly grey heads, shells, and flat-bladed limbs inside mingle so completely it is impossible to separate one from another.

33

They must have emerged during the night. The first were unlucky, having poked their heads through holes only to have them bitten off, by a fox perhaps, or maybe the ghost crabs that haunt this beach after nightfall. I ease the crate upwards to free the young, which start instantly and surprisingly quickly for the sea. I spare them the effort and relay thirty-two to the water's edge by hand. They switch from ungainly crawl to skilful swimming the moment they touch water, such is the power of instinct.

The reef platform is only thirty or forty metres wide and I swim to the edge before the hatchlings. Stopping there to see the moment they find the open sea, I am oblivious of the drop beneath. Soon the tiny flapping turtles arrive, flying in a loose, bobbing formation at the surface. They pass offshore without hesitation, dwindling to fluttering pinpricks before disappearing. Only then do I look down and see that I have unwittingly followed them offshore and am suspended above a dimensionless abyss. I scan below for something to anchor by – a fish, a coral – but only blank and shapeless blue lies beyond the play of sunbeams. Starved of perspective, I shift focus to the close-up world of drifting plankton. Next to my mask, minuscule hairy crab larvae, barbed arrow-worms and iridescent, pulsing comb jellies take on the mantle of giants and monsters. It feels like the ocean has swallowed me and I am a drifting particle in its immensity.

A prickle of fear drags me from my planktonic reverie but with only a slight lift of my head I find reassurance in the buff line of distant cliffs, our camp and the faraway cement factory. The trance broken I hurry back to the reef pursued by tiger sharks of the imagination, slowing only as vague outlines of corals and flickering fish emerge from the shadows ahead. The scene resolves with proximity, as if lights are being turned up in a darkened room, and I find myself back among friends. Later that evening, I pen a letter home by the white hiss of paraffin light:

'The structure of the reef here is magnificent with many buttresses, channels and inlets. There are sweeping arches of living coral through which you can snorkel into hidden recesses of life, the only clue to their existence being the shafts of light illuminating in ethereal blue rays the coral and sand of the mini lagoons. Some corals are huge here. One vast domed coral rose two metres high and was three across.'

'Rupert', I ask, 'what are you going to do with our fish counts?'

In the manner of all good teachers, he throws the question back: 'What do you think?'

'Well, I know that I want to find out whether fish with similar needs share space or divide it up between them. But how is that going to help the Saudis?'

'It isn't, really,' Rupert replies, 'They want to know where the best reefs are – the ones that might be worth protecting in marine parks. We can find them by counting fish and measuring coral cover.'

'So we are bean counters?'

'Not exactly. Knowing where species are found and how many are there tells us about how reefs are put together. Charles Darwin and Alfred Wallace,' he continues, 'each saw patterns in the distribution of species that led them to the theory of evolution by natural selection. Different but related animals lived on different islands, suggesting that they had common ancestors.'

Rupert goes back to his notes and we fall into silence. I resolve to try and discover something important. Flicking through my notebook, the pages of fish counts appear as an unknown code. I must find the cipher. My throbbing ears prevent further scientific thought. The cleaning regimen is not working. I had perforated an eardrum the previous year in a swimming-pool hockey game and am worried, so I give them another thorough clean.

Later that evening when the others are in bed, too tired to stalk turtles, Mick and I creep back along the beach. 'I found twenty-three nests today,' he whispers excitedly, 'and saw twelve turtles on the reef.' We find one that has just begun to lay, and we settle behind her tail to watch. An egg the size of a ping-pong ball swells her oviduct and plops onto damp sand, glistening in the muffled torchlight. Half a minute later another drops beside it. Gradually the chamber fills, accumulating 130 porcelain eggs over the next hour. Then a hind flipper, which has been still throughout laying, takes a scoop of sand and, with unexpected tenderness, places it onto the eggs. More scoops follow, which she firms into a dome with utmost care, all the while testing its consistency with her tail. When satisfied, she begins to flick sand backwards with her front flippers to conceal the egg chamber. She edges forward as she does this until she is several shell lengths from the nest. For three or four metres the disturbed ground is now level with the rest of the beach. Only an experienced human eye could tell where the egg chamber is, or a predator lying in wait. Earlier that evening our torchlight had startled a fox, its eyes glowing like headlamps. We saw their tracks earlier in the day, but the few scattered shells suggested that turtle eggs are difficult to find even for foxes.

The next day, Mick and I are snorkelling the edge of the reef just opposite the turtle beach. Peering into a thicket of coral, I'm straining to see the internal structure of the cups that hold the polyps, the key to its identity. Suddenly, Mick is beside me shaking my arm and making strangled noises through his snorkel. I follow his pointing arm to a patch of sand at the bottom of the coral cliff, lit by a sunbeam. Two turtles entwine, if that is possible, the male across the female's back at a jaunty angle, the thumbs of his front flippers hooked inside the ridge of shell behind her neck. His muscular tail presses beneath hers. There is no obvious movement, no thrusting or sweaty climax. Turtle sex, like much else in their lives, is a leisurely affair. The female looks anxious at our unembarrassed scrutiny. With strong, slow, strokes of her front flippers she lifts off with the male still in position. They pass within metres of us, their reptilian faces expressionless, although I imagine the flicker of a smile in the curve of his mouth as he sails past. We watch until their bodies fade to obscurity. The timeless, tranquil beauty of the act feels almost like a religious vision.

We spend another week by the cement factory before going north. Our destination is the Wedj Bank, a reef that loops far offshore, the Red Sea's only barrier reef. Most Red Sea reefs fringe the mainland or islands, but barrier reefs, like the Great Barrier Reef of Australia, rise from submerged offshore ridges. Parched from hours of driving, we break the journey where a bright finger of sand draws the eye towards a small island from which it is separated by a slash of dark blue. Mick and I take our snorkel gear, hoping to swim the channel and reach the island, while Alec and Rupert head in the opposite direction for a rapid shoreline survey. We walk, then wade and are halfway when a dark blotch materialises from the sand at our feet, rushes sidelong and vanishes into the seagrass that edges the spit. 'Stingray!' shouts Mick, adding, 'That was close.' I have yet to see one this size underwater; it must have been a couple of metres long. Screwing my eyes against the sun glare, I search the sand for slight blemishes that might give away the presence of others. Not far ahead, the sand is spotty, so I slip on mask and snorkel and glide forward.

Two periscope eyes watch from underneath sand that covers the beast's broad wings like an invisibility cloak. It remains motionless until I am a few metres away when a slight fin quiver betrays unease. The knobbed eyes are separated by a curve of forehead that narrows to a frown. Each gleaming pupil is shaped like the face of a horned owl, giving the ray a deeply sinister look. At a guess, it is three quarters of a metre from wing tip to wing tip and the whip tail adds another metre of length. A poisonous gimlet spine juts from the base of the tail, cocked and ready, it seems. The spine is there to deter would-be predators like sharks, but looks like it could more easily penetrate tender human flesh. The ray rises slowly into a hover, sand spilling from undulating fins, like a sprinter in the blocks waiting for the gun; then it starts to approach. I feel I should back off but am held by its unblinking gaze. About an arm's length away, still hovering, it stops. We contemplate one another. The standoff lasts less than a minute but feels longer before the ray edges sideways, and then, in a magician's flourish of puffed sand, disappears. I look up from the shallow water to find Mick looming over me chuckling, 'That ray didn't look like it's used to other animals not getting out of its way.' At the end of the spit, we find the current too strong to pass the channel, but the ray made it worth the trip.

Birrim Island lies at the edge of the Wedj Bank barrier reef, 650 kilometres north of Jeddah. After protracted negotiation with the local coastguard commander and eventual intervention from his bosses in Jeddah, we are taken there in a large patrol boat. The crew are not Saudi Arabians. Those I talk to come from Tunisia, Palestine and Jordan. I am beginning to realise that Saudi Arabia is run by other nationalities, even in the security services. We choose a small bay for our camp, ferrying supplies ashore in a rubber tender. The beach is made entirely of rounded coral pieces, like peanuts with the shells on. At one end, there is a crude lean-to of bleached drift-wood sticks and planks surrounded by fish heads and bones and a vapour of flies. This fishing camp looks like it hasn't been used for months although the stink lingers. We pitch the tent at the other end of the beach to avoid the flies.

It is late afternoon by the time we are free to explore. Rupert and I head for the outer barrier reef while Mick goes in search of turtle tracks. A Goliath heron, the biggest of its kind at a metre and a half tall, lifts off heavily as we approach, flashing chestnut feathers beneath great grey wings. Flopping down a hundred metres further on it resumes fishing. Further offshore, a tiny green-backed heron stalks the reef flat, the breeze ruffling metallic shimmers from its plumage as it steadies for a strike. We make a note of them before wading into the sea towards a line of grumbling breakers at the lagoon's distant outer edge. Rupert grabs my arm excitedly and points offshore, 'Sharks!' I squint to make out anything against the low sun, but following his finger see four triangles trailing ripples. My heart is pounding now. We expect sharks to be common on this remote, deep-water reef, but none of us is sure how many or whether they will be troublesome.

As we put on our equipment, Rupert runs through his shark advice once more.

'Remember, if you look a shark in the eye it's less likely to attack. It knows you'll put up a fight having seen it and won't want to risk injury. If it approaches, swim towards it.'

I swim across the lagoon in a state of anxious tension, hanging a little behind Rupert. Should it be necessary, he will need space to demonstrate his technique. 'Look it in the eye, swim towards it,' plays through my head all the way to the surf line, but we reach the edge without having put it to the test. The waves are shoulder-high here and knock me backwards several times before there is a brief gap of smaller swells and I charge offshore. Below me huge spurs of reef intersected by deep channels slope towards the open sea like the parallel buttresses of a medieval city wall. Their upper surfaces are covered by a mossy and pinkish algal mosaic and are strangely devoid of coral. Just then a grey reef shark appears and swims directly for us. Its pale chest is broad and deep, bigger than my own, larger even than Rupert's waist. I freeze at its bold approach, but the shark veers off at the last moment and curls into the distance, leaving me quivering with exhilaration.

Rupert seems unfazed and comes to tell me that the strange look of the reef here is because huge swells this far offshore tear off much of the shallow coral. The richest region is deeper down. To see it he leads me further offshore following the knobbled crocodile back of a buttress as it slips towards the ocean. A small black-tip shark passes underneath us and then another, but they don't approach. By now, the top of the reef is five metres below and hard to make out in the fading light. There is a dark and menacing atmosphere I haven't experienced in previous dives, making me feel small and vulnerable. I am about to ask Rupert whether we should go back when the first shark, or one very like it, reappears, circling us slowly at a distance of a few metres. It turns towards Rupert then swings away only to return moments later. This time Rupert is ready and I watch him swim directly for the shark, which sheers off only to come back faster than before, by which time Rupert is at my side, blue eyes wide inside his mask, suggesting in hurried gasps that we exit. I expect a razor grip on my leg any moment as we swim for the breaking waves, but the shark has gone.

Later that evening I am writing notes, notebook on one knee, underwater writing board on the other. The sea breeze is soft with moisture and the night black beyond the circle of our paraffin lamp. A hermit crab heaves itself onto my bare foot and tickles its way to the other side. The beach has come alive with them since the sun went down.

'Rupert,' I ask, 'When we were swimming back across the lagoon, what were those pale fish with the yellow tail and black stripe that we saw following the blue-spotted stingray?'

He carries on scribbling in his own notebook for a few moments before looking up. 'Red Sea goatfish,' he replies, 'They were following the ray in the hope of a free dinner. When the ray digs in the sand for food, it disturbs tiny worms and crustaceans that the goatfish snap up.' He pauses for a long moment, as if distracted. 'Its scientific name is *Parupeneus forsskåli*, named after Peter Forsskål. He was a Swedish naturalist who explored the Red Sea in the 1760s on a Danish-led expedition. They collected hundreds of plants and animals as they travelled through Egypt and Arabia on to Yemen.' Rupert stops to slap a mosquito that has landed on his forearm. 'It didn't end happily though. Five of the six men on it died, including Forsskål. Malaria probably. His notes made it back to Denmark with Carsten Niebuhr, the sole survivor. We know from Forsskål's diary that he spent six weeks in Jeddah collecting fish. The goatfish was one of a handful of fish skins that made it back to Copenhagen. The others were destroyed after customs officials in the city of Mocha poured away the alcohol preservative.'

Although dog-tired from the long day, I am wakeful after lights out. It had been exhilarating on the barrier reef, snorkelling through powerful swells and dodging sharks. But Forsskål's expedition faced immeasurably greater risks. I wonder if he saw this island as he sailed from Egypt to Jeddah? Far from land, a torrent of stars ignites the universe as the Milky Way spills from horizon to horizon. I fall asleep to an oceanic duet: waves softly lap the shore while distant breakers expend their might at the reef edge.

On the way across from the mainland, Alec managed to charm the coastguards into the offer of a smaller boat to take us to the south end of the island. A launch arrives mid-morning, driven by a tiny Bedouin. His coppered frame is wiry as a saltbush and evidently sustained by equally meagre desert fare. We are ready to leave, but the driver has other ideas. Squatting in the middle of the beach, he fires up a sheesha pipe, taking a long gurgling lungful before blowing thin streams of smoke from his nostrils.

The sun's heat is scalding in the beach glare. After an hour, by this time nearly insensible, the driver signals his readiness to leave, wobbling to his feet. I ask Mick whether it is wise to leave with him in this state. 'It will probably improve his driving,' he laughs, 'and anyway, we can always swim back.' But after our shark encounters the previous evening, the swimming option doesn't appeal. Nor does another minute in this solar barbecue, so I jump aboard and we depart in a choking cloud of engine smoke.

We arrive without mishap an hour later. Mick heads for a large stand of mangroves, Rupert and I for the reef. Two black-tipped fins cut the surface as we fit mask, fins and snorkel and I feel an unexpected shiver. I swim the channel on high alert, but the sharks have gone. We elbow through breakers before plunging into the surge. The water beyond is startling in its transparency, revealing a grandiose seascape; broad ridges thrust seaward, topped with layered table corals, some metres across, like giant leaves in a rainforest. Fish rise from them in their thousands, like curling mist, more than I have ever seen before, almost beyond imagining.

Four groupers skulk above a ledge several metres down, their fat bodies spangled with livid blue spots that stand out from the skin like an optical illusion. I dive towards them and am surprised they let me approach so close that I can see the teeth gleam inside their twisted mouths. At thirty kilometres offshore, this reef is the most isolated I have seen and the fish more prolific and less wary than those near Jeddah. For the first time, I wonder about the effects fishing might have on the make-up of life on a reef. Other reefs I've seen have felt pristine and primordial, but were they all that they seemed?

Rupert swims over to tell me that I should start my fish count here and follow the reef edge, then heads off to look at corals. He looks like a bathtub duck, bobbing away in his yellow swimming shorts. Where to begin, though, amid this disorientating confusion of bodies? At least I don't have to count everything. We've settled on two families – butterflyfish and damselfish – for their close association with corals and broad diversity of life styles, which narrows my list to just under fifty species. Butterflyfish are the most instantly recognisable of coral reef fish, with their flamboyant primary colours and heraldic liveries. All are active by day and about the size of a child's hand. My favourite is lemon all over, with water-coloured orange stripes on its flanks and daubs of blue on its cheeks. This goes by the name *Chaetodon semilarvatus* and is found only in the Red Sea. Like most butterflyfish, it lives in monogamous pairs that are touching in their fidelity. If you spot one fish, its mate is sure to be nearby.

Damselfish are more varied in size and shape; the biggest are butterflyfish-sized, but the most common are just five or six centimetres long and live in dense schools. Some rival butterflyfish in their colours with flanks of emerald, sulphur, cornflower, orange, or chess-board black and white. But there are, to my consternation, more than a few dull brown jobs, which I'm struggling to distinguish. Latin names aside (which Rupert insists upon because the common names are unreliable, shifting from place to place and book to book), learning the fish feels like a new language, or reading hieroglyphics perhaps, every species a unique cartouche.

We have two kinds of fish counts: timed swims of fifteen minutes and counts along a pre-measured distance of two hundred metres. In both I have to count fish within five-metre wide bands, estimating the two and a half metres either side of me by eye. This one is a timed swim, so I move forward slowly, pencilling in a group of four blacktail butterflyfish milling about my feet. I'm soon deeply absorbed as I wrestle to estimate – guesstimate might be a better word – the numbers of tiny damselfish picking plankton from the current flowing from the open sea. They hover a metre or two above the coral in mixed species schools, usually hundreds strong, but here in their thousands. The best method, I've found, is to count a patch of fish in a shoal and then multiply up based on how many times the patch fits into the whole. Packs of hunting jacks make the fish counter's life difficult, creating spectacular Mexican waves as the tiny fish just ahead of them dive for cover and those behind rise up again.

Yesterday's brush with the shark has left me uneasy so every now and again, prompted by some movement at the periphery of vision, I pause to look around. A Neil Young song is playing on a loop in my head: 'What could be stranger than the unknown danger that lies on the ocean floor...' Two small white-tip sharks have swum past since I began counting. With their beady myopic eyes and elongate cylindrical bodies, they look like overgrown dogfish and show no interest. Towards the end of the count I spot Rupert some thirty metres ahead when he abruptly kicks hard and disappears around a spur, camera at the ready. A few minutes later, I round the same spur, still engrossed in counting, when there is a sudden shout, muffled by water: 'Callum, look down!' I do so, reflexively tucking my legs in. At that second, a chunky black-tip shark races below my feet. It is smaller than me, but not much. Rupert hurries over and pulls his snorkel out. 'I thought it was going to take a bite out of you!' he says, then adds, 'It probably just didn't see you.' Trembling with adrenalin and less than reassured, I spend the next few minutes gulping lungfuls of air until calm enough to finish the count. But promenading butterflyfish are interrupted by thoughts of how long it would take to summon help here: too long. Much like Forsskål, Niebuhr and other explorers of old, we are on our own.

The next day is our last here and Mick comes along as shark lookout. I spot three and he sees four during my fifteen-minute count. They seem indifferent, although it is hard to tell through the veil of inscrutability that sharks wear. At the end, Mick gets out to fetch a water sample bottle. Bathed in morning light, the reef seems less intimidating and more beautiful than on the first evening. A coral at the edge of a surge channel six metres down catches my eye. Its criss-crossing fawn branches are broad and flat, reaching above the understory like a solitary tree on a bracken-covered hill. I make a quick scan for sharks and, seeing none, take a breath and dive. Thumb-size gobies grasp branches within the coral lattice with prehensile pelvic fins, their bodies yellow as sweetcorn and crackled with blue lightning. I watch them watching me before turning to swim along the upward sloping surge channel to surface close to the reef crest, still calm this early in the day. From down here the surface is a bright strip of sky between dark buttresses close enough to touch if I spread my arms fully. Halfway to the crest, a loud knock above the general background of squeaks, scrapes, crackles and pops, makes me turn. Approaching fast, a large grey shark almost fills the channel, its down-curving mouth menacing inside the chevron frame of fins. I react with two huge fin strokes, by which time the shark is only a metre away. But it responds faster, turning in less than a body length and charging back to the open sea. I surface at the ridge, leaping out of the water with what feels like a penguin's athleticism and shout for Mick, my voice halfway between cry for help and whoop of excitement. Instead I find Rupert who has just arrived to take some pictures and is busy kitting up.

Rather than putting him off, Rupert is enthusiastic. 'I've been trying to get some good shark pictures for ages,' he says, before his snorkel prevents further conversation and he jumps into the sea. To prove I'm less perturbed than I feel, I follow. By the time I have my mask on again, Rupert is at the reef edge where he has found a black-tip shark – or perhaps it has found him. My fins won't quite do what I want them to, the underwater equivalent of wobbly legs. But thoughts of sharks are quickly banished by hundreds of surgeonfish churning around a pinnacle like breaking waves against a sea stack. Everything here seems more prolific or bigger than I have seen before. There is nothing subtle or understated. This reef is all grandeur and power. I leave the water half an hour later, sorry this will be my last look at one of the Red Sea's wonders.

Back in Jeddah, Rupert and the team have a couple of weeks of meetings with our Saudi paymasters. Actually, they have a few days of meetings and a great deal of sitting around, waiting to be seen, like supplicants come to pay homage. The meetings make Alec and Rich irritable, but Rupert thrives on mint tea and Arabian pleasantry.

Alec and Rich's administrative frustration is my chance for some final research. So Mick and I take the jeep to Shu'aiba, a hundred kilometres south of Jeddah, for a week's camp. We arrive in late afternoon, the wind strong and sea rough. Even from a kilometre away I can almost feel the rumble through my feet of the pounding surf line where reef edge meets open sea.

I rise early next morning after fitful sleep. The wind has blown hard all night filling my bed with grit, and the surf looks no less daunting. It takes half an hour to swim to the reef crest against a stiff current. Close up, the waves topple in murderous thunderclaps that churn across the ridge I stand on. I hesitate. Mick is a faraway figure on the beach relaxing with a book. I edge across the ridge until the rush of water threatens to sweep me away. I brace for a drenching wave but a second hurls me backwards, pressing me to the bottom. Shaken but unscathed, I struggle up and try again, this time making it through by diving underneath the breakers and clawing my way along the bottom. Beyond, the water is smooth, and I float there to catch my breath. Below is a maze of channels and ridges from which stiff coral clumps rise like termite mounds on a savannah. I settle quickly into watching the daily struggle of damselfish, all fury and neon fin-flash as they defend their territories, my body rising and falling to the rhythm of passing swells.

Lunchtime comes and goes but I have no appetite for the swim back. Finally, after eight hours I can squeeze no more notes onto my two boards. I have been visited by several sharks, a curious turtle and a group of devil rays, formation flying on chevron wings. Reluctantly, I contemplate the narrowing wedge where the bottom rises towards the reef crest and the surf white-out. I hang back waiting for a gap, but a toppling swell throws me into the spume, grounding me on the bottom in a burst of foam. A shooting pain tears through my head with a squeal like the noise from a blown blade of grass. There is a cold flush of water into my middle ear, which sets off a disorienting attack of vertigo. I roll helplessly in the surf, unable to tell up from down, until the water pushes me onto the ridge and I drag myself out of trouble. I have felt this pain before: the compressed air from the wave has ripped my eardrum.

Badly scratched and dejected, I cross the lagoon in agony. Overnight the pain eases and, driven by a compulsion to collect more data and against Mick's advice, I pack my ear with cotton wool and vaseline and begin to study the behaviour of a tiny grey damselfish in bathtub hot water near shore. For three more days I plot territories and watch border scuffles, but the pain returns with a fury that cannot be ignored, driving us back to Jeddah. There I am told that I have contracted a vicious antibiotic-resistant bacterium and spend my last week making daily visits to a clinic for injections in the bum. On the plane home, the anguish returns as pressure changes squeeze thick green pus through the rupture into a handkerchief held to my ear. My dreams of becoming a marine biologist feel like they are dripping away.

CHAPTER TWO

Voyage to the end of the world

Saudi Arabia, 1983

AFTER THE PREVIOUS SUMMER'S EXPEDITION, I threw myself into study at York University, determined to become a coral reef scientist. My burst eardrum took months to heal, but was now intact and hopefully ready to sustain a diving career. I would need a PhD, which would in turn require an excellent degree, so for months I practically lived in the library, reading everything my lecturers had recommended and far more besides. I met my future wife Julie, a biology student in her first year at York who, amazingly, tolerated such antisocial behaviour. I was smitten.

One sunny July afternoon, soon after the degree results were out, the Head of Department called me into his office and offered me a PhD scholarship to study coral reef fish behaviour and ecology for the next three years with Rupert Ormond, leader of last year's expedition to Arabia. Seven weeks before, I had arrived in Jeddah for a second expedition, this time to travel by sea and land to the wilds of northern Arabia. The journey across had been tough. The 'one or two things' that Rupert had asked me to carry on the plane turned out to be a six-man tent in two colossal bags and twenty kilograms of lead diving weights. There was no mention of excess baggage payment, so I was left to plead student poverty at the check-in desk and to carry the weights in my hand luggage, listing to the gate.

This year we will survey by sea and land, thanks to the loan of a yacht. *Hattan* is berthed in a coastal inlet just north of Jeddah. The name means 'light drizzle', a blessing in Arabia rather than the scourge of British winter days. The boat is a catamaran whose single mast is planted in the centre of a deck that straddles twin fibreglass hulls. Down below, the main cabin spans the hulls, giving plenty of space to live and work. Two hulls mean more stability with the shallow draft necessary to penetrate dangerous reef complexes, while also offering the safety of two engines. She is, according to Andrew who will captain the boat, a perfect coral reef research vessel. Andrew is in his early thirties, stocky and deeply tanned with tousled hair, bushy black beard and twinkling eyes. My first impression is of Sindbad himself, which is fitting since he has recently sailed across the Indian Ocean using only traditional methods in a replica of an ancient Arabian dhow. Before taking this job with Rupert, he spent several years doing biological surveys for an American oil company on the Arabian Gulf coast of Saudi Arabia, so he knows the country well and has a smattering of Arabic. The plan is that Rupert and Rich will head north in the boat with Andrew to survey offshore reefs for the first month. I will join the boat for the second month, meeting them at a town far to the north.

With a summer of fieldwork under my belt, Rupert has given me the chance to lead my own field trips while he is on the boat, taking with me Tim, one of his undergraduates. After they set sail, our first venture is 170 kilometres north of Jeddah. After a hectic week buying provisions and cleaning and repairing equipment left in storage, we reach our destination parched and crusted with dust from the drive. We set up camp on a narrow scoop of coral beach set between cinnamon bluffs of fossil reef. The Red Sea is edged with the remains of prehistoric coral reefs, long ago uplifted by tectonics. The wind-etched remains of long-dead corals on their rock faces look as crisp and sharp as on the living reef. Looking closely, many species are still present on the living reefs, but a few are unfamiliar. What differences, I wonder, led some to disappear, while others thrived? Were they maladapted, or was it just bad luck? A few stunted bushes break the inorganic monotony of rock and sand, clawing a living from unforthcoming dust.

My pride in getting here is badly dented when, lying on my foam mattress that evening, humbled by stars, I realise with a sickening feeling that our dive regulators are still hanging on the back of the bathroom door in Jeddah. As this leaves us with nothing to breathe through underwater, we drive five hours the next day to fetch them. Tim seems unperturbed by this setback, which somehow deepens my annoyance. Tim is the embodiment of middle-class Englishness, tall and lean with floppy blond hair. I eagerly anticipated taking him onto the reef for the first time in Jeddah, expecting the same thunderclap of wonder that struck me the year before. But he emerged strangely unmoved, displaying the deadpan insouciance of a fighter pilot or astronaut.

The shallow reef edge at Rabigh is crowded with tessellated fire coral, yellow as sharp English mustard and with a bite to match: their translucent hair-like tentacles are armed with powerful stinging cells. The previous year I watched Rupert accidentally back into a clump on a dive and a piece plopped down the neck of his T-shirt making him writhe comically as he tried to pull it from beneath his air tank. By the time I arrived to help, struggling to suppress giggles, all the stings had discharged leaving angry welts. They didn't seem as funny above water.

The Red Sea has just a half metre of tide, sometimes less, but unusually, in Rabigh the corals bristle dangerously above the surface when the tide falls.[1] I tread carefully, having felt the fire of this coral many times. Finding a smoother gap at the edge, I sit

---

1. There is also a seasonal 'tide' generated by wind and air pressure differences that heap up water at one season, and push it away at another.

down to put on mask and fins. As I write later in a letter home to Julie: 'This place is exquisite underwater. The reef edge plunges vertical as a cliff into the depths and is alive with corals. There is something eerie about dangling your legs into nothingness. I felt rather apprehensive about diving here but once you get far enough down and see what is there, a sandy slope from about forty metres deep, your fears dissolve.'

Tim seems less excited. I begin to suspect that rather than suppressing the emotions I feel, he isn't feeling them at all. Forced into each other's company, conversation soon dries up.

After running the usual fish counts, I have the luxury of extra days to study the behaviour of the fish that tend 'algal lawns' in the shallows. Having spent a childhood poking around Scottish shores slippery with seaweed, watching the tide raise them into forests, I was greatly surprised to find seaweed in short supply on coral reefs. Where one might expect vegetated banks, a thin crust of flesh-coloured coralline algae fills the spaces between corals, sponges and sea fans. Its dominance is assured by multitudes of parrotfish, surgeonfish and urchins that mow the tastier leafy and filamentous seaweeds to near invisibility. But on the shallow reef platform, large areas of the bottom sustain a billiard table fuzz of green. They are the work of territory-holding surgeonfish and damselfish that drive away other herbivores, promoting the growth of a more nutritious lawn whose uniformity would satisfy the most fastidious gardener.

The largest and most beautiful of these gardeners is the Red Sea surgeonfish, the creature whose bold charge gave me such a shock on my first sight of a reef. From side-on it is the size of a honeydew melon, with a broad face and laugh-line squiggles about the eyes. Bright orange splashes its sides and the base of a tail where scalpel-like blades project, hence the name. A black fin runs like a crest along a parchment body etched with dark lines, flashing electric blue as it scuds past with pursed lip concentration. To make sense of their lives, I plot the movements of the fish in pencil on a plastic board on which I have sketched a map of the reef.

As I watch each animal for twenty minutes, patterns form from the confusing blur of activity. Instead of ranging freely, as it seems from their energetic sallies, the movements of individual fish are circumscribed as if by invisible walls. They pace back and forth within a few square metres, visiting and revisiting each coral head and dip of lawn, here and there plucking hurried bites. They know the limits of their farms exactly. Ever eager for a scrap, they scan constantly for interlopers, chasing off unwary parrotfish three times their own size and living in a state of uneasy truce with neighbours of the same species whose territories abut their own. Occasionally other grazing fish conspire to overwhelm the defensive shield, descending on a territory in irresistible numbers to gorge their appetites in frenzied cropping while the occupier looks on in helpless frustration.

I soon discover that as furious as surgeonfish defences are, they have a blind spot. While any number of different herbivores would swiftly be dashed from the territory, a few live below their radar. Several species of seaweed-munching damselfish are ignored. They go by tongue-twisting names like *Plectroglyphidodon leucozona* and *Chrysiptera unimaculata* that seemed to have been devised as an ichthyological test of sobriety. I watch them rip brazen tufts from the algal lawn in full view of the adrenaline-pumped proprietor, and, to my amazement, get away with it. Granted, with a length range that spans six to eight centimetres, they are less than a tenth the weight of a Red Sea surgeonfish. But a surgeonfish territory might hold three or four damselfish; too many to overlook, surely? The damselfish, in turn, defend territories vigorously against one other. And then there are the blennies, smaller still and even more numerous. These finger-sized fish dart out of the holes in which they live, snatch a few bites and disappear again, ignored by damselfish and surgeonfish alike. Blennies particularly favour as homes the empty cylinders of twisting, tubular molluscs smashed open by triggerfish with their can-opener teeth. Chocolate blennies with delicately red-spotted cheeks, and others with extravagant tufted eyebrows, watch me from the safety of these tubes. Might I find some clue to the secret of the great richness of coral reefs among these fish?

I spend my days floating near motionless while hurried lives unfold. My arrival in the morning is met with an alarm that spreads like wind as waves of fish seek refuge ahead of me. But they soon settle, resuming their activities. Minutes and hours tick by. I become a part of the reef, one fish among many, or perhaps a floating log. At least that must be how I look to a booby that one day explodes into the water a body length in front of me. This tropical gannet narrowly misses its target and flaps back to the surface, its leathery black feet peddling. For a moment, we are eye to eye, his beak a wedge of slate, the dark pupils unfathomable. He looks surprised, then anxious, lifting off in a clatter of wings and spray. Fish that live in open water are drawn to floating objects. For some they offer a semblance of cover from predators amid the emptiness, for others they signify better hunting. I notice now that in my stillness I have gathered a silver halo of baitfish, around which lurks a corona of predatory needlefish and tiny jacks. I am still reliving the thrill of the booby's strike when another blast of bubbles erupts in front of me; this time the gimlet beak holds a writhing shard of silver.

Fish fill my days and haunt my dreams. They weave psychedelic patterns in the sea and sow perplexity in the mind. I return to Jeddah with a notebook filled with palimpsest maps on which I have picked out the movements of individual fish with different colours and symbols. Complex annotations mark every chase and the identity of the species pursued. But like the fragmentary remains of some ancient manuscript, the meaning is hard to decipher. Poring over these maps, I wonder whether I can discover any greater sense concealed in the criss-crossing trails of points written by the fish I have watched.

Last year's findings were tantalising but inconclusive. Similar species of fish, like coral-eating butterflyfish, did seem to occupy different parts of the reef, conforming to the ecological dogma that they divide up food and space to reduce competition. But I had found some compelling counterexamples, like my surgeonfish-damselfish-blenny troika, where species that seem near identical in needs share the same spaces. Their coexistence appears to trounce prevailing theory, which holds that ecosystems are assembled according to long-established rules fixed by evolution. But to some scientists, such examples suggest that reefs are ruled by chance: whichever fish first finds a newly vacated spot gets to keep it. This summer I want to find out which view is right, if indeed either of them is.

Our flat in Jeddah is the same as last year. Returning after our camping trip, we find the air inside stale and oppressively hot. The living room is sparsely furnished with a few foam mattresses covered in garish patterned cotton. One wall is papered floor to ceiling with a photograph of a rushing mountain stream in the Swiss Alps, cooling for the soul if not the body. The shiny almond bodies of a dozen cockroaches scramble for cover in the bathroom when I flick on the light; several disappear into the shower plug only to reappear and race up my legs when I later turn the water on.

Tim and I have bedrooms to ourselves for once as the rest of the team are aboard the yacht. From my bed, I keep an eye on the saucer-sized camel spider that skulks in a corner of the ceiling, its hairy limbs flattened to the wall. In another corner, a pale gecko with soulful caviar eyes chirps evening sonatas between throat-expanding meals of moth and cockroach. We have six days to resupply before heading north to Al Wedj. At 700 kilometres north of Jeddah, it marks the point where the tarmac coastal road turns to sand.

The drive to Al Wedj is arduous, our Land Rover crammed floor to roof with the paraphernalia of camping and diving. This time, I remember the regulators. Sun scorches through the metal body-work and the black vinyl seats become unbearably hot after even the briefest of stops. We arrive ten hours later, tired and gritty, the wind roar singing in our ears.

We find the beach after winding through one of the parched river valleys that cut through the gilded cliffs fronting this coast. The sea is sombre and restless under a stiff westerly. Waves worry at the reef edge just offshore, expending in noisy bursts onto a black and uneven ridge that appears and disappears with each suck and blow of surge. The encrusting coralline algae that built it only thrive above water by constant wetting from big swells. My shins will soon carry the scars of combat and I pray for leniency.

Next morning, steep curling waves still spume angrily onto the ridge, but Tim and I find a safe entry through a short channel. We separate underwater. He has to plot butterflyfish territories near the surface, while I am to count fish on the deep slope. I descend slowly to spare my eardrum, still worried it might rupture again. This time I have left the cotton buds at home. According to the doctor, Rupert's 'helpful' advice led me to strip my ear canals of their wax protection last year, making infection a near certainty[1].

Like most of the reefs I have seen so far, this one takes a giddying plummet into deep water, losing itself in velvet obscurity. I wear a depth gauge but by now can almost sense the depth by the play of light and colour. I stop descending when reds turn greenish black, yellows become greens and sunbeams bathe the seabed in soft blue. A group of unicornfish, their improbable horns set above smooth brown noses and pouting lips, hovers close above a coral pillar. They flare their gills, offering the crimson arches within to a tiny blue-striped cleaner fish that pops inside. This year, with more experience, I have several new fish families to count, so I write the species name and number of fish on my board and begin to swim slowly along the depth contour.

A shark passes in the vague distance of open water. It is hard to tell whether it is a small shark nearby or a large one far away. Several scars disfigure this one's grey flank and by the slow beat of its tail I guess it is large, maybe three metres or more. A slight nod

---

1. This doctor's better advice was, 'never put anything in your ear that is smaller than your elbow'.

of its head suggests I have been seen, but it passes without further acknowledgement. By now I am used to the abrupt appearances of little reef sharks, although they still excite an adrenaline rush, but I'd rather not see any whose bite could rob me of limb or head.

There is a constant hiss and crackle underwater, like radio static. This is no silent world, nor are the noises the mumbled gurglings of a swimming pool, but crisp snaps and chattered grunts of deliberate communications overlaid upon a background cacophony of rasps, scratches and thumps. The water reverberates with reports from pistol shrimps, the whiplash cavitation of predatory attack, or the harsh scrape of a grazing fish beak on rock. Sound travels five times faster in water than in air and is the primary sense for many species here. Fish use the soundscape to create an image of their world that is heard and felt. As well as with their ears, most fish feel sound with a line of sensors on each flank. I wonder how differently reef creatures might behave if I weren't exhaling rumbling clouds at every breath. Would fish approach more closely? Might new species appear that had been frightened away by my clamorous approach?[1]

For a week we count fish and map their territories, waiting for *Hattan*'s arrival. At last, we board the yacht in Wedj harbour as the afterglow of sunset burnishes the minarets of the old town. Rich has gone ashore to settle the paperwork with local coastguards while Rupert gives Tim and me instructions for the next four weeks, perched on the bow like a Bedouin sage, skin dark bronze, hair stiffened into untidy peaks by wind and salt. Also with us, sitting slightly apart reading a book, is Trevor, another of Rupert's students who has been on board with him and will carry on north with us.

The following morning, as Rupert and Rich leave for Jeddah, we set sail north-west, leaving the protection of the cliffs that hem Wedj Bay. *Hattan* immediately begins to buck and pitch into choppy waves driven by a brisk northerly. Three flying fish leap from the bow and glide away on translucent wings like huge dragonflies, their metallic

---

1. Today's natural history film-makers use rebreathers that produce no bubbles.

bodies almost scuffing the wave crests until they dip their heads and are gone. The closest anchorage is in the lee of a crescent of reef fifty kilometres north. It will be a long day. Although other reefs are closer, none is secure. The chart shows that they drop almost vertically into deep water. You would have to set anchor so close to the edge that a short swing on the line would ground the boat onto the reef platform. The much larger reef that is our goal for the day shelters an extensive sandy lagoon in its lee, albeit one peppered with coral outcrops; we will have to reach it in daylight to be safe.

By late morning, the wind has whipped the waves to steep peaks that lift the bow sharply only to slam it into the trough that follows, throwing a cascade of spray over the deck. The constant jarring has us queasy, so I find a shady spot and settle into a fitful doze. A shrill alarm from the cockpit has me scramble up again. 'The port engine has overheated,' Andrew shouts above the alarm. Cutting the engine stops the alarm and *Hattan* slows as the starboard engine takes the strain. Andrew is soon waist-deep in the engine compartment, frowning at a spurt of hot water hissing from the radiator.

Northerly winds gust the full length of the Red Sea in summer. They strengthen into early afternoon as intense heat lifts air above the desert coast, sucking cooler air off the sea, and slacken into the evening as the land cools. It is two o'clock and we are battling wind and waves at the point of maximum resistance. *Hattan* struggles on for another half hour before the temperature alarm shrills for the second engine. Without power, we raise the sail and begin to tack.

It is in the evening, when the sun is low and the water settles to glassy tranquillity, that this sea is at its most dangerous. When winds tear across the surface, every threatening reef and shoal is rendered visible by a nimbus of breaking foam. Even when there is unusual midday calm, the high sun picks out reefs as vivid smudges of green, ochre and brown that contrast with the indigo density of deep sea. As this afternoon lengthens into evening, the wind falls away and reefs melt into invisibility. We're in trouble.

This sea is carbuncled with reef patches, some charted, others not, or at least not where they should be. I have with me an 1838 volume of *Travels in Arabia*, by the British hydrographer James Wellsted. This second-hand bookshop discovery is a perfect companion for our voyage. Wellsted was sent by the British Navy to produce an accurate map of the Red Sea and describes his travails over several years, including a detailed account of this coast. His map rendered coasts and islands with great precision given the tools of the age. But brilliant as he was, large spaces on Wellsted's charts were left blank. Judging by the dates of the various depth soundings on our Admiralty Chart much of this coast appears not to have been revisited since the nineteenth century, to my astonishment and consternation. The golden rule for navigating these waters, as Wellsted knew, is trust only your eyes.

The water is too deep to anchor and the least movement might drift us onto some unseen shoal if we try to hold a position in open water. Precious time has been lost restarting the engines and, as the sun slips below the horizon, the anchorage is still five kilometres away: we are cruising blind. Two hours after sunset, we nose *Hattan* into the lee of Uwainidhiya Reef, Tim chugging ahead in the inflatable Zodiac, straining his eyes for danger beneath the spot-lit pool thrown by our searchlight.

I'm up before the sun and Andrew is already on deck washing his face and bushy black beard with fresh water from a plastic bottle, the red glow of dawn building in the east. I revise my earlier impression: he's not Sindbad, but a dead ringer for Captain Haddock from *Tintin*. 'We were lucky last night!' he says. Around us is a labyrinth of reef outcrops. A sooty tern bounces lightly on slender wing tips from the direction of a low islet, its sand luminous and pristine.

I feel that familiar pull of a new reef, unexplored and enticing. What lies beneath? Grey chub play about the hull, flashing fat bellies as they mingle with a fish whose white sides are barred with black, like flags waving in a crowd. The barred fish are another collected by Forsskål and still bear the name he knew them by, *Abudefduf*, or 'the one with the striped vest' according to Rupert's translation from the Arabic.

An hour later we are chugging along the back of the reef in the Zodiac, looking for a passage to its deep northern side. The tide is low and the reef crest visible above water as a low ridge, the line of which can be followed by tumbled slabs of long-dead coral. We moor the boat to one of these slabs and cross on foot, picking a careful line to avoid skin-shredding coral thickets and clusters of urchins waving black spines as long as knitting needles but slender as hypodermics.

I pull on mask and fins and slip over the edge, savouring the cool water. A rusty parrotfish sculls away in alarm, its turquoise pectorals beating like butterfly wings. Buttresses loom upward intercut by deep channels, like the ridges between valleys eroded into a tropical ravine. A dozen eagle rays pass beyond the drop-off, their goblin faces oddly mismatched to smooth trapezoid bodies. I want to follow them; the draw of the deep is almost irresistible. But there are fish counts to do and with two more sites to survey today, we must reach the next anchorage before dark.

Back on board, the sea is picking up. White caps gasp and rush beside the hull. I try my luck on the front deck, but halfway there slip on a greasy patch and am pitched headlong. I slide to a halt beside Trevor who is slathering his buck-naked body with coconut oil. A fat drop falls from the end of his penis, now at eye level, and plops onto the deck. I berate him for putting us all in danger by greasing the deck, but with a defiant toss of his head he insists that he must get an all-over tan. What for, I wonder? I take my case to the captain but find him stark naked at the wheel. This never happened in *Tintin*.

Days pass and we acquire the grizzled aspect of hardened sailors, bodies salt-rimed and dark, hair lighter. Reefs come and go, each a rhapsody to life, like stepping from gallery to gallery in a museum of masterpieces. The confusion of fish slowly takes shape into repeated patterns, just as a mosaic forms from individual fragments. Each species has characteristic preferences, living only in particular places. Some like the turbulent reef platform, others the sultry lagoon, or the current-flushed outer edge or shadowed slopes deep down. I can now begin to predict where to find them, wresting a semblance of order from the apparent chaos. Sulphur damselfish bob like lemons above the reef edge; jewelled damsels shrug their sapphired flanks at the bottom of the reef face; white-barred damsels with greenish bodies court invisibility among the weeds of the seaward reef flat. The armful of scientific papers I have with me reads like an intellectual tennis game, each author firing what they believe is a killer shot to nail the argument about whether life on reefs is ordered or chaotic. For the moment, I am tending towards ordered, but am beginning to suspect that, as with all heated arguments, there is truth on both sides.

Yuba Island has been visible for the last two days, a wedge of desert anchored on our horizon. We approach at last in early evening on a silvered sea whose surface occludes the world beneath. From the east, only the rounded backs of limestone hills are visible, but from the west the aftermath of geological upheaval is laid bare. Cliffs soar upward, their rough beds of limestone and sandstone bewitched by the setting sun into layers of cream, umber and saffron. Somewhere far above, the shrill cry of a sooty falcon bounces from the rocks. We sup for a while on its time-worn majesty, then circle the north end to Yuba's less dramatic face and find a safe anchorage for the night in a shallow bay.

Next morning we are back, this time in the inflatable. The reef is no more than a thin green line along the bottom of the rock face, now in deep shade. I'm first in the water, eager to see whether Yuba's grandeur continues underwater. It does not disappoint, sheering off vertiginously in echo of the soaring face above. Passing over this precipice I feel like a sooty falcon myself, motionless in the updraft, looking for any unusual shape, colour or motion, before tilting my wings to stoop.

The light mellows quickly, like gathering night. Clumps of coral and sea fan sprout like shrubs from clefts, but much of the shadowed rock is blank or encrusted by thin layers of sponge and algae, lichen scabs to these stones. Here and there a blacker patch gives away the presence of a cave. I peer into one to find a twinkling wall of glassfish, their bones and organs visible through translucent flesh. A hefty grouper glowers from within their midst, a brooding sage among acolytes. Teeth appear and disappear behind thick fleshy lips with each gulped breath. I expected more fish, but they are sparse compared to the profusion and variety in places with gentler slopes. Submarine cliffs, like those above water, seem to be uncompromising places to live, too steep and gloomy for most creatures.

For days, our new satellite navigation system has been playing games in this maze of reefs and islands. Several times it had placed us firmly on dry land according to the chart, while demonstrably we were still afloat.[1] Like much else on this boat, it is probably broken. So out comes the sextant. Andrew stands on the rocking deck, feet splayed like a pharaoh. Peering into the lens, the sextant's triangle half buried in his beard, he struggles to fix the positions of horizon and sun. To our surprise, sextant and sat-nav agree. It is the chart that can't be trusted.

We have made heavy use of the engines because of contrary winds and a tight schedule and continue to be plagued by overheating. As we near our anchorage for the evening in another glass-calm sea, the alarm sounds and we are without power again. Andrew and Tim rush to raise the sails while I head to the bow to watch for reefs. Trevor is there as usual, his now mocha body slick with oil. He raises his head slightly to see what the commotion is about, reassures himself that there is nothing he can do and returns to his nap.

Now raised, the sail hangs limp in the breathless air. Adrift without power, I can see far down into the still sea. Beams of sunlight play through layers of deepening blue, picking out drifting plankton and particles like dust motes. I strain to distinguish real from imagined

---

1. It is hard to remember in these days of smartphones and GPS, that satellite maps were not available in the early 1980s. Our satellite navigation system merely told us our latitude and longitude, which we plotted onto a paper chart.

danger in this ghostly world; deeper shadows that might be reef appear then melt away. Noises from the back of the boat tell me that Andrew and Tim are getting the inflatable ready. We will have to push *Hattan* to our anchorage, still more than a kilometre off. Just then, a shadow appears that doesn't go away, followed by another, then an indistinct landscape lightens rapidly and mushrooms into coral heads: a reef is rising towards me through the water and passing sideways underneath the boat. *Hattan* had seemed motionless moments before, but I now realise we are drifting fast on a current that is dragging us onto a concealed reef. 'Reef, reef!' I yell. At the same moment, there is a splash: the boat is in the water with Tim in it, scrambling to fit the outboard engine.

This reef is at once gorgeous and terrible; running aground here would be disaster. I feel a new appreciation for the sailors of old. Wellsted faced the same peril:

It is by no means pleasant at any time to be in the vicinity of coral reefs, but when there is no wind, it is particularly dangerous. The smooth and glassy surface of the water then prevents any distant view of the rocks lurking beneath: on this part of the coast we remained utterly unconscious of our proximity to such destructive neighbours, until it became evident that the current was sweeping us slowly over an extensive bed of rock. Through the bright blue and pellucid water, we could then discern the minutest objects at an immense depth, and the secrets of the reef thus laid open to us afforded the most magnificent spectacle which can be conceived. Although there were neither 'Wedges of gold, vast anchors, heaps of pearls',[1] nor other treasures of the vast deep, yet the productions of nature, valueless but far more beautiful, were before us; every formation of the coral was exposed to view: on the one hand we had

---

1. Methought I saw a thousand fearful wrecks;
    Ten thousand men that fishes gnaw'd upon;
    Wedges of gold, great anchors, heaps of pearl,
    Inestimable stones, unvalued jewels,
    All scatter'd in the bottom of the sea...
    Shakespeare, *Richard III*, Act I Scene 4

a huge and shapeless pile, formed by thin horizontal layers; on the other a ponderous, and widely-spread mass, like a huge blossoming plant, supported by a thin cylinder, or stem. Successive circular fragments reared themselves aloft, or assumed the fantastic, tortuous forms of gnarled and knotted forest trees: how varied, how beautiful.

Grounding on this reef might be gentle now, but when the waves next get up they will pound us to pieces. Mercifully, we have recourse to a power source the sailors of old did not. By pushing us to safety, our inflatable boat again spares us ignominy.

Within a few weeks of arrival in Saudi Arabia the previous year, I had been diving on my own. Although proscribed as dangerous by the diving establishment, solo dives were normal practice for Rupert and he expected the same from his team. Since most of the time we had to collect different kinds of data, it was more efficient, he said, and the fish would be less disturbed by a solo diver. I soon discovered that I loved to dive alone and now, halfway through the voyage, I do it whenever I can. When not counting fish, or logging their activities, I let my mind drift. Half-seen movements tempt me into the darkness of caves. Lobsters guard clefts with parrying antennae. Overhanging corals form avenues that wind among monolithic columns, their faces creeping with creatures whose rococo bodies shimmer like coins seen through the rippling surface of a fountain. Coarse sand fills the bottom of the channels and flows downslope in smooth sheets, puckered with the pits and eruptions of fish and burrowing invertebrates. I dig up handfuls of this sand and watch close-up the coralline trickle of body parts run through my fingers: urchin spines, shell fragments, flakes of calcareous algae, rounded coral grains, discarded crab armour, discoid coccolithophores. Here is a reef reduced to its essence.

Despite taking what I believe is great care, over the course of weeks I twice almost put my hand onto a piece of reef that moves a fraction of a second before contact, revealing itself as a deadly poisonous stonefish. Its camouflage as a weed-covered rock is near flawless, save for beady eyes and glum expression. The fish's sullen

Top left: In 1983, northern Arabia felt like the end of the world (*Ch. 2*). Bottom left: Callum at the helm of *Hattan* (*Ch. 2*). Top right: Andrew Price checks a Red Sea osprey nest, 1983 (*Ch. 2*). Centre right: Red Sea cliffs were made by long-dead corals (*Ch. 2*). Bottom right: Rupert Ormond with a new-born green turtle, 1982 (*Ch. 1*).

Top: Wild Arabia (*Ch. 4*). Centre: Charles Sheppard (left) and Rupert Ormond, exploring southern Saudi Arabia in 1984 (*Ch. 4*). Bottom: Callum and his wife Julie Hawkins, on an expedition to the Gulf of Suez, Egypt, 1988 (*Ch. 7*).

Top: Dead *Acropora cervicornis* branches litter the seabed on Bonaire ten years after a 1980s Caribbean-wide epidemic devasted the species (*Ch. 6*). Bottom: *Cyphastrea* corallites close up. Each cup is only a few millimetres wide (*Ch. 1*).

Top left: Suez Canal University's Marine Research Centre overlooking Na'ama Bay, Egypt, 1988 (*Ch. 7*). Bottom left: Callum counting fish, Caribbean 1993 (*Ch. 12*). Bottom right: Callum in southern Saudi Arabia, delighted to be exploring the Red Sea, 1984 (*Ch. 4*).

Top left: UNESCO experts search for spilled oil in Iran, 1993 (*Ch. 11*). Top right: Callum lost in Tehran, 1993 (*Ch. 11*). Centre left: Oiled beach hardened to a tarmac pavement, Arabian Gulf 1992 (*Ch. 10*). Bottom: Callum and Julie celebrate finishing fieldwork in Saba, Caribbean 1996 (*Ch.12*).

Top: I was stunned to discover this picture of St Thomas harbour in a *National Geographic* from 1956; by the 1990s, most fish this size had disappeared (*Ch. 12*). Bottom: 'Tub', who introduced me to Abbot Point wetlands, Australia, and the late Flic Wishart, to whom this book is dedicated, campaigning for reefs in 2013 (*Ch. 13*).

Top: Julie in 1987 on her first open-water dive at One Tree Reef, Great Barrier Reef (*Ch. 13*). Centre: Callum with Susan White, US Fish and Wildlife Service, on Palmyra, Pacific Remote Islands Marine National Monument, and (right) Palmyra Atoll. Bottom: Coconut crabs have rebounded on Palmyra since rats were eliminated (*Ch. 16*).

Top: Maaga Reef, paragon of a many-wondered corner of Faafu Atoll, Maldives, before the El Niño bleaching of 2016. Bottom: The same reef in 2017. Following the bleaching, crown-of-thorns starfish (centre) feasted on the remains until almost all the corals were dead, then starved to death. The reef is now recovering (*Ch. 17*).

immobility reminds me of a character from Greek mythology, turned to rock for looking at the Medusa and ever after brooding in petrified resentment. Other times, when I put a hand down to steady myself I am surprised by the bee-sting percussive shock of a snapping shrimp punch. Although only a few centimetres long, these creatures have one huge claw, like a boxing-gloved hand. The 'snap' shut is so fast it cavitates the water, making a loud pistol crack that stuns prey or jolts divers.[1]

Fish have little fear of us, unlike most creatures on land. Schools enclose me in giddying walls of bodies, close enough to touch but never touching. A curious wrasse attacks its own reflection in the lens of my face mask, bashing its nose repeatedly on the glass. Other fish pull leg hairs, perhaps mistaking them for weed. Predators, like peacock groupers, eye me with curiosity and sometimes tag along like dogs, hoping I will flush out an easy meal. There is always something new.

Weeks pass and our chart track criss-crosses north from island to reef to island. Our maps have filled with lists of birds, the locations of turtle nesting beaches, numbers of sharks seen and long catalogues of fish and coral. Today, we attain the northern limit of our survey, Ras Fartak. This desolate hook of land overlooks the entrance to the Gulf of Aqaba, a deep rift between the mountains of Arabia and Egypt's Sinai Peninsula. After a gruelling day beating into a brutal chop, we draw into the lee of this headland with relief. We've seen little evidence of human life along the way, so Ras Fartak feels like the end of the world.

We manoeuvre as close as we dare to the base of sheer cliffs, their sandstone faces honey-gold in the afternoon sun. The triangular

---

1.   It can even, believe it or not, produce a spark underwater!

outline of an island rises in the distance, blue-grey above a quicksilver sea: Tiran. At a signal from the helm I fling the anchor into the water and the chain roars from the locker. Craning over the rail I watch it wiggle towards the bottom, expecting that I will soon see the arc of chain from the other end. But the thought is interrupted. On the cliff top above, a vehicle skids to a halt in a rumble of dust and a disembodied, over-amplified voice begins to bellow incomprehensible orders in crackling Arabic. Moments later, a navy launch rounds a headland from what we can now make out as a well-concealed but heavily fortified military installation. Ras Fartak is a strategic crossroads past which all traffic into and out of the Gulf must pass, including that from Israel, which has a northern toehold on the Aqaba coast. From the look of the armed men on board, we are evidently not welcome.

The boat pulls alongside and a man grabs our rail, his uniform baggy on a scrawny frame. We try to explain in fragmentary Arabic and elaborate sign language that we have permission to be there (even if it isn't theirs). But they bundle Tim onto their boat at gunpoint, indicating for us to follow in our inflatable. One points his gun at us as they bounce ahead from wave to wave; I pray he won't accidentally shoot.

On the beach, we are corralled by eight armed men while Andrew, clutching the folder of permits from Jeddah, is escorted through lines of barbed wire and sandbags into a low concrete building. The soldiers stare with unconcealed curiosity, touched with hostility, exchanging muttered comments and nudges. Sweat beads their foreheads and shines on their hands. I watch nervously as the youngest, no more than eighteen, grips his rifle, finger hovering above the trigger. A fly lands on my cheek and begins a tickling exploration, but I don't dare move.

Contemplating the guns around me, I hope fervently that the soldiers now searching *Hattan* will not confiscate our notes. We have only Tiran Island left to survey and it would be a disaster to lose everything now. After a tense hour, Andrew reappears with an officer, both smiling. Our papers have checked out and everyone can relax. I'm glad he had his shorts on when we were arrested, although Trevor had to scuttle below deck for his. Now that they are no longer needed, one of the soldiers casually empties the bullets from his magazine onto the sand. We leave amicably an hour later, after enjoying the healing power of cardamom coffee served in dainty china cups.

Free to explore, we head for Tiran whose steep peak has beckoned for several days from the edge of our water world. The chart shows sheltered anchorages on both sides, but we go west as the name 'Foul Bay' suggests that the eastern inlet is dangerous with shoals and we've had enough excitement.

From the west, Tiran is at its most imposing. An opaline sea ripples below a fan of scree and tumbled blocks from which tan cliffs sheer upward to the cragged summit. Below water, the reef extends south in a long green finger whose tip marks the point where a submarine escarpment plunges a thousand metres into the Red Sea. It encloses a broad lagoon of cobalt and turquoise, like the glaze of Iznik pottery, giving us complete protection from the relentless winds. As night falls, a distant lighthouse blinks awake and begins its nocturnal sweep of the empty sea. A handful of lights punctuate the heavy line of the Egyptian coast on the other side of the Gulf of Aqaba, the nearest just five kilometres away. Aside from our recent encounter with the Saudi navy, they are the first signs of human life we have seen in weeks.

Possession of Tiran Island is disputed between Egypt and Saudi Arabia, but geology presumes in favour of Saudi ownership, so we include it in our survey.[1] I join the shore party first thing in the morning, glad of a chance to stretch my legs. The beach glows in

---

1. Egypt's claim to Tiran eventually won out. However, a more recent deal sought to 'give' the islands back to the Saudis in return for a land bridge across the Strait to Arabia. But the Egyptian people protested the loss of the islands and the deal was rescinded. In 2017, political changes in Saudi Arabia have seen the revival of this proposal, with plans unveiled for the wilds of Ras Fartak to become the hub of an enormous economic centre.

the early light, its graceful sweep interrupted in the distance by the scruffy mound of an osprey nest. Ospreys are common, often swooping low over our boat. I have learned to imitate their shrill whistle, enjoying the puzzled looks as they search for another bird. These offshore islands are treeless and lack foxes or rats, so ospreys nest on the ground on teetering piles of driftwood and skeletal fish remains built up by generations of birds. This nest is different though, its upper layers stuffed with bits of polypropylene rope, crumbling plastic bottles, fragments of fishing net, and even the bleached remains of a plastic Action Man. You can read in the strata of this nest the emergence of our throwaway society.

As we walk north, the beach steepens under the influence of northern swells, and the scatter of junk congeals into a continuous drift metres thick. Plastic bottles, cans and wrappers printed in fading Hebrew, Arabic and a dozen other languages mingle in sickening testament of carelessness and waste. Two container ships have crawled by in the time we have spent walking the shoreline. Approached from Arabia, this place seems like the end of the world, but the populous coasts of Jordan and Israel are not far away.

A great submarine river pours past Tiran Island into the Gulf of Aqaba to replace water lost by evaporation. Moving shapes below water sharpen anticipation of the coming dive but give little away, the waves flaking bodies into dappling blocks of colour. On entry, the tension explodes in a concealing mass of bubbles, which clear slowly like a theatre curtain drawn back to reveal the players and set. A spooked shark scuds off, its body gleaming bronze. The current pulls like a torrent and I have to kick hard to stay by the boat until Andrew jumps in. Underneath us the reef tumbles off steeply, deepening to indigo far below. We descend the escarpment like eagles, water ruffling our hair as the current blows us through parting clouds of fish. Dense shoals of fish hug the cliff face, feeding on plankton drawn by the flow from the Red Sea, thinning into open water where watchful barracudas, jacks and tuna lurk. We are wafted into a blue-steel vortex of jacks, all razor teeth and sour faces, like the piranhas of legend closing in to strip their prey. But they separate and let us through. A giant trevally passes further out, deep-bodied, heavy-shouldered and menacing. Its Latin name is *Caranx ignobilis*, but there is nothing ignoble about its imperious bearing. The water here thrums with predatory energy.

Returning to *Hattan*, we find a lateen-rigged sailing boat tied alongside. It is open-decked and little bigger than our inflatable, made of worn wooden planking sealed inside with tar. It fits the exact description of the boat that James Wellsted used to navigate the more dangerous sections of this coast in the 1830s. The three Egyptian fishermen on board, all sunburn and sinew from weeks at sea, could have stepped directly from his world. The man at the tiller looks to be in his sixties and wears only a twist of white cotton cloth on his head and a pair of frayed shorts stiff with fish blood. The others are younger, though it is hard to tell by how much after a lifetime in the sun. They have come in hope of water. We fill their jerrycans and in return they press upon us the dried feet of spider conch, whose aphrodisiac powers they indicate with lewd gestures and throaty laughter. 'Very good for the ladies,' the captain adds in broken English. Quite why five men on a boat in the middle of nowhere should need them isn't clear. Chewing on mine later, I make no impression on the hardened salty flesh. Perhaps eating them is a test of virility.

After two more days diving we turn south, our work complete, setting sail for Jeddah as the sun passes behind the agate folds of Sinai's mountains. Fifty dolphins join us, gasping hellos about the bows, and then are gone. With wind and waves behind at last, we raise the sails and head for deep water where few reefs threaten. The boat falls into each wave trough with an easy rush that carries it up the slope of the next wave and over the crest, breathing the rhythm of the open sea. Taking the first night watch, with the swash of water beneath and creak of canvas above, I lie on deck probing for enlightenment as I revisit in my thoughts scenes from the reefs we have dived.

CHAPTER THREE

Looking back

York, UK, 2014

SUN HAS LIFTED THE MIST, driving away the early chill and touching the trees beyond my office window with autumn copper and gold. It is the beginning of a new academic year and there is an energy and excitement about campus today. Friends greet one another on the walkway outside and share stories of their summers in noisy laughter. Other faces, hesitant, expectant, lost, consult maps and smartphones. In half an hour I will meet twenty-five new students enrolled on our Masters course in Marine Environmental Management. Julie, the course director and my wife of twenty-seven years, has just passed by to check I am ready.

It feels almost like yesterday, looking back. That first taste of a coral reef remains as vivid today as it was in 1982, so often have I replayed it in my mind: the cobalt intensity of sea, the pause at the reef crest, the plunge, then revelation. Few moments in life can compare with that of sudden arrival on a reef; that headlong rush from the realm of air and people, buildings and cars, into the fluid domain of creatures that crowd and jostle, fearless and unconcerned.

After over thirty years of diving, I have never lost the sense of excitement on entering the water, but I no longer dive alone. I miss the solitude and freedom, but my university would never allow it today. Mind you, the thought of letting my own students do the things I once did brings on a cold sweat. I would happily head for the reef edge, tank strapped to my back, with little more than a wave and a 'back in a couple of hours!' shout. I wasn't even certified to dive on my first trip to Saudi, not having completed the open-water tests. One time I reached the reef crest after a hazardous wade through churning breakers only to find I had left my fins on the beach. I went for the dive anyway, wading along the seabed like the hard helmet divers of old. Another entry in my dive log reads: 'Unfortunately the compressor had been playing up, so the tank was only 20 per cent full. Fortunately, the reefs are very shallow here (6 m) so the efficiency of the census was not impaired. No buddy.'

To help write this book, I retrieved a horde of letters home to Julie, then my girlfriend, from a tin box in the attic. I am lucky to have married her for many reasons, but now have another: my letters were spared the bonfire of departed love. Rereading them, the memories flood back. So many things have changed. The letters show how fascinated I was by sharks, and frightened too. The movie *Jaws* had recently kindled the primal horror of becoming prey, reminding me that I was a clumsy intruder in a medium the sharks had mastered millions of years before. Moreover, the derring-do stories of pioneer divers like Hans Hass and Jacques Cousteau were full of encounters with 'man-eaters', many of which ended with a length of steel through the shark! So I savoured the excitement and unpredictability of their appearances. I am still drawn to sharks, all the more so because there are so few today compared to then: man eats shark happens millions of times more often every year than the other way around.[1] But because of the recent collapse in shark numbers, it is hard to separate hype from reality in the accounts of early explorers.

Were they really so dangerous? I recently came across a telling passage in William Beebe's *The Arcturus Adventure*. Born in New York

---

1.   An estimated 100 million sharks are killed by people each year, compared to an average of six people killed by sharks. Only one in twelve shark attacks is fatal.

in 1877, Beebe was a scientist at the New York Zoological Society and a great writer of natural history. His books were bestsellers and if anyone had an incentive to spice descriptions of sharks with machismo, it would be him. Published in 1926, *The Arcturus Adventure* tells the story of Beebe's expedition to the eastern Pacific and of his visit to Cocos Island, 500 kilometres from the coast of Costa Rica. Cocos is a jungle-clad shard of land that had, and still has in depleted numbers, some of the sharkiest seas on the planet.

By coincidence, Beebe visited the same year as the big game fisherman Zane Grey, also a writer, and quotes Grey's description of encounters with Cocos sharks: 'It was a marvellous sight to peer down into that exquisitely clear water and see fish as thickly laid as fence pickets... We saw yellow-tail and amberjack swim among the sharks as if they were all friendly. But the instant we hooked a poor, luckless fish he was set upon by these voracious monsters and devoured.' Having caught and killed a shark, Grey disposes of the corpse over the side of the boat: 'A cloud of blood spread like smoke. Then I watched a performance that beggared description. Sharks came thick upon the scene from everywhere. Some far down seemed as long as our boat. They massed around the carcass of their slain comrade and a terrible battle ensued. Such swift action, such ferocity, such unparalleled instinct to kill and eat!'

Less than a month later, William Beebe anchored in the same bay where he and the rest of his staff 'were diving in helmets and walking about on the bottom, with these self-same 'man-eating' sharks swimming by and around and over us, dashing at and taking our hooked fish, but, except for a mild curiosity, paying no attention to ourselves. It was as unexpected to me as to anyone, yet I will go on record as saying it is perfectly safe.'

So that settles it. It isn't sharks that have changed so much as the way we see them. The bold adventurers of today don't fight sharks underwater but commune with them, cageless and exposed, even among the most feared tigers and great whites. I once sat next to a South African on a plane who had pioneered out-of-the-cage encounters with great whites, which he somewhat disconcertingly called his 'puppies'. Rupert has joined this shark-loving band. After a long stint at the University of York and then as director of a Scottish marine station, he joined the Save our Seas Foundation as chief scientist. In a pleasing about-turn from the indifference which many Saudis showed to marine life in the early 1980s, Save our Seas was established by a rich Saudi Arabian and is dedicated to studying and saving ocean giants. Its work is desperately needed today.

The unalloyed optimism that flies off the pages of my letters home has been tempered by experience. When was it that I first sensed something big happening to coral reefs? Right from the start I remember an argument raging among established scientists about whether coral reefs were robust or fragile. Certainly, there was plenty of evidence that reefs could easily be damaged by careless use. It is telling that in my very first letter home, back in 1982, I write of the damage done by construction of Jeddah's Corniche road. In 1980, the International Union for the Conservation of Nature had just established a group to consider the protection of coral reefs. I met its chairman in 1983 at a conference, an elegant, white-jacketed Frenchman named Bernard Salvat who was kind enough to invite me to his research station on the French Polynesian island of Moorea two years later. In his first statement of the group's purpose, published in 1980 and titled 'Death for the coral reefs' (which sounds more like a message of intent than a clarion call for protection; something lost in translation, one hopes), he listed his main coral reef worries as fishing, shell collecting, coastal development and mining for building materials. There is no hint of the trouble ahead.

The robust/fragile debate burned out after a few years when people noticed that members of the robust camp were mostly geologists, while those taking the fragile view were ecologists who spent their time with living reefs. Coral reefs might be prone to local damage and collapse, but over the long run they would endure, or so we believed.

Looking back, it seems that the first events to rock our confidence in the permanence of coral reefs, in their solid, vibrant immortality, were unfolding at the time of my first trip to Saudi Arabia. This was in the eastern Pacific and Caribbean in late 1982 and early 1983, when an almighty El Niño, a periodic reversal of ocean currents and airflow over the tropical Pacific, stewed reefs in a pool of overheated water. The corals lost their bright colours and turned deathly white when water temperatures rose to excess, a phenomenon soon dubbed 'mass bleaching'. Hot water causes the delicate symbiosis of the coral animal and their plant-like microbes to break down. Mutual benefit turns to cost and the coral either kills or expels its zooxanthellae. A bleached coral is a starving coral; if conditions don't soon swing back to normal, it dies. Excessive warmth led to the almost complete annihilation of corals in the Galápagos, a catastrophe from which they have never recovered.

Meanwhile, an unknown affliction was sweeping the Caribbean that would destroy almost every long-spine sea urchin by the end of 1984. To those who have ever been impaled by an urchin, this might seem a matter of little regret, but it unleashed a chain of events with terrible consequences that would only be fully appreciated years later. For the moment, untroubled by such news, I was content to follow my ambition to understand how reefs could sustain so many species. It would not be until 2001 that I would adopt the moniker of Professor of Marine Conservation at the University of York, substituting the word 'Conservation' for 'Science'.

As in past years, I find the new students on our course united by a passion for the ocean. They share my younger self's love of the sea, but where I was unconcerned by any sense that this world might be threatened, they know it is and are here to learn how to protect and look after it better. In just thirty years, humanity has gained the upper hand in planetary affairs and the environment is suffering. But still they bubble with enthusiasm and hope. I am careful not to dent their optimism.

CHAPTER FOUR

Seaweed and lava

Saudi Arabia, 1984

SUMMER 1984 AND I'M BACK IN SAUDI ARABIA for our last Red Sea expedition. This year we explore southwards by land from Jeddah to the Yemen border, one of the least travelled parts of the country. I have four months to collect the evidence from which to piece together my solution to the species diversity riddle. I have a hunch from the sailing charts that the reefs here will be different from those in the central and northern Red Sea. Instead of precipitous descents into limpid water, the south has a wide, shallow continental shelf that extends far offshore. There must be clues concealed in these differences, but can I find them?

When I arrive in Jeddah with Trevor to searing August heat, Rich is already here, looking harried after days of administrative combat. Trevor and I have a couple of weeks to unpack and clean stored equipment while the rest of the team flies in one by one, which means, I suspect from last summer's experience, that I'll be doing most of the labour while he works on his tan.

Before the middle of the twentieth century, Jeddah was a compact square of buildings on a headland, enclosed by an ancient wall. The old heart survives, but only just. By day the streets here are near deserted, their life shuttered behind crumbling plaster facades and projecting mashrabiyah windows. Blocks of coral mined from nearby reefs are exposed where plaster has fallen away, some roughly hewn, others sawn into neat slabs. Bisected by the saw, long-stemmed corallites crawl over their faces and blossom in floral bouquets. Some buildings rise four or five stories and have been patched many times, imparting a hoary and despondent look.

After dark, the zigzagging alleys come alive as shutters are raised on shops. Heavy scents of sandalwood and frankincense drift into the passageways and the streets fill with people, mostly men, dressed in traditional thobe and gutra or Western clothes. The few women are immersed in flowing black, their veiled faces hidden. Aluminium pots and pans hang in bundles from walls and there are shops full of multicoloured plastic bowls, jerrycans and mats. We soon find all the camping supplies that we need.

Between preparations, I spend afternoons in the sea, probing the secret of peaceful coexistence between the damselfish and surgeonfish that farm algal lawns. Last year's observations suggest that these fish tolerate one another because the benefits of mutual defence are greater than the costs of sharing the seaweed within their territories. While surgeonfish see off big herbivores like parrotfish, damselfish maintain a defensive shield against the smaller ones. It seems like a winning partnership, the kind of mutualistic support network that if multiplied many times over, might explain the great richness of coral reefs. But I need more data to be sure.

Every day I return to a place just seaward of the reef crest, no bigger than the ground floor of a modest house. The water beyond the breakers is a couple of metres deep and the seabed plush with the lawns of surgeonfish and damselfish. Scattered coral heads hold their branches close to survive rough weather. I lose all sense of time in the mundane repetition of fish lives. Days pass and this place yields up secrets. Midas blennies, their slender bodies golden, fins like long braided cloaks, hide in plain sight within flitting schools of rosy *Anthias*. A tasselled carpet shark appears one day pressed like a stone to the centre of a table coral. Its flattened crocodilian body is near invisible, wrinkled, spotted and feathered with dozens of appendages; perhaps it was there all along? A sabretooth blenny with a racing blue stripe hawks a living from within a coral's petticoat folds by pretending to be a cleaner wrasse. Instead of plucking parasites it grabs hasty bites of fin or scales, or me. Every now and again I feel a horse-fly nip and, spinning around, see the tiny fish dart off. Sometimes, when two surgeonfish chase each other, the blenny takes advantage of their preoccupation, scooting out to rip off a bite. The victim immediately breaks off the pursuit to race after the blenny, venting its fury in fruitless chase.

This is a place of chimeric blends of texture and appearance. The silky look of coral belies hardness and edge. Giant algal cells look like green soap bubbles but are rigid with pressurised water. Hydroids appear like feathered tufts but sting like nettles, tingling for days. The shag pile knap of an anemone has an unexpected adhesive grasp. Stones on the shallow back reef, rolled about by waves, are, in fact, nodules of living seaweed. It would take a dozen lifetimes to unravel a tenth of the mystery here.

Our team this year is six strong, including me. Alec arrives in late August and joins Rich in the permit merry-go-round, which soon gives him many good reasons for a long face. But their persistence pays off and even Alec can't help smiling as they return one day waving the last permit we need. I am reunited with Andrew, the 'Captain Haddock' of our yacht *Hattan* last year. This time he is land-bound as chief surveyor of mangroves and seagrasses. Finally, a new member of our team, Charles Sheppard, flies in at the beginning of September and we are ready to go. Rupert is not due for another month, detained at home by university business. Charles, our coral expert, is tall, blond and bearded. He has spent two years at the Australian Institute of Marine Science, one of the foremost centres of coral research in the world, which to me bestows him with god-like powers.

Our first destination is 250 kilometres south of Jeddah, not far beyond the coastal village of Al Lith. Jacques Cousteau came here in 1952 and landed a party of geologists. They spent several days enjoying the hospitality of the local Emir, who lived in an Ottoman castle surrounded by a scatter of houses and date palm groves. Enjoying is perhaps the wrong word. They soon discovered that the Emir had no intention of letting them travel to the volcanoes they longed to study. What they found instead was a window into an antique world. The Emir kept slaves to attend to his every need, in an echo of a comment made of this region by the author of the *Periplus of the Erythrean Sea*, a first-century Greco-Roman guide to travel and trade: 'The country inland is peopled by rascally men speaking two languages, who live in villages and nomadic camps, by whom those sailing off the middle course [of the sea] are plundered, and those surviving shipwrecks are taken for slaves.'

Haroun Tazieff, one of Cousteau's geologists, recalled a night scene in the Emir's castle:

Crouching in the much-trodden ground in the reddish flame of an oil lamp were about a dozen men, bearded, glittering-eyed, thin beneath their dirty rags. Sitting on their heels in a ring, trunk bent forward, one hand hanging open between the feet but the other closed at the end of the emaciated arm that rested on the knee, they were playing some enigmatic game of chance... But what petrified me about the scene was this: all these wretches, gathered in this circular well of the castle like the Forty Thieves in their cave, were fastened together, one to the next. From neck to neck hung the heavy shining links of an iron chain... Behind the men moved their enormous, tragic shadows, as if in a separate life, on the curve of the reddish wall.

It is hard to believe that, at this point, a mere thirty-two years separates us from that scene. Might there still be slaves in Al Lith, or chained prisoners languishing in filth? In the punishing midafternoon heat the streets are deserted, save for a couple of boys in ragged clothes herding goats with sticks.

The coastal plain is broad where we camp and the level ground, seasonally inundated by the sea, is baked into a glittering saline crust. It sustains a thicker cover of saltbushes than coasts further north, which as the sun drops we discover means maddening clouds of mosquitoes. In the morning, I find the reef unlike any I've seen in thousands of kilometres of travel in central and northern regions. Things start normally as I wade, then swim, across the shallow reef platform. But on reaching the crest, instead of a narrow band of low seaweed, there is a dense forest of swaying Sargassum more than fifty metres wide. With stems as long as kelp the weed damps incoming waves so there are no breakers. The water simply rises and falls with a slithering vegetable hiss.

The seaweed wraps like tendrils, pulling tighter as I struggle, so I slide onto my front to wriggle, a wall of weed against my mask. It is rough and spiky to deter herbivores and rasps like a loofah as the plants writhe back and forth with each incoming wave. At last I burst through the forest's seaward edge, nauseous and exfoliated. The water is murky and there is no reef edge, just a shadowy incline of coral knobs and knolls above a dusky carpet of weed. It is very unlike the billiard-table baize of surgeonfish lawns, so I dive and tear up a handful, raising a cloud of silt. It has the wiry texture of a kitchen scourer and immediately draws dozens of tiny fish into a miniature feeding frenzy as they fall upon the worms, shrimps and snails I have exposed. The wrasses arrive first, slender and dainty-lipped, with harlequin, zigzag, or red-barred flanks, and a glorious creature with rows of azure dots, peacock-spots above and below the tail, and a chin of sunshine yellow. Bigger fish barrel in, attracted by the commotion, and snatch the larger morsels. In less time than it takes me to run out of breath the food is gone and the fish disperse.

Further on, an eel hunts in the open, its creamy skin smutted with soot flakes and flecked with gold, sinuous as it probes myopically along a scent trail. Walls of resting snappers almost conceal coral hummocks, their yellow flanks and neon-blue stripes glowing in the murk. Loose gatherings of groupers, hump-backed and round-bellied, hang suspended under coral tables. They appear surly and watchful with their glowering rubbery lips and beady eyes. I have never seen so many kinds together: snowflake-dusted groupers rub shoulders with darkly speckled ones, sapphire spotted with crimson-barred, ivory-barred with teal-faced. While some fish are familiar, there are new species aplenty. And among the known, many that were rare in the north are common here, while others that were common are scarce. Yet this reef, so different from all I have seen, is just an hour's drive south of Shu'aiba, the reef with the towering breakers and steeply plunging underwater cliff where I perforated my eardrum two years before.

The scene seems perfectly peaceful as thousands of creatures go about their lives, unhurried, untroubled. Surgeonfish and damselfish champ their algal lawns; schools of *Anthias* pluck invisible plankton from the passing flow, their tangerine fins flowing like silk scarves; snappers rub shoulders peaceably around coral towers, their would-be prey mingling unconcerned nearby. But the feeding frenzy I unwittingly set off reveals a different side to life. This harmony is illusory, for the coral reef is a simmering cauldron of carnivory, every day lived a small miracle of luck and instinct. While some predators chip away for hours at a mollusc or sponge, the act of predation is often so fleeting it is little wonder that peace appears to predominate over violence: a momentary lightning bolt acceleration by barracuda or jack and a shoal of fish numbers one less; a split-second yawn by grouper or scorpionfish and a wrasse vanishes so instantly, you wonder if it was ever there. In thousands of hours, only two or three times have I seen the instant of predation, watched the look of surprise on one face and the calculated intent on the other. To some scientists, the voracious efficiency of reef predators weeds out animals ill-suited to a particular habitat and leaves behind those best adapted, creating order. To others it is a disorganising force that promotes coexistence of many species: the constant removals are a source of opportunity, opening space for others to fill in a chaotic sequence of lottery winners. I wonder which view is right, and how can I tell?

The coral levels into sand seven or eight metres down, although the visibility is so bad that I have to duck-dive to see it. Back in the shallows I begin counting fish. The flood of new faces requires feverish concentration, sketching patterns and noting colours for later identification. Several hours later, I slither back through the seaweed, ideas tumbling through my head, trying to make sense of it all.

The sun is ferocious now. Even the flies have retreated from its unblinking stare. Charles is rummaging in our stores for biscuits, still dripping from the sea.

'What do you make of this reef?' I ask, taking a swig of hot water decanted from a jerrycan. It does little to quench the thirst.

'Nothing like I've seen before,' he says, taking a bite. 'So many new corals. The structure is completely unlike the reefs up north.'

Charles had until recently worked for an oil company in Yanbu, close to the cement factory where we saw the nesting turtles. We swap experiences over tasteless biscuits until the stifling heat drives us back to sea.

This sudden shift in reef composition has me puzzled. The obvious explanation is that the conditions favour different species. But there is a hitch. All the fish and many corals have an egg or larval dispersal phase in which they spend their very early lives drifting or swimming in the plankton of open water, away from the reef. For much of the summer, currents flow south under the influence of northerly winds. Many animals breed year-round so there must be a steady river of eggs and larvae of northerly species streaming south: so why don't they show up here, at least as juveniles? Even if the habitat isn't ideal, it would surely be preferable for a larva to settle from the plankton and take its chances than wait for inevitable death in the open sea.

For the next week, we snorkel and dive our way along a hundred kilometres of coast. Our new Nissan Patrol vehicle, while more luxurious than the Land Rover, is a liability, constantly bogging in deep sand. One day we dig it out three times. I can't understand why anybody would be idiotic enough to create an off-road vehicle with a spare wheel slung underneath the chassis, guaranteeing trouble on soft ground.[1] Andrew is happy though. Being sheltered, low-lying and muddy, this coast has much more mangrove and seagrass than regions to the north, so he and Trevor are gone for most of the day with our much more reliable jeep. Alec and Rich have the Land Rover, driving off early with an armful of aerial photographs to 'ground truth' them, matching features on the ground to the images. Alec's forays into the sea are brief and frequent, no more than a series of snapshots from which he builds a habitat map of the coast. From our evening conversations, it's clear he is unimpressed by this coast, having recently discovered much richer, deeper reefs from our yacht *Hattan*, far out to sea at the edge of this broad continental shelf.

Charles, on the other hand, is enthusiastic. Science thrives on novelty and many species and forms of coral here are new to him, and a few possibly new to science. 'One of the problems a coral biologist has,' he tells me one evening, 'is that the same species can look completely different depending on where it grows. Take this *Pocillopora*,' he says, picking up a fist-sized clump he collected earlier in the day. 'In shallow water this is robust and knobby to withstand the waves. Deeper down its branches are slender and delicate, spreading wide to catch the light.'

---

1. I realise now that the Nissan Patrol was one of the first in a new generation of 'off-road' vehicles built for city dwellers for whom going off-road means mounting the kerb on the school run.

'I thought parrotfish were hard,' I reply (males, females and juveniles of the same species all look different), 'but corals are beyond me.'

We work our way south in steps, setting up camp for a week then moving on. We're far from any city and the stars are so dense that even on moonless nights there is light to see by. In the brief time before sleep comes, outside in the balmy air, I watch the slow rotating blinks of orbiting satellites and wish on meteorites.

The desert comes alive at night, even in places that appeared sterile in the broiling sun. Lumbering beetles tiptoe along trails, while quick-eyed gerbils, light-footed and silent, scamper from bush to bush. Hermit crabs drag scribbles in the dust with their shells, to be read by daylight. At one camp, ghost crabs have raised a cordillera of sand volcanoes along the beach, each conical mound paired with a burrow. They slink from these holes after dark on pale spindly legs. Black-bean eyes glint on upright stalks that can be folded flat in a moment. Watchful and tentative, they freeze at the slightest provocation, then scuttle off. I am woken in the night by the needle patter of feet across my chest and lurch upright, scattering a dozen crabs. Around the bed rows of crab eyes shine in the torchlight. As soon as the light is off, they edge closer again. Later on I am woken by a nip as a crab tests my ear lobe and I send them running again. The next evening, I prop my camp bed on stones.

Come first light, the fly alarm clock wakes me. Fat, black tormentors alight on lips and investigate nose and ears. The sheet is dew-damp and my back prickles with salt and sunburn. Persistent and relentless, the flies have me out of bed in minutes. I shake accumulated hermit crabs from the food box and breakfast on cereal and warm UHT milk. 'It's the breakfast with *get-up-and-go*,' Andrew jokes every morning. The heat builds fast when the sun clears the horizon. Within an hour I am in the water to escape its power. Sometimes the fringing reef is a long wade and swim away, and then a struggle through the dense seaweed barrier.

But most of the time it is little more than a hundred metres from beach to crest.

As we move south, the extraordinary differences from northern waters coalesce, reef by reef, into a consistent pattern. The reefs are muddy, darkly mysterious and their coral patchy. Corals love light, or at least the zooxanthellae in their tissues do, so turbid water is not ideal, just as forest shade deters understory plants. But there are ancient oaks in this forest, pillowy colonies five metres across and several tall that must be hundreds of years old. The veil of suspended mud makes me nervous: might there be a bull shark, sawfish, perhaps even tiger shark, nearby? Pearl divers, I have read, feared sawfish more than any shark. One slash of their blade, double-edged with razor teeth, could slice a man in half. My eyes play tricks in the half light, rendering fish at the edge of visibility as disembodied stripes and dots, a scatter of punctuation marks in search of words. But the thrill of discovery is stronger than fear, so I linger whenever I can, searching for clues to the diversity riddle. I never do see a tiger shark in Arabia, although I am convinced some see me. But when reef sharks appear their entrance is dramatic, literally popping up alongside in the low visibility, leaving an adrenalin surge that carries on long after their departure.

Heading south, the daytime heat soars above 40°C. After a quick break for a spam and cracker lunch in the midday furnace, I dance back through shallow water so hot it stings. Even here there are fish, tiny creatures that glisten like black leeches in the film of water over the rocks. An eel slips between wet stones like a snake. The sea offshore is steamy too and I sweat underwater for the first time, a prickling tingle for which the only relief is to duck-dive several metres to a cooler layer.

My data collection complete after five or six hours, I emerge from the sea in late afternoon. We dine early on tinned food with rice or pasta: food for fuel. By seven the sun has set and paraffin lamps are lit. There are still several hours work transcribing notes from boards to notebook, trying to ignore the storm of flies and moths buffeting the light.

The stars are hard and crystalline and shine without twinkling in the desert air, the atmosphere invisible. Adrift on this phosphorescent night sea, the immensity of space feels almost overwhelming.

Data collection has become routine again, now I have mastered the thirty or forty unfamiliar fish species that live here. Science is not really what I expected. Those eureka moments that are the staple of schoolbooks and encyclopaedias are rare and must be hard won. There are long stretches of boredom. I have endless time to remind myself of Edison's epithet that genius is one per cent inspiration and ninety-nine per cent perspiration. Fortune favours a prepared mind, said someone else whose name I forget.[1] By the end of this trip, mine will surely be primed.

Several weeks into our expedition, Rupert flies out to join us for a couple of weeks. By now we are camped beside a group of extinct volcanoes, the ones Jacques Cousteau's team never reached. I climb the nearest to a cinder peak hundreds of metres above the plain. The heat radiating from its brimstone is almost intolerable but sweat evaporates instantly in the hot wind, leaving the skin barely damp. Not for the first time I wonder how swiftly death might come in this desert, lost and out of water. I squat on my haunches like an Arab, the rock too fiery and sharp to sit. Far below a maze of reefs, islets, lagoons and lush mangrove meander along the coast, colouring the sea with the palette of life in arresting contrast to the elemental rock and dust onshore. A raven chuckles overhead and alights on an outcrop lower down. Several dozen pink spots creep across the turquoise face of a distant lagoon: flamingos. I have already watched spoonbills sifting the mangrove edge early in the morning, while pelicans bigger than swans worked a shoal of fish further offshore. Silhouetted against

---

1.   Louis Pasteur.

the hard sun shimmer, droplets thrown from their beaks glittered like diamonds as they downed fish. Chocolate rivers of hardened lava snake from the mountains to the coast, producing gaps in the mottled line of reef at the water's edge where corals were incinerated long ago.

By the time I get back, Rupert has arrived and is in deep conversation with his field lieutenants, maps and photographs spread across the bonnet of the Land Rover. I say a quick hello and head for the sea. Returning several hours later, my board dense with notes, Rupert is still on the go. Flopping into a chair next to Alec with a glass of hot orange squash, I watch in puzzlement as Rupert picks up a brush and begins to sweep sand from inside the tent. As there is no groundsheet I wonder when, or even if, he will stop. Alec leans over and with a shadow of a smile, whispers, 'I'm not sure how this is going to end.' In Jeddah, Rupert is always fastidious about the equipment, meting out endless cleaning tasks but seeming to avoid them himself. Having raised a berm of sand across the front of the tent, he notices the state of the food box. 'Just look at these tins,' he says, picking up a grimy can of peas from the crate at the back of the tent, 'They're thick with dust.'

'We just give them a wipe before we open them,' Charles replies.

Undaunted, Rupert picks up a handy rag, which might be Trevor's shirt, and begins to polish. One by one the contents of the crate are buffed and stacked onto the camp table. He then calls me over to help. Carrying the crate outside, we shake out several kilos of sand and about a hundred hermit crabs. 'You see how unhygienic this is?' I haven't noticed any of these hermit crabs opening tins, but keep my mouth shut.

Later that evening, satisfied at last with the cleanliness of the tent and by now well fed, Rupert makes an announcement.

'I've been looking at progress and at this rate it will be touch and go whether we make it to the Yemen border in time. You're going to have to work faster.'

Andrew looks surprised, Alec winces and Charles argues: 'We've been surveying two sites a day, I don't think we can fit any more in.'

'You need to do three,' Rupert says flatly, 'I'll show you how tomorrow.'

Come bedtime, I find Alec and Rich conferring in hushed whispers at the edge of camp 'Bloody Rupert, coming out here with his dikctats. I just wish he'd let us get on with things…' They fall silent and smile weakly as I pass.

Next morning Rupert wakes everybody at first light by banging a saucepan. Having mustered a reluctant team, he tells us he will come to the reef with Charles and me first, then join the mangrove team for the afternoon. He will accompany Alec and Rich on the habitat survey the following day. I am glad of the chance to quiz Rupert on some of the many questions I have stored up. Once in the water he is as absorbed as I am by the strangeness of these reefs and the three of us enjoy a morning of spluttered conversation through snorkels.

Come noon, Rupert swims off to join the mangrove survey. After half an hour watching a new damselfish species, I am ready to begin counting but my pencil breaks, necessitating a tedious swim to the camp. Wading across the shallow reef, I spot something large floating near the shore. It is Rupert, fast asleep, his pale belly rising above the water like a half-submerged hippopotamus. He doesn't notice me creep past, nor when I slip back into the sea.

All afternoon, clouds have been coiling about the mountain range that follows the coast, darkening to the colour of wet slate. They erupt into violence as night falls, forking lightning into dry valleys. As the storm edges closer the wind strengthens, flapping tent canvas and strafing us with blown grit. Flashes ignite gargantuan thunderclaps and illuminate the desert like a B-movie set. The coming squall threatens to tear loose the tent, so we park all three vehicles close in, secure extra ropes and gather belongings. The air is now so thick with dust it is hard to see and we retreat inside, hanging onto roof and poles to stop the tent disintegrating in the lashing wind.

The following morning drifted sand lies over everything and the food crate is half full of dust. Charles cheerily picks up the brush and offers it to Rupert: 'If you get started now, you might finish by lunchtime.' Rupert gives him a sideways glance, then pulls a cereal box from a mini dune by the cooking gas bottle. Nothing more is said of cleaning.

For the next several days, Rupert flits between reef team and mangrove, mangrove team and ground survey, causing dismay and mild mayhem. After a week in the field, he declares himself satisfied. The odd thing is that, at last, the heat and activity have finally sapped enough of his energy to slow him to the pace we were working at before he arrived.

We have camped for nearly a month when Charles, passing me struggling out of bed on the way to breakfast, says, referring to my pillow, 'Is that a towel or an engine rag?' After a few days in the field, we all gain a gritty patina of sand and salt crust that can't be washed off with seawater, and freshwater is too precious for anything but face washing. On the other hand, Charles has a point; my towel and bed sheet stink. So I volunteer to accompany him to the local coastguard station to get more water. Later on, I hop into the Land Rover with him, wearing only a swimming costume, a decision I will come to regret.

At the station, instead of being shown around the side to fill up from a tap in the wall, the duty guard insists we meet the captain. He is having a siesta, but no matter: he will see us in his bedroom. I feel underdressed and grab a towel from the back seat to wrap around my waist. It's worse than my own and might well be an engine rag.

The curtains are shut in the captain's bedroom and the air musty. A ceiling fan creaks lazy, pointless circles overhead. The captain sits on the edge of his bed wearing a vest and something resembling a sarong. He looks me up and down, raises one eyebrow slightly, then addresses Charles: 'Show me your papers.' Charles hands them over.

'Are you the manager?'

'No.'

'Where is your manager then?'

'He's in the sea at the moment.'

'Go and get him.'

We both get up to go but the captain calls me back.

'Not you, just him.'

I give Charles a pleading look, which swiftly turns to panicked glare when he breezily says, 'Don't worry, I won't be long.'

With Charles gone, the captain beckons me, patting the spot beside him. The sheets are unkempt, the pillowcase grey and shiny from long use.

'You have a nice face,' he says.

I wish I'd put on some clothes. He stands up and walks to the wardrobe, the only other item of furniture, and takes out his captain's jacket.

'You like?'

'Very smart,' I reply, warily.

He places it back in the wardrobe, takes out a bottle of aftershave and gives himself a lavish spray. 'One Man Show. Very good.'

He brandishes the bottle near my face and releases a choking cloud. I certainly hope that a 'One Man Show' is all this will be. He sits down again, this time so close I can feel his breath on my cheek. He leans over and lifts the edge of my towel.

'No, no... please! I have a wife in England,' I lie, picking up his hand and restoring it to his own knee, a bad move since he now begins to rub his crotch.

I stand up and tell him I must leave, but he orders me to sit or he will have to handcuff me. Things are awkward.

'Mafi mushkellah, no problem, no problem,' he tries to reassure, unsuccessfully.

Another ten minutes of entreaty and rejection ensue, until finally he gives up, perhaps put off more by the crustiness of my towel than my reticence. Soon after, Charles returns and announces that Rupert can't be found. This time the captain allows us to go.

I explain what happened as we fill the jerrycans, omitting the bit about 'One Man Show'. Instead of being contrite, Charles finds it funny. We drive back, windows wide open to the desert.

'Can you smell anything odd?' he asks after a few kilometres, sniffing the air. I glower back. He leans over and sniffs closer to me.

'Are you wearing perfume? You are wearing perfume! Didn't the captain like the smell of your towel?'

He throws back his head and roars with laughter. He is still hooting when we get back to camp, tears streaming down his cheeks, and by now I am chuckling too. The scent of 'One Man Show' lingers on in camp that evening, even after I've spent a couple of hours in the sea.

As we press south, the habitats shift from hard bottom to soft sediment. Reefs become smaller, more widely spaced and further offshore, while mangrove, seagrass and mud come to dominate. While this means more work for the others, Charles and I charge to the Yemen border ahead of schedule. Back in Jeddah, with free time on my hands, I return to mapping fish movements, counting bites of seaweed and watching fish vent their fury on neighbours. Day after day, metre by metre, my maps expand and my mind turns to mashed potato. The repetitious banality of scientific research is numbing, even amid such splendour. But there is satisfaction in seeing notebooks fill, and for some peculiar reason, counting bites of food going into a fish seems superior to watching it poop. I have a study with me which begins: 'The fates of 5,975 faeces produced by 88 species of reef fishes were monitored at Palau (western Pacific Ocean). At least 45 fishes ate fish faeces in addition to other foods.' But after reading it I have to revise my views, for herein lies an unsung wonder of the reef. A predator's poop rarely falls to the bottom. It is evidently delicious, judging by the enthusiasm with which it is devoured by wrasse, parrotfish and a plethora of others. The poop of herbivores is just muck though, which no other fish will touch. That pleasure falls to shrimps, worms and microbes. Coral reefs are a miracle of nutrient recycling, which explains the paradox of plenty in the midst of such nutrient-deficient seas.

After learning of the peculiarities of fish crap, I take a closer interest in the pufferfish that lurks at the edge of a reef patch I've been studying. Its body is like a balloon half-filled with water propelled by three clunky fins at the rear end. A black stripe covers its eyes like a cartoon bank robber's mask. It begins the day smooth-bellied, almost svelte by pufferfish standards, but as the sun arcs overhead the fish ambles about, snapping off coral branch tips, and by early afternoon its stomach bulges oddly, like a restaurant diner who has inadvertently eaten the cutlery with his food. By late afternoon, the coralline breakfast has worked its way through and the fish begins to pass sharply pointed fragments, slowly and quite possibly very uncomfortably. The pieces fall to the reef untouched by any other fish, in my imagination tinkling as they hit the bottom.

With three Red Sea summers under my belt I have started to form my own ideas about the processes that generate richness on coral reefs. The scientists espousing a chaotic view of reef life are mostly Australian and work on small patch reefs on the Great Barrier Reef. Schooled in experimental science, they see manipulation as key to picking apart the forces at play on the reef, so they build tiny patch reefs from living and dead corals on areas of open sand, and then watch as fish move in. After several years of effort, their findings show little pattern in the sequence of the arrivals or in the final make-up of the communities. But is that surprising, I wonder? If you documented the inhabitants of a single tree, would the numbers and types of birds or insects have greater consistency? But at the scale of the forest, there would be far more similarity from year to year. My counts cover a large chunk of each reef and reveal regular patterns of habitat use by nearly all the species present. Yes, there is variability from place to place, but underlying this ecological noise, there seem to be broad forces at work structuring the community of life.

I chose well with the herbivores too. The long days watching their lives unfold have revealed an exquisite pattern of resource sharing, mutual benefit and parasitism among a loose collective of fish that all depend on the algal lawn for food. Big and aggressive surgeonfish keep out stocky herbivores such as parrotfish, but tolerate small and aggressive damselfish that drive away small grazers, saving them work. Neither kind of fish can do anything about the blennies, whose diminutive size, elusive habits and modest needs make it energetically senseless to exclude them, so they are ignored. These species coexist amicably according to rules written by evolution.

Over the next two weeks the field teams come back from the south, stow their gear, pack their bags and leave. It is the beginning of November and Trevor and I are on our own. Both of us are anxious to squeeze this trip for every page of data we can get. We settle into a routine of long days in the sea, Trevor pacing the shallow reef, me diving alone. I have just enough time to study the jewelled damselfish that form tight-knit colonies at the base of the reef cliff. The seaweed within their patches is lush, but living five to ten metres deep, they have no surgeonfish to help with defence as the latter occupy the shallow reef platform. Instead, it seems that living in a crowd so increases defensive strength that even small damselfish can drive off a large parrotfish if several cooperate in the attack. I need data to settle the case.

The dives are long, one over three hours. Science like this takes patience, but there is something else; I can hardly bear to leave. The last entry in my dive log reads: 'I sucked the bottle flat on this dive, finishing just as breathing started getting difficult.' Science to the last gasp.

CHAPTER FIVE

Country under construction

Qatar, 1986

RUPERT KEEPS AN UNTIDY OFFICE, scruffy even by academic standards. Piles of papers teeter on one side of his desk and continue onto the floor, making it hard to open the door. A row of stacked trays occupies the full extent of the back of his desk suggesting that his solution to never managing to clear his in-tray has been to buy more.

It hasn't worked. All the trays are full and, except for a space the size of a blotting pad at which he works, the rest of the desk is covered by a thick detritus of papers that constantly encroaches. Here the latest scientific studies rub shoulders with lecture notes, invoices, scribbled reminders and drifts of unopened mail. In a late-night conversation on the shores of the Red Sea he admitted to me that he once had to plead with the publisher of his coral reef book to reissue a royalty cheque, the one they had sent having expired before he got around to opening it. A small Arabian rug lends the room an exotic splash, relieving the institutional monotony of pine shelving and nylon carpet. Rupert is sitting in the middle of it, rocking back in a deep leather armchair. 'How would you like to go to Qatar?' he says.

It is 1986 and for the last two years I have been trying to wrestle the mountains of data collected in the Red Sea into a passable thesis. Having spent months hunched over a computer, I'm overjoyed at the prospect of getting wet again. Besides, for years I have wondered how reefs in the Arabian Gulf differ from those of the Red Sea, snapping up titbits gleaned from the stories of returning travellers. The Arabian Gulf and Red Sea bracket the Arabian Peninsula, east and west. During the Ice Ages when sea levels dropped, the Gulf had been a fertile valley but now is a shallow inlet of the Indian Ocean. I know that conditions there are highly stressful for reefs, experiencing extremes of temperature and salinity well beyond those in the Red Sea. Perhaps they can help me shed light on the crucial factors that determine the richness of reef life? 'When do I leave?' I reply, unable to suppress a huge smile.

For the next half hour we discuss the practicalities of getting to Qatar and what I would be expected to do. The project will look at the environmental impact of a proposed coastal development and recommend ways to reduce its adverse effects. The prospect is daunting as well as exciting. I've never done an environmental impact assessment before and the country and habitats will be new to me. But Rupert assures me that I would be assistant to a highly experienced international consultant who will take care of all the details. Noticing the time, he suddenly begins rifling through one of the teetering piles on the floor, starting about two thirds of the way down. After a few minutes search, he pulls out a dog-eared brown folder, takes a quick look inside, tells me he has to rush to give a lecture and is gone.

Alec is in his usual spot in the corner of the lab outside Rupert's office, his desk strewn with photographic slides, which he is labelling. 'Are you going to go then?' he asks.

'You bet', I reply 'but why aren't you doing it?'

'I would but I have to go to Yemen next week for a couple of months.'

After our surveys in Saudi Arabia, Rupert had landed a contract to inventory coastal habitats along the Yemen coast. I had so much wanted to join them, but Rupert more sensibly decided that I had plenty of material for a PhD, especially as I had squeezed in a trip to French Polynesia and Australia's Great Barrier Reef in the interim. Australia's seaweed-eating blennies, I discovered, coexisted amicably with damselfish much like those of the Red Sea. This time, though, rather than just watching them, I had done an experiment, removing damselfish from some areas, and blennies from others and watching the outcomes. While the damselfish coped just fine with their territories full of blennies, there wasn't much evidence that they benefited from blenny removal, which I would have expected if the algae had been in limited supply. An inconclusive result.

Alec picks up a slide and holds it to the light: 'Recognise this?'

I peer at it over his shoulder and make out the shape of a volcano separated from the sea by a green slash of mangrove. 'Is it that place where we had the storm? What was its name?'

'Al Qahma. We're going to recommend the Saudis make it a marine park. The habitat variety is fantastic and the birdlife some of the richest in the country.'

Memories of crackling heat, spoonbills, flamingos, ravens and mosquitoes flood back. We chat for a while until Rich arrives, looking harassed as usual, to talk with Alec about progress getting Yemeni visas.

A couple of weeks later I'm at Heathrow Airport waiting for my travel partner. Brian Mackinnon is a serious man in his late forties with heavy rimmed glasses and a dark beard frosted with grey. He seems friendly and we fall into easy conversation on the plane. He has worked across most of Africa and Arabia and from his stories appears to have seen it all. I feel in good hands. After lunch and cognac he settles into his seat to get some sleep, but not before asking the stewardess for a whisky. This he downs in one with a tablet, telling me that he can never sleep on planes without a little help. Is this wise, I wonder? Qatar is five hours from London and there are only two and half left. He must have done this many times, I reassure myself.

When the announcement comes that we are about to land, Brian doesn't stir. We hit the runway with a thump; still no movement. The seat-belt sign goes off and the cabin comes alive. Nothing. 'Brian... Brian, we're here. Brian!' I shake him but he only grunts. The plane empties and Brian remains insensible. A stewardess asks if there is anything wrong. We both shake him vigorously. Brian's eyes open slightly and he says something that sounds drunken and rambling. 'I'm so sorry, my friend took a sleeping pill...' I tell the stewardess, dying inside. Brian is manhandled off the plane by two stewards and half dragged to the terminal. I hold him up while waiting for our luggage wondering what the hell I am going to say to the welcome party from the coastal engineering company.

In arrivals, it is not hard to find Tony, the project manager, among the sea of Qataris with their white dishdashas and gutras. A tall English expatriate, he looks aghast as I introduce myself with Brian propped at a dangerous angle against my left shoulder, his head slumped forward, mouth ajar. 'He's a little tired after the flight,' I venture, 'Perhaps a few hours rest will help?' Not sure what to make of us, he whisks us to our hotel, promising to return for an evening briefing. With Tony gone, I walk Brian painstakingly through check-in. His eyes are rolling upward as he signs the card and there is spittle at one corner of his mouth. The receptionist shoots us a disapproving look as I steer him to the lift. His shuffling mechanical walk and half-mad expression give him the look of a character from *Night of the Living Dead*. When we reach his room he flops onto the bed like a ragdoll and passes out.

Mercifully, by the time Tony returns with a colleague from his company, Brian is up and about. 'How on Earth did I get here?' he asks after answering my knock, 'The last thing I remember was going to sleep on the plane.' I take him through our nightmare arrival, sparing nothing as we head to the lobby for the meeting. He shrugs it off with hardly a trace of embarrassment, greeting Tony and Anwar, a Jordanian engineer, with steel-plated confidence. Glad to assume the role of sidekick once more, I look on as Tony outlines the project with the help of a large plan of the coast which he unrolls onto a coffee table.

'This is where the West Bay Lagoon will be built,' says Tony, indicating a blank area just north of Doha. 'Sheikh Khalifa wants an upmarket residential area with an exciting new waterfront so we will have marinas, beaches and islands, all connected by bridges. Obviously, we want a high-quality environment, which is why we need your help.' Sheikh Khalifa is the Emir of Qatar, ruling over the nation since 1972, a year after the British withdrew having presided over Qatar and much of the rest of the Gulf since the First World War. As conversation progresses, it becomes clear that my idea of a high-quality environment doesn't match theirs. Their main concern seems to be that the lagoon does not become a slime-filled, methane-belching backwater, whereas I am more worried about what they plan to destroy. 'What's in this area at the moment?' I ask.

'Nothing – just sand and mud,' Anwar replies.

'What will happen to the material you excavate?' Brian asks.

'None will go to waste,' Tony explains, an engineer's gleam in his eye. 'Some will be used to extend the airport runway,' he says, pointing to a rectangular section of coast just south of the city, 'while the rest will be used to create another island.' He waves his hand over the sea just offshore.

'What will this island cover?' I ask.

'There's nothing much there,' Anwar chips in, 'The water is shallow and stagnant. Some fishermen use it from time to time, but I think it is only mud.'

Only mud – to these developers, mere clay from which they can conjure whatever dreams their paymasters can afford. But to me mud is the lifeblood of these coastal seas. Packed with billions upon billions of tiny worms, snails, clams, crustaceans, microbes and a host of other scuttling, scratching, sucking invertebrates. Mudflats power marine ecosystems. They feed fish and shellfish and are nurseries for their young; they support millions of migrating birds; they recycle nutrients and assimilate and neutralise coastal pollution. But to Tony and Anwar it was dirt. I wonder if this was how the engineers of Jeddah's Corniche road saw coral reefs, as mere rock, no more than a convenient foundation and cheap source of water features? We leave after arranging to meet in the morning for a drive along the coast. I can't help but feel slightly depressed.

Tony picks us up at 8 a.m. Within a few blocks of the hotel, the road opens onto the coast where it joins a broad palm-lined boulevard that follows the graceful curve of the shore. Or rather, the shore follows the curve of the road, as Tony explains, since by now not much of Doha's coast is natural. This corniche road runs from the airport, itself claimed from the sea, to an even larger squared-off section of flat land that juts offshore north of town. The West Bay, as it is called, is not a bay at all, but the site of a former bay, and, perplexingly, is not west of anything except sea. Now it is a twenty- square-kilometre canvas on which an exciting new, and doubtless extremely expensive, part of Doha will be painted in. At the seaward tip a solitary building draws the eye, appropriately enough a pyramid: the new Sheraton Hotel. Inland and separated by kilometres of emptiness, the grey skeletons of several high-rise buildings already clamber upward.

Tony drives us through the middle of this blank of fill material, most of it sand and rock trucked from the desert, although some was sediment sucked from the sea to deepen the approach to the harbour. The roads are complete, even down to street lamps, giving the place an expectant if forlorn air. The slightest wind lifts clouds of dust and flaps surveyors' tape tied to scattered stakes. A few kilometres further on the metalled road ends abruptly and we at last reach something that looks like natural coast, heading off across a smooth mudflat baked hard by sun. Tony stops the car a few hundred metres from the sea and we get out. This is it, the West

Bay Lagoon,' he says, waving his arm in the direction of nothing in particular. The land is flat and mostly empty, aside from low patches of saltbush. 'We're standing where the yacht club will be. Over there will be luxury villas, all with private beaches, and we want some islands too, several of them...' Tony's chest seems to swell a little as he runs through the plan, describing enthusiastically all the things they will do. In the distance, a group of redshank work their way along the shoreline on spindly orange legs, probing the mud every few steps. You're not part of the plan, I'm afraid, I'm thinking. The sea behind them is the blue of duck eggs, lucent and enticing. I can't wait to see what lies below.

'What happens if we discover something important offshore, Brian?' I ask over dinner that evening. 'I mean, something that the development would destroy that is irreplaceable, like a coral reef or bank of pearl oysters. Could we stop the development from happening?' Brian gives me a surprised look, then pops another forkful in his mouth, perhaps to give him more time to decide whether I am serious. He wipes his beard with a napkin, 'You know, this will go ahead regardless of what we find or say. There is so much money behind it, so many vested interests. Not even a gold-plated oyster bank would put them off!' He takes another mouthful. 'All they want from us is advice on how to keep their bay from fouling up.' My feeling of depression returns.

The following day, we have a meeting at Tony's office in the heart of downtown Doha near the corniche. Qatar is a country under construction. The city bristles with cranes as a new skyline asserts itself above the old. On the way we pass once imposing buildings, like mosques, that now squat in shadow, robbed of their airy birth right by concrete and glass, vulgar or stylish according to taste.

At the office, explaining how the West Bay Lagoon fits into a grander scheme, Tony and Anwar show us the master plan for the city. For ten kilometres either side of Doha the coast is a mix of straight lines and curves too perfect to be natural. Qatar has only been independent for fifteen years, but its rulers haven't wasted time. Newly enriched by vast reserves of gas, they are intent on transforming this quiet desert cul-de-sac into something lively. The country is low-lying and largely featureless so they have a virtual blank canvas. Nor have they felt any compunction about letting history or tradition get in the way. Anwar tells us that the town of Al Khor, a sizeable fishing community not far north of Doha, was one of the first places to be redeveloped after independence. Bulldozers levelled the entire town.

Not content with limiting their ambitions to borders that geology and happenstance have given them, Qatar's rulers are intent on sculpting a new identity by hollowing out areas of sea and creating new land elsewhere. The West Bay Lagoon is just one part of this national remodelling, and a relatively modest one seen alongside other schemes, like the island that the new lagoon's excavated material will create further offshore.

Tony's takes us to the window of his office, high in a tower block, to explain the layout of the coming city, pointing out landmarks not yet visible in the world outside. Through the tinted glass, the sea glitters in the noon sun. Smudges of sepia and green reveal the pulsing life of the underworld, like veins seen through skin. Seagrass, shellfish beds, sandbanks and coral reveal their presence in swirls of colour and the rippling patterns of refracted waves. Two sandy islets sit in the middle of the bay, Alya and Safliyah, each surrounded by a corona of hidden marine life.

Tony has arranged for a boat and diving cylinders and we meet the driver on the seafront early the next morning. Hameed is a local fisherman, albeit one of a new generation that has swopped wood and sail for fibreglass and outboard engine. He is in his early thirties and speaks good English, welcoming us with enthusiasm. The air is cool and still and the sea like a mirror. There is something almost dreamlike about days like this. Over the side, I watch seagrass meadows, coral heads, thickets of seaweed, rippled muddy bottoms and shoals of squid skim past. But then the bottom shelves away and suspended silt draws a curtain on the entertainment.

Halfbeaks erupt from the water at the bow, glinting like polished chrome. They look like exclamation marks as, half upright, the slender cylindrical fish beat urgent trails across the surface with their tails before disappearing in a cascade of leaps. Part way to becoming flying fish, halfbeaks lack the wings to glide but their frenzied paddling is effective nonetheless.

Hameed slows as we approach Alya Island. A group of flamingos, rose-pink in the early light, lift off on cumbersome wings. Brian is not a diver, so I am on my own again. The water is murky and I can't see the bottom when I roll in. As I descend, the world above seems to cloud over and the light dims until I am in a silty cocoon whose visible edge is four or five metres distant all around. Scattered coral clumps dot the bottom, seven or eight metres down, each with a halo of fish flickering in the half-light. A crocodile fish, flat-headed, fat-lipped and swivel-eyed, leaps off the bottom in an indignant puff of sand and speeds off. Its mimicry of seabed rubble is near perfect. Shadows at the edge of visibility entice me onward, coalescing into solidity at my approach as if teleported from somewhere else. A sinuous 'S' emerges from the gloom a metre above the bottom, resolving into a lithe and muscular sea snake, its black and white bars glowing, tail flattened into a paddle. We consider one another before the snake resumes its business, leaving my heart racing. An outcrop of pearl oysters tops a ledge, reminding me of the source of Qatar's more modest wealth in centuries past. Now surplus to requirements, they might soon be scooped up or paved over, their pearls disregarded.

On the next dive, thickets of branching corals sprout from a basement of ancient limestone, stone giving forth stone. Although there are familiar faces from the Red Sea, the fish are mostly new. Tiny blennies, extravagantly tufted and ornamented, blend into invisibility against the agitation of the reef. Snappers form stacks of golden bars above coral tables, while eels skulk beneath. Slim green fish are half-glimpsed among dense seagrass, matching their stop-start swimming to the warp and flex of the grass blades. Cloaking fins crackle with electric blue as their owners slide unseen beneath rocks. I've often wondered why so many reef creatures carry flashes of electric blue or purple. Here I find a possible answer. Sometimes the electric patterns are all you can see in the murk or the grey light of dawn and dusk. I disturb a small hawksbill turtle demolishing a soft coral, its plate-like copper face trailing a mane of mucus strands squeezed from the coral that fills its mouth. It pauses momentarily to consider my intrusion, looking at me through goggling reptilian eyes, before resuming the destruction.

We pull onto Alya Island for lunch, raising a clamour of terns. This early in the year the sun is pleasantly warm and a light breeze has picked up since the morning, riffling the water. In the distance, Doha's nascent high rises stand tall above an understory of flat-topped apartment blocks and offices, while the Sheraton's pyramid squats alone on its synthetic headland. Brian is eager to know what I have seen so I run through the cast of creatures, lingering on the sea snake. But flies have found us and are soon running amok over our lunch and buzzing our faces in excited mobs. We carry on the conversation walking the beach. At regular intervals there are hairy patches of skin and picked bones, all that remain of goats or sheep, each surrounded by a circle of empty drink cans, plastic bags and more energetic flies. The old Arabian attitude, that the desert will swallow all, has yet to be sloughed off in this modern world. During our expeditions to the Red Sea, we avoided camping by palm groves near cities and towns because of the drifts of filth left by day trippers.

Our next stop is closer to the mainland, shallow enough to see the bottom over the side of the boat. The seabed is obscured by a stubby forest of crinkly sargassum weed from which rocky outcrops rise like mountain tops through clouds. Putting on mask and snorkel, I slip into the water. Young parrotfish flit among the fronds while round-bellied grunts retreat at my approach. I am drawn into their world, forgetting for a brief hour the city above that will soon change it forever.

Nobody could claim the reefs here are extraordinary. They are not really reefs at all by the standards of the Red Sea, no more than a veneer of life on a rock foundation. The Gulf is an exceptionally stressful environment, baking in summer and often chilled in winter, its silt-occluded water concentrated into brine. Stands of dead coral are testament to past episodes of excessive heat or cold. Human impacts layer upon these natural stresses, as evidenced by the remains of fishing nets tangled amid the corals, anchor scars and trenches ploughed by boats running aground, and the litter of plastic bottles and cans on the bottom. But life here is prolific and varied. The places that our architects plan to sweep away are far from being stagnant shoals.

The reefs are fascinating in another way. They look like stripped-down versions of those in the southern Red Sea. Most of the fish families I expect to see are present, but represented by fewer species. On a Red Sea fish count there would be thirty-five to fifty different kinds of fish, whereas here there are fifteen or twenty. While corals do grow, they are not luxuriant or vigorous enough to construct reefs. Extreme conditions knock them back too often to build a lasting framework. The cocktail of stresses has pruned diversity and scaled back function.

It feels, as I dive these waters over the ensuing days, that I am documenting a world condemned, like a linguist sent to record a tribal language before its last ageing speakers die. By the end of the trip I am certain the environmental cost of the West Bay development will be high. Our report is a damage limitation exercise, explaining to the developers how to play a more benign God with nature. We distil the parameters necessary for each habitat to survive into terms that engineers can understand – depth range, slope, bottom type, water temperature, salinity tolerance – in the hope that they will create new opportunities for life in the aftermath of its destruction. I leave with a heavy heart though, knowing I am one of the last to see this sea at its best.

CHAPTER SIX

Reflections

York, UK, 2016

QATAR WENT AHEAD WITH ITS COASTAL REMODELLING, despite our misgivings, just like a hundred other schemes around the Gulf rim have done since. I recently overflew Qatar's coast with Google Earth. What a gift for the armchair explorer! On so many occasions in the 1980s I wished that I could take wing above the shores we tramped, to trace the curve of a reef, distinguish hidden coral patches offshore or find lagoons concealed by dense mangrove. Now it has become trivial to soar uninvited above any place on the planet and swoop in to uncover its intimate secrets.

The West Bay has been carved out and the fill material used to extend the coast in a flourish of islets named The Pearl – after the pearl banks entombed beneath, perhaps? The oysters must feel honoured. The two main islands of The Pearl have been hollowed into circular lagoons surrounded by tower blocks and marinas. At the seaward end there is a string of islets, each joined to an artificial peninsula by a short causeway; a pearl necklace according to the developers, but more like a sprig of tomatoes. Only four islets have so far grown palaces, making the Qataris remarkably tardy compared to neighbouring Dubai where the flamboyant Palm Jumeira sprouted offshore faster than a real palm tree would grow.

This is more lavish than anything I saw on Qatar's master plan. Flush with oil money, for the last forty years Gulf States have been locked in a gigantic pissing contest with their neighbours, each concocting ever more extreme ways to parade its wealth.

Qatar was little known when I visited but has become a household name, although not for all the right reasons. In the mid-eighties, it had just a quarter of a million people, no more than a modest city. Today with ten times more it is still small, but Al Jazeera ensures global influence. However, Qatar's new influence borders on notoriety. An old Qatari proverb says 'Open your hand (be generous) and all people will be your slaves'. Some might have taken this too much to heart. Great wealth can fund great deeds, but often it exposes the worst in people. Qatar's 2022 World Cup is mired in controversy, tainted by allegations of corruption, lax safety, bonded labour and modern-day slavery. Qatari money has been linked to support for religious extremism, including the 'Islamic State' fundamentalists of Iraq and Syria, although connections are vigorously denied by its rulers.

Qatar's airport is complete but somewhere in the span of years it ballooned from a simple runway extension to an entire new airport built across the sea. A corner of the reef it obliterates pokes from underneath a runway, a poignant reminder of a loss that need never have happened. Qatar has enough flat and empty desert to accommodate dozens of airports. On my 1980s map of Qatar, Ras Abu Aboud was a coral reef south-east of Doha. Now it is the name of the city district under which it is interred.

What irony that a country so empty and lifeless on land should concentrate development on the narrow coastal strip where wildlife thrives. But I suppose it is exactly this harsh and unforgiving desert that draws people to the shore. The sea ameliorates the torrid climate and beautifies the scene; hardly surprising that people want a piece for themselves. In the struggle for foreshore real estate in Qatar and the rest of the Gulf, developers create new land from sea, stranding inland those who once had a front row seat on the ocean and blocking their views behind towering cliffs of steel, concrete and glass. The Gulf's shallow waters encourage such maritime urban sprawl.

I see that Alya and Safliyah, the islands in the middle of Doha Bay, have not yet been developed but they still have no formal protection. Peering from their glass eyries in the West Bay, Qatar's dreamers and financiers can hardly resist such tempting parcels of land for long. Who knows what gilded towers, what gardens and pleasure palaces have been imagined for them? Plans to develop Alya were drafted some years ago, I discover from an internet search, but then shelved, perhaps because they were insufficiently ostentatious for this prime location. It can't be many years before these islands change forever.

While I have the helm of the Google spacecraft, I head for Jeddah to see what has become of the Corniche road on the Red Sea coast. How much more of the reef has been sacrificed by misguided highway builders? The road itself has not extended much farther, but the shore to north and south has been built up for tens of kilometres with an almost unbroken chain of mansions and palaces. Each has gouged its own marina from living reef, like chunks carved from cheese. I can imagine what I would find were I able to drop into the water: holes too murky and dirty to support any but the hardiest creatures. And to seaward, where once I gloried in frenzied, surging life, the coral will be entombed under the tailings of aspirational lifestyles.

It was this kind of damage that I fretted about as a student in the 1980s, and my space- gazing tells me I was right to. But such harm was only an aperitif to the degradation spiral into which reefs would soon be sucked. I had no inkling of it then. Why would I? Reefs had been around for millions of years. Their history was written in the cliffs that bordered the Red Sea. They were eternal.

Reef history is also written into the cliffs of many Caribbean islands, like Bonaire, a Dutch island just north of Venezuela. I visited Bonaire in 1994 with Julie, by then a published scientist, who had been invited by the local marine park manager Kalli de Meyer. Kalli was concerned about damage from the thousands of scuba divers attracted by the island's unusually accessible coral reefs. Bonaire's reefs are no more than twenty to forty metres from shore to edge, reachable by a short swim across a platform of swimming-pool depth and, on most days, tranquillity. We were to repeat a survey of the corals made a decade earlier by a Dutch scientist and, by comparing results, would see how the reefs were coping with this touristic adoration. In the interval between morning and afternoon dives, we basked in the sunshine on beaches of coral bones, the smoothed remains of elkhorn corals torn from reefs just offshore, flat-bladed and heavy as their namesake.

We were too late to see Bonaire's reefs at their best, although Julie's research cleared scuba divers of culpability. The disease epidemics that wiped out elkhorn and staghorn corals across the Caribbean in the 1980s had already done their worst here. Where these corals once forested the shallow reef, now there were ruins. staghorn branches littered the seabed in a thick bed of fragments. Here and there columns of living star coral and the angular trunks of dead elkhorn corals rose above the wreckage. It looked like a city in the aftermath of a bombing campaign: scattered walls and chimneys stand erect above mounds of rubble, while here and there a building, a church or house perhaps, survives intact. Before the plague, staghorn and elkhorn corals dominated the shallows, leaving the place strangely empty now. But on the slope below this death zone, where different species of coral held sway, Bonaire's reefs still thrummed with life, apparently unaltered.

The southern half of Bonaire is a low expanse of desert and blinding crystalline salt pans. But its north end is a dense cactus scrub that deters all except goats, the descendants of animals left centuries ago by pirates and seamen. A limestone ridge rises above the barbed thicket, the remains of coral reefs long ago thrust above sea level by tectonic forces. At the shoreline, the lower flank of these fossil hills meets its living counterpart. Slabs of ancient seabed lie in the water, exposing on the cliffs from which they have fallen the petrified heart of a long-dead world. Engraved in the cliff face, coral skeletons clamber over one another in a multi-millennial cutaway of history. Despite such great age, their forms are familiar. Rounded pillows of star coral press upon two metre columns of elkhorn, muscular as trees. Jumbled cylinders, their surfaces pitted with corallites, fill the spaces in between. They remind me of the cuneiform cylinders of an ancient Babylonian library and, in their own way, they tell the story of this reef.

Just above one picnic spot, a star coral had split apart when a block fell from the cliff. Inside I could trace its growth in band after band of polyps, like tree rings but laid one on top of another, from the single polyp that first settled onto the reef through to the boulder-like immobility of old age. But much like a tree, a coral is never really old. The living polyps at the surface, like fresh wood beneath bark, are forever renewed, youthful and vigorous. What finally brings a coral's life to senescence and death is the vigour of others that overtop and shade it, eventually entombing its skeleton within a chalk sarcophagus.

A coral reef grows when three vital ingredients come together: framework building corals, the stones and bricks of the reef; fill material, the hardcore that plugs the spaces in between; and cement, the binder that holds it all together. Here the framework builders were unquestionably the Star and elkhorn corals. The fill consisted mainly of sand and the cylindrical fragments of staghorn coral, with a sundry assortment of bits and pieces. The cement is only obvious on close inspection. Tucked among the corals and joining one to another are thin chalky crusts stacked like layers of puff pastry: coralline algae, one and the same as the purplish-grey layer that covers much of the living reef below water. This humble seaweed is vital to reef growth, binding and consolidating loose material to build the structure upward. There is another kind of binder here that only becomes obvious when you try to scratch sand grains from the cliff. They are stuck together by an aragonite[1] cement chemically precipitated from the rich carbonate broth of the pore water percolating inside the reef rock when it lay below sea level.

To a trained eye, the scenes written into this cliff are as nuanced and revealing as any temple frieze from Ancient Greece or India. Mine was not such an eye. I could pick out obvious features, like an observant tourist recognising the cartouches of certain Egyptian Pharaohs on tomb walls. The kings and emperors of this reef were unmistakable. But a skilled palaeontologist can recall a reef to life from its remains. Their science, one might call it an art, is taphonomy, which derives from 'taphos', the Greek word for grave. John Pandolfi and Jeremy Jackson, then respectively at Australia's University of Queensland and the Smithsonian Tropical Research Institute in Panama, were masters of the art. In the first few years of the twenty-first century, they tapped and chipped their way across the limestone flanks of Barbados, a thousand kilometres east of Bonaire. Their geological transects mirrored the ones we had swum on living Red Sea reefs, noting which species lived where and how many there were. After the application of various corrections that account for the tendency of some species to preserve better than others, they described the communities of corals inhabiting reefs going back 220,000 years.

The results were startling. These reefs had existed virtually unchanged throughout an expanse of years that encompassed almost the whole of human history, beginning as our species emerged in Africa. Across this immense stretch of time, which took in an Ice Age as well as our own more clement times, staghorn and elkhorn corals had dominated shallow waters. As sea levels rose and fell, they marched up and down in step, a constant presence at the edge of the sea. The greater shock of these findings lies in what they mean: the recent mass coral mortality has no precedent

---

1. Aragonite is the chemical form of carbonate from which corals construct their chalky skeletons.

in history. It is unique, a one-off, and so the finger of blame points to us.

Whatever killed these corals was extraordinarily virulent. The bubonic plague that swept Europe in the Middle Ages killed 70 to 99 per cent of those it afflicted. Left untreated, Ebola carries off 70 per cent or more. The malady that sickened staghorn and elkhorn corals destroyed 95 to 99 per cent of them. The cause was a mystery for decades. How strange that something so devastating in consequences should be so hard to apprehend. But it killed swiftly, leaving no trace that the analytical methods of the time could detect. Recent flare-ups in places where the species have begun to make a comeback gave us a second chance with more advanced molecular probes.

Nobody expected the blame to point so directly to us. The pathogen turns out to be a human gut bacterium that made the leap from people to coral. We have grown familiar with the species-hopping tendencies of diseases, like Ebola, from bats to people, or swine flu. But it feels peculiar to be donor rather than recipient. The epidemic most likely began with untreated sewage sloshed into the sea. How many other diseases lurk in the shadows, waiting for an opportunity to strike?

The 1980s was also a bad decade for coral on the other side of the Panamanian Isthmus, in the Pacific Ocean. The giant El Niño climate disruption of late 1982 to early 1983 was the biggest for at least a century and a half and was catastrophic for coral reefs. An El Niño happens roughly once every three to seven years when equatorial winds that blow across the surface of the Pacific reverse, blowing west to east rather than the usual east to west. This pushes a pool of warm water far into the eastern Pacific, flooding through the Galápagos Islands and causing a near shutdown of the cold water upwelling off the coast of Peru that fuels its spectacular anchoveta fishery with nutrients drawn from deep water. As a result, the anchoveta fishery dwindles and predatory seabirds, mammals and a host of others starve. By early 1983, after several months sweltering in the hot water pool, Galápagos beaches were strewn with the carcasses of starved sea lions, while emaciated marine iguanas littered its rocks. The rare Galápagos penguins failed to produce young and thousands died.

Corals usually like it hot, preferring sea temperatures above 20°C. But the water soared above 30°C in late 1982 and stayed there for months. Corals turned deathly white as they lost their zooxanthellae, the internal microbes that photosynthesise to make their food, and then died themselves. When the winds swung back to their usual patterns and temperatures fell, most of the coral on Galápagos reefs was dead. The survivors quickly found themselves under attack by coral-eating crown-of-thorns starfish scrabbling for their last meals. And with the reefs now blanketed with green algae, the numbers of grazing sea urchins boomed. Urchins are short-lived, fast-growing and prolific, so are quick to take advantage when conditions turn in their favour. Before long, what remained of the reefs disappeared beneath black mats of waving needle spines as tens of thousands of urchins swarmed across the bottom, like maggots on a carcass.

Urchins are not delicate eaters. Their mouths contain a star-shaped cluster of self-sharpening chisel teeth whose tips are hardened by magnesium. With each mouthful of algae, they ingest a little bit of the rock it grows on. In less than a year, what was left of Galápagos reefs began to be worn down under the onslaught. In truth, the reefs were patchy, poorly developed and never very strong, nothing like the Red Sea's monumental coral cliffs. I had the chance to see them for myself in 1999 when Julie and I went to the Galápagos on behalf of the World Wildlife Fund to appraise the design of its new marine park. I soon discovered that diving the Galápagos can be bracing. The dive usually starts cosily in the warm lens of water floating at the surface. Then, with little warning, fish wobble and quiver, the sharp outlines of rocks blur and seem to uproot and dance, while colours smear and blend. This is the layer where warm and cold waters mix, and when you break through, the world suddenly comes into sharp, vivid focus and the temperature plunges half a dozen degrees. In this chill clarity, the boundaries of the visible world retreat and a huge seascape opens up. The upwelling of cold, nutrient-rich water makes this place special. The Galápagos once went by another name: Islas Encantadas or Enchanted Isles. It was fitting, for in this bizarre and wondrous place there are strange bedfellows. Creatures from colder climes, like playful fur seals or penguins, may join you on your dive, mingling incongruously with wizened iguanas and purposeful columns of multi-coloured fish familiar from coral reefs.

But the reefs here, what was left of them, were almost unrecognisable, no more than an eroded and scalloped layer of carbonate smeared across volcanic rock. It felt like looking at the dead bones of a much-loved companion and Shakespeare's famous line played in my head, 'Alas poor Yorick... Where be your gibes now? Your gambols? Your songs? Your flashes of merriment...' All gone.

Even when at their best, Galápagos reefs were stunted by the tough environment. Temperature lows and highs were one part of the stress they experienced. The other problem was extracting enough carbonate from seawater to build skeletons. The eastern Pacific is short on dissolved carbonate because its water is more acidic than most of the rest of the ocean. Standing on the cliffs of Santa Cruz Island, watching the green waves steepen and crash over naked volcanic rock, seeing foam streamers snake and twist on the currents just offshore, it is hard to think of these seas as anything less than well mixed. But deep down the eastern Pacific is one of the global ocean's stagnant corners.

This is because, all over the planet, the deep ocean is refreshed by exceptionally cold, dense water sinking near the poles. For hundreds of years this polar water gurgles and trickles its way unseen through deep sea canyons and abyssal darkness, before upwelling to the surface again far away. Over the course of this long perambulation, the oxygen it contains is breathed by a fantastic menagerie that inhabits the abyss and is replaced by their exhaled carbon dioxide. When carbon dioxide dissolves, it creates carbonic acid, which is where fizzy drinks get their bite. The eastern Pacific backwaters of the deep sea are bypassed by these currents and languish unventilated by fresh oxygen, meaning they have more carbon dioxide. The acid produced reacts with dissolved carbonate, the raw material of coral skeletons, locking it away as bicarbonate which corals can't use. So corals in the eastern Pacific had a hard time of it long before the 198283 El Niño.

The precipitous collapse into oblivion of Galápagos reefs begs further explanation. Of the three elements needed to make a reef, building materials were in short supply due to limited coral growth, which meant that fill material was too. Most of the fill consists of broken-down coral fragments and sand produced by the scrape and rasp of urchins and parrotfish on reef rock. But crucially, the last element – cement – was scarce too. Coralline algae, the glue that binds it all together, are more sensitive to the effects of acidity than corals and struggled to thrive. And reduced carbonate levels in the water inside the pores and crevices of the reef rock meant that chemical precipitation of cement was low too. These reefs were poorly made from bad materials, and like shoddy buildings thrown up by rogue constructors, they disintegrated quickly under stress.

Over thirty years on from the Pacific El Niño and Caribbean coral plagues, neither region shows any sign of recovery. I returned to the Galápagos in 2010 with the famous American oceanographer, Sylvia Earle, and her 'Mission Blue' voyage to raise funds for a massive global expansion of marine protection. Sylvia is small and slight, with sea-blue eyes and an impish smile. She had been famous for decades by the time we met, having trail-blazed a career as a female marine biologist and oceanographer in the male-dominated America of the 1960s and 1970s. Not only has she had a distinguished career as a deep-sea explorer and scientist, she led the US National Oceanic and Atmospheric Administration in the early 1990s, and was named a *Time* magazine 'Hero of the Planet' in 1998. Sylvia had won the TED Prize the previous year and our ship was full of scientists, explorers, industrialists, philanthropists, entrepreneurs and movie stars. I felt a little overawed by the company, but any barriers there might have been soon fell away as we lost ourselves in a shared passion for the sea. Sylvia celebrated her seventy-fifth birthday that year, but her girlish enthusiasm bubbled brightly as she mingled with the likes of Leonardo Di Caprio, Ed Norton and the home computer magnate Ted Waitt.

After a morning of presentations, my own included, on the urgent need to protect the ocean, we went diving. Back in my twenties, I never expected that one day my dive buddy would be Cousteau, albeit the great man's grand-daughter Celine. I was glad to be back in seas buzzing with life, positively jumping with it, in fact. The marine park had been up and running for a decade and I soon saw the benefits of protection in one of the marine reserve zones that had been closed to all fishing. The fish had multiplied since my last visit and were bigger too, just as I would expect from a well-defended park. Fur seals and sea lions chased one another and swam loops around us as we drifted with the current along a rock wall, streaming bubble trails from their nostrils and dense pelts. On our seaward side there was a living wall of goggle-eyed jacks with scimitar pectoral fins drawn onto shining steel bodies, kept in constant motion by the rushing passages of seals. Beyond the jacks, the silhouettes of burly hammerhead sharks could be seen cruising further offshore. We spotted dark lava slabs with incandescent splashes of sea stars, some orange and shaped like a Star of David, others blue or purple with smooth, long-fingered limbs. Knobbed tube corals crusted the rocks like yellow fists. The water around the boulders was filled with flapping yellow tails attached to hundreds of angelfish and surgeonfish. The angelfish were square-bodied with deep indigo flanks marked with a vivid white slash, the surgeonfish were pastel blue ovals with two dusky facial bars and puckered lips with which they kissed weed from the rocks. There were corals too, here and there, scattered colonies none much bigger than a cauliflower. This spot once had a well-known reef, but the best it could muster now was a whitish cast of coral carbonate, all that was left after the urchins had finished their work. At the end we surfaced unsure whether to laugh or cry. If this were my first ever dive I could not have been happier at the wild exuberance of life. But Celine and I were burdened by the ghosts of the disappeared.

There is one last element that helped seal the fate of reefs in both the Galápagos and Caribbean: they are much less rich than those of the Red Sea or western Pacific. Where the Red Sea has several tens of different coral species that all contribute bulk material for reef construction, the eastern Pacific and Caribbean have just a handful. Isolation, clashing continents and evolution have dealt these places a limited hand, which renders them especially vulnerable to loss of species. With the disappearance of elkhorn and staghorn corals, the Caribbean lost two of its three most significant reef builders. The third – star coral – is faltering too, falling victim to a slower acting but nonetheless devastating disease dubbed 'white plague'. The epidemic has slain towering colonies metres wide that were alive when Columbus crossed the Atlantic. When they are gone, what then?

Looking back, it is hard to believe how much coral reefs in these places have altered in such a brief moment, no more than a camera flash in the span of geological time. elkhorn and staghorn corals are now on the US Endangered Species List, something utterly unthinkable when I began my career. How the mighty are fallen. Their collapse from supremacy is on a par with the slaughter of buffalo, or the extinction of the passenger pigeon, once the most abundant bird in North America.

In 1986 I finished my PhD, but not my quest. The secrets of reef diversity remained obscure. One thing I had discovered from sifting through hundreds of our Saudi Arabian expedition surveys was that turtle and shark numbers declined as you neared fishing villages. I wrote my findings up and submitted them to a scientific journal, pleased and expectant. A few months later a letter of regret from the editor arrived, accompanied by the scathing comments of two reviewers. I was unprepared for and anguished by their words. 'This paper has nothing of merit,' condemned one. 'You cannot survey sharks and turtles simply by watching them,'[1] reproached the other, pointing out the superiority of fishing surveys in which sharks are counted after being caught and killed.[2] Re-reading the reviews now brings back the heartache and insecurity of those early years when I was trying to make it as a scientist.

Since my paper's rejection many studies have reported the signature of fishing in the falling abundance of big fish, turtles and a host of other edible fauna. In fact, you could call the discovery of what a profound impact hunting and fishing have had on the sea one of the greatest shifts in understanding of the last thirty years of marine science.[3] The further we got from habitation on our Red Sea expeditions, the more crowded reefs seemed to be with stout groupers, emperors and snappers, battered and scarred by age. They were utterly unconcerned at my approach, never having seen the glint of hook or spear. It surprised me later, when collecting fish for research, how quickly they learn to fear the spear. Before long every fish in the neighbourhood has singled you out as a predator, so you can't get near them. No wonder so many predators use stealth rather than speed to snatch their prey.

I had more luck with a different study from our Red Sea expeditions, which was published in the proceedings of an international coral reef meeting in 1988. Over several years we reached hundreds of places up and down the Red Sea coast, scoring every site for the abundance and diversity of fish and for characteristics of the reef such as living coral cover, the steepness

---

1. You can, of course, but I was too insecure then to challenge their prejudices.

2. Many fisheries scientists still prefer to kill first and count later, but with large and often rare species, non-lethal surveys are much preferable.

3. I later wrote a book on the influence of hunting and fishing on the oceans: *The Unnatural History of the Sea* (Island Press, 2007).

of the slope, the architectural complexity of the structures present, water clarity, and even how beautiful the reef appeared. By comparing these features one against another, you can begin to understand the forces that shape reef communities. Reefs with the highest cover of living coral tend to be the most architecturally complex, with a rugged, convoluted appearance produced by layer upon layer of corals of different shapes and sizes, pitted with crevices, caves and fissures. In turn, structural complexity begets abundance and diversity, with complex reefs supporting more prolific fish and a greater variety of species. Amid complexity, there is greater scope for creatures to make a living by different means, and more opportunity to escape being eaten. And yes, for us at least, the most beautiful reefs were also the most complex, varied and exuberant, set in water of crystalline clarity.

What drove that complexity though? Why were some reefs rich and complex and others less so? The most complex reefs, it turned out, were in places most favourable for coral growth, which meant close to deep, clear water, strong currents and a ready supply of planktonic food. So here, at last, were some of the keys to reef diversity. These patterns didn't explain global geographic gradients in underwater richness, but they said much about what made reefs tick at a local scale.

Although there is much to lament about the state of coral reefs and the sea in general, there is also hope. In the early days of our Red Sea exploration we were joined several times by young Saudis from the Meteorology and Environmental Protection Administration, our paymasters. But they came and went within a day or two. My adventure was their penance. Arabian seafarers were once admired across the known world, but these Saudis had little understanding or love for the underwater realm. Pearl divers aside (none of whom were left by the time of my expeditions), most kept their feet firmly planted on desert or deck timber. Seafaring fell into decline in the nineteenth and twentieth centuries as trade moved elsewhere and bigger ships supplanted dhows. Most Saudi Arabians I met therefore had no idea that there was anything of value beneath the sea. Our map of marine habitats was the first accounting of their treasures, but at the time we made it few people in Saudi Arabia saw them that way. In the years since, several rich Saudi princes have fallen in love with scuba diving and have established philanthropic foundations, such as Save our Seas, dedicated to saving ocean life. And the good news is that Saudi Arabia still has enormous tracts of unspoiled reefs, many of which remain much as they were thirty years ago.

Attitudes are changing for the better too. Researching this book, I read Haroun Tazieff's account of Jacques Cousteau's expedition to the Red Sea in 1951. A couple of throwaway lines rooted me to my chair: 'People on land would hardly imagine the vast amount of rubbish and filth that a ship in dry dock can accumulate. Fortunately ships are able to use the whole ocean as their dustbin, and we soon learnt the pleasure of throwing things overboard – one way of getting rid of lumber irrevocably and without regrets.' At the time, even Cousteau thought of the sea as big enough to swallow anything dropped into it with no comeback. More surprising still, at this point they were in the Ionian Sea, not exactly an ocean away from hundreds of islands where their floating muck would doubtless soon wash ashore. Much later, Cousteau changed his mind, writing: 'Water and air, the two essential fluids on which all life depends, have become global garbage cans.' Nobody who visits the seaside today, who sees the high-tide scum line of trash, needs much convincing that something must be done.

CHAPTER SEVEN

Science diving for Muslim ladies

Egypt, 1987–88

KHODAIR'S OFFICE, ON THE ISMAILIA CAMPUS of Suez Canal University, is as spacious as the ballroom of a small country house. Chairs and sofas line three walls, their arms gilded, ornately carved and battered from long use. A man I assume to be Khodair, president of the university, sits at the far end behind a vast desk flanked by two Egyptian flags. From behind his broad shoulders a large portrait of the Egyptian president, Hosni Mubarak, glares at the room, his expression an ambiguous mix of ruthlessness and munificence.

It is 1987 and Charles Sheppard, our coral expert in Saudi Arabia three years ago, is with me, now as my boss. Most of the chairs are occupied with what seems to be a complete cross section of the university's staff: three groundsmen in gallabiyahs with hands like tree roots and faces dark as walnuts, various suited men and a scattering of smartly dressed women. Some appear to be academics, others administrators. Several of them are nervously fingering pieces of paper. It has the feel of a doctor's waiting room, but with the consultations being held in public.

Judging by his dismissive tone, Khodair seems to be finishing a meeting. The man in front of him begins to shuffle backwards in the direction of the door, giving a series of little bows and muttered thanks. He couldn't look more servile if he had tugged his forelock and offered grovelling appreciation for some minor favour to the squire of an English estate. Without looking around the room, Khodair barks 'Mona!' A slender woman in her early twenties wearing a red, figure-hugging skirt scurries to his side with a box of tissues. He takes one, dabs his forehead, places the tissue in her manicured hand, and turns to the next in the queue. A harassed-looking man in a dark suit stands up and walks to the front. Khodair curls his lip, exposing yellow teeth behind his toothbrush moustache. He begins talking in a barely audible whisper but quickly builds to a shouted staccato. The man flinches submissively as Khodair works his way to crescendo, purple and breathless. At some unseen gesture, the man turns on his heel and hurries out. 'Mona!' The tissues arrive again and he takes one, blows his nose noisily and drops it into her outstretched hand.

For the next hour, I watch in mounting alarm as Khodair lurches between extremes of anger and pleasantry. By the time our turn comes I feel as if we are in the court of Henry VIII, unsure whether we will be praised or sent to the Tower. Unusually, Khodair stands up to greet us, the top of his head rising to the level of my chin, making him barely more than five feet tall. But his barrel chest is more rugby player than bureaucrat. He shoots Charles a critical glance, then looks me up and down. 'So Chippr'd, this is the new man for Sharm-el-Sheikh?'

'Yes, he's just arrived from England.'

'Are the buildings in Sharm-el-Sheikh ready yet?'

'Actually, that's what I wanted to talk to you about.' Charles replies. 'The renovations should be complete by now, but they haven't even begun yet.'

Khodair's expression sours. The marine station in Sharm-el-Sheikh is a leftover from the Israeli occupation. Sinai was annexed by Israel during the Six Day War of 1967 and returned in the early

1980s as part of a peace deal. The Israelis built a marine science station in Sharm that was abandoned on withdrawal and has slowly gathered dust. Our project, a collaboration between Suez Canal University and Britain's Liverpool University, will renovate the centre and spearhead a marine science renaissance in Egypt. At least that is the plan, but spending the money is proving difficult, as Charles had begun to explain to me earlier in the day. The project aims to build up marine research capacity in both Ismailia and Sharm-el-Sheikh, a tiny town on the Red Sea coast at the foot of the Sinai Peninsula. I had recently been appointed 'Team Leader' for the Sharm-el-Sheikh marine station, which had reunited me with Charles. With funding of more than a million pounds sterling to pump into Egypt in four years, it should have been easy. But Charles found himself battling two giant bureaucracies: in one corner the European Economic Community, and in the other Egypt. Both were beset by Byzantine rules on spending to prevent fraud. Nearly a year had passed with little to show except for the grim lines that had appeared on Charles's face.

Charles badly needs Khodair to unblock bureaucratic pipes and let the money flow. But Khodair is reacting badly to the implied criticism of his staff and of Egypt itself. As his expression darkens and his voice rises, Charles matches him with a belligerence that surprises me. Is this the same easy-going fellow from our southern Arabia trip? Our audience suddenly ends and we are on our way. A shout of 'Mona!' follows us down the corridor.

Outside, the heat and smell of sewage hits us with a one–two punch. A man in a dirty gallabiyah and a pair of orange wellingtons dozes in the shade of a palm while a hose glugs fetid water from a tanker over a flower bed before flowing ineffectually into a pool across the road. We skirt the edge of this lake as Charles takes me to see Abdul Aal, the project administrator and the blockage he was hoping that Khodair might shift. Aal jumps up from his desk when we arrive and enthusiastically pumps my hand as Charles introduces me, vigorously resisting several attempts to release his grip.

Aal winces visibly as Charles launches the latest salvo in his battle to spend money. It turns out that the villa at the field centre that Julie and I are to live in is still derelict. To get it into a liveable state will take the production of three tenders from contractors before any plaster can be slapped onto walls or windows repaired; a small matter, Aal explains, which will take two weeks, or perhaps four, six at the most. His bald head is round and shiny and his face has the rubbery expressiveness of a circus clown, passing rapidly from optimism to fatalism and finishing on empathetic concern. I leave feeling dejected. Instead of soon being immersed in the Red Sea, Julie and I must endure weeks – perhaps months – of limbo in Ismailia.

It isn't as if Ismailia is unpleasant. The town lies halfway between the Red Sea and Mediterranean on the banks of Lake Timsah – Crocodile Lake, although there are none left today, so far as anyone can tell. The town is bright and airy, with broad streets lined with palms, flamboyant trees and pink and purple flourishes of bougainvillea. Floral scents leaven the notes of drain in its municipal bouquet. The place has the sedate gentility of a mid-size university town and nothing of the polluted, noisy claustrophobia I had briefly experienced in Cairo on arrival with Julie.

Charles lives with his wife Anne and their young son and baby daughter on the first floor of a small apartment block on the edge of town, five minutes' walk from campus. He enjoys pointing out that he chose his wife by interview, hiring her as a research assistant for an expedition to the Chagos Islands in 1979. This reminds me of Hans Hass, one of the pioneers of scuba diving, who reluctantly took his glamorous secretary Lotte to Sudan in the 1950s and then found he couldn't live without her, proposing marriage at the end of the expedition. Anne welcomes us enthusiastically, glad to have more company after being kept at home by her young family for much of the last year. She speaks with a precisely enunciated Scottish accent, choosing her words

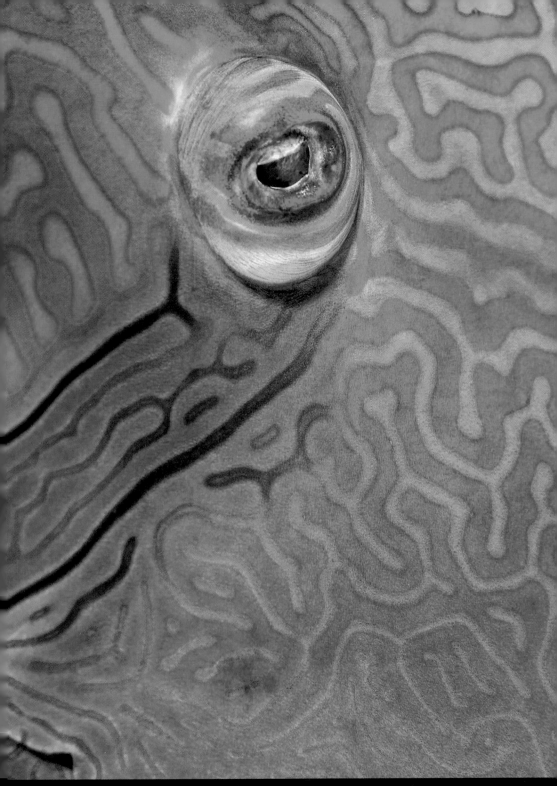

Coral reef fish are renowned for their brilliant colours and abstract patterns, as in this intimate humphead wrasse portrait (*Cheilinus undulatus*); these fish reach nearly two metres long and dine on clams and needle-spined sea urchins. Red Sea (*Ch.1*).

Top: Maldivian anemonefish (*Amphiprion nigripes*) live in garrulous groups in their anemone hosts, dominated by a single matriarch (*Preface*). Bottom: Lemon gobies (*Gobiodon citrinus*) are shy and stay within the interstices of branching corals; Red Sea (*Ch. 2*).

The reef wall, like this one from the Red Sea, faces the open sea and is where the greatest richness and abundance of life is found. The blizzard of orange fish are scalefin Anthias (*Pseudanthias squamipinnis*) (*Ch. 1*).

Moray eels spend their days in fissures, only their gaping mouth and beady eyes visible. This one, *Gymnothorax javanicus*, is being picked over by a cleaner wrasse (*Labroides dimidiatus*) that has no fear of being eaten, Red Sea (*Ch.1*).

Shallow reef corals must withstand punishing waves in the central Red Sea. I spent hundreds of hours in places like this, floating at the surface watching fish behaviour just beyond the reach of the breakers (*Ch. 1*).

Top: Sometimes fish surround you so completely, it feels like a storm of bodies, as with these Bohar snappers (*Lutjanus bohar*) (*Ch. 14*). Bottom: Predatory coral trout (*Plectropomus pessuliferus*) with

A crab (*Paguritta* species) hides in a living coral branch, its lair lined with pink coralline algae (Similan Islands, Thailand, part of the Coral Triangle) (*Ch. 9*). To survive on reefs packed with predators, small creatures rely on concealment or crevices.

Top: Scissortail damselfish (*Abudefduf sexfasciatus*). *Abudefduf* means 'the one with the striped vest'. Red Sea (*Ch. 2*). Bottom: Twice a deadly poisonous stonefish (*Synanceia verrucosa*) moved just before I put my hand on it, thinking it was a rock (*Ch. 2*).

with same methodical care she applies to the complex puzzle of coral classification, her speciality. Tubs of bone-white coral pieces are stacked in their apartment, each specimen labelled in her neat hand.

Julie and I, as temporary residents here, are consigned to a windowless, airless basement of the apartment block where Charles and Anne live. It was meant to be only a week or two before we moved to the Red Sea coast, but after six weeks of bureaucratic inertia, Julie is being driven quietly mad by confinement and the muffled noise of babies through the ceiling, threatening bodily harm or flight from Egypt unless we get to Sharm. So Charles musters an expeditionary party bringing Anne and their children in their car, while Professor Ghobashy, the Dean of Science, travels with Julie and me in the university Land Rover. For an hour, the road follows the Suez Canal until the horizon turns dark blue, blossoming at the next rise into a broad finger of sea that beckons like an old friend. We skirt the Gulf of Suez — one of two northern cul-de-sacs of the Red Sea — for four parching hours, windows rolled down to ameliorate the late summer heat. For the last two hours, we are hemmed in on our left by a towering sawtooth of naked rock, the mountains of South Sinai.

Sharm appears suddenly as we descend into a valley having just passed through two military checkpoints and a rocky landscape scarred by trenches, sandbags and barbed wire, a legacy of the conflict with Israel. A one-pump petrol station stands on its own halfway between the sea and a row of sheds that I later discover is the town market. Dust devils curl across the open space and a shimmering haze crackles from hot earth. It has the look of Wim Wenders' *Paris, Texas*, which to me is not a recommendation. The land beyond rises to a headland capped by a concrete rind of Israeli blockhouses, pierced at one end by a mosque's minaret.

We continue to Na'ama Bay, twenty minutes further on, driving to the top of a cliff at its northern edge, pausing briefly at a gap in a fence where a painted sign announces in wobbly Arabic and English that we have reached the Madrassat el Bea, Research Centre of Suez Canal University. We pull up outside a nondescript single-storey building. 'Welcome to your new home!' Anne shouts, getting out of the car in front. 'The villa on the right is yours, the one on the left ours.'

'Not much of a villa,' I whisper to Julie as we walk towards what looks like four buff concrete boxes bolted together. There is a hole in the wall where a window should be, while the back door is wedged open by a pile of debris. We make for the door but Anne intercepts us, taking Julie by the arm: 'Don't go in there yet. Come and see the view.'

From its cliff-top perch the house commands a sublime outlook across the sweeping curve of Na'ama Bay, south towards the heart of the Red Sea. To our east, Tiran Island rises from the other side of the strait that bears its name, behind it a fawn haze of Saudi Arabian dust. Its familiar triangular peak brings memories rushing back. It is hard to believe that so slight a distance separates us from Ras Fartak, the site of my arrest four years before, a place that at the time felt like world's end. Nearer to hand, a ribbon of dappled ochre cliff and emerald reef traces the interlacing of sea and land, separating water from dry earth. The pull of these reefs is almost irresistible; I feel like abandoning everyone and running headlong into the sea.

Anne's voice snaps me back to the present. There are two hotels in the bay, a campsite and another hotel under construction, she is explaining. Otherwise the desert is a blank of sand and pebble trails that merge with distance into a gravel plain, which crawls into foothills before losing itself in a mountainous carcass of geological upheaval. Steps lead down from the cliff top to a broad rock platform backed by a crescent of identical concrete boxes. 'Students and visiting Egyptian staff will stay in those rooms,' Anne continues, 'while the four buildings in front' (all from the same concrete mould, I note) 'will be the teaching labs, the classrooms, the diving centre and the admin office.'

Turning back to our 'villa', it is clear that there is a long way to go before this dream can be realised. Pushing through the door, we pick our way carefully across the floor, crunching broken glass. Inside the air stinks of shit and stale urine. Anne recoils as two wraith-thin cats bolt for the door.

Outside we rejoin Charles, who until now has been deep in conversation with Ghobashy. There are four more pairs of semi-detached villas spaced along the cliff top. 'That one belongs to the governor of South Sinai,' Charles tells us, 'and President Mubarak has the two at the far end.' I am trying to take this in when he says, 'Come and see the rest of the place,' and whisks us through 100,000 years of coral history as we descend the fossil cliff to the lower level. Corals inscribe the rock face either side of the steps, petrified in their growth positions and stained a uniform russet by time. The experience of neglect and dereliction continues in the buildings below and we leave as buoyed up by possibility as we are weighed down by reality.

We are staying at an old Israeli hotel in town that has seen better days. The curtains in the lobby are grubby and frayed. Lumps of plaster have fallen off walls that nobody has thought to repair. Caked in dust I try to wash, but instead of producing water the taps in our room give a long, gasping inhalation when I turn them on. The mood at dinner is as sombre as Anne and Charles's two small children will allow.

'The place looks just the same as when we arrived in Egypt,' Anne says, pushing another scoop of mashed potato into her daughter's unwilling mouth.

'At least the tenders for renovations are due in next week,' Charles says.

In truth, none of us can imagine the work being completed for months. But Anne has heard from friends here that a new hotel in Na'ama Bay will open in two weeks. Several beers later we have a plan. Julie and I will come and live in the hotel until the Research Centre is finished, while Charles and Anne will make monthly visits. That way we can keep an eye on the renovations. Two days later we return to Ismailia in high spirits, knowing that the next time we come to Sharm it will be for good.

There is only so much piped hotel muzak that one can stand in a lifetime. After three months at the Ghazala Hotel, Julie and I have heard enough for several lives. But by early February 1988, we know our torment is nearly over. The villa is finished and we are to move imminently. There is a last-minute complication though. Khodair has assigned the villa promised to Anne and Charles to his new Research Centre manager, Captain Wessam Hafez. I am recalled to Ismailia urgently to help resolve the problem.

There comes a point where it is hard to ignore the possibility that malicious intent has infiltrated itself into the sluggish and impenetrable machinery of Egyptian bureaucracy. Charles has long since passed this point and scents the breath of schemers behind every setback and delay, whereas I still ascribe them to innocent cock-up and the legacy of British rule. When Egypt overthrew the British, instead of purging their complex and officious bureaucracy, Egyptians embraced it. Already tortuous procedures were elaborated – ostensibly to deter corruption – until they became oppressive.

I could see in the rash and slightly mad look in Charles's eyes this morning that the time he has spent here has taken its toll. 'They've known all along that we need two villas in Sharm!' Charles fumes as we stride towards Khodair's office. Is this just regular incompetence or an effort to lever Charles out? He is convinced of the latter. A more charitable explanation is that the university has simply failed to secure the space it needs at the Centre. But nobody will give us a straight answer. Instead, Abdul Aal insists, with his usual slipperiness, that there was never any agreement in the first place to hand over two villas.

Unexpectedly, Khodair is the only person in his office when we arrive. He glances up and his face hardens. 'Chippr'd, Roberts, how is your project?' Charles is so wound up that he unloads a furious outburst instead of exchanging pleasantries. It is a dreadful misjudgement. Khodair's base colour is rust, but over the course of two minutes his face flushes to temple-busting maroon. His neck swells so it overflows his collar, veins like strangler vines. Charles seems not to notice, or he doesn't care. The gates of his anger are open. I watch in panic. 'You're fired!' Khodair bellows. 'Clear your office and get off campus immediately.' Charles looks stunned for a moment, then oddly triumphant, having said exactly what he thought to Khodair for the first time, and the last.

We walk across campus in silence, lost in thought. It is mid-winter, but this morning has the feel of an English summer day. A fresh breeze has cleared the air and rustles flamboyant trees beside the road.

The next few weeks are hectic. Messages fly back and forth between Liverpool and Suez Canal universities and a visit by my bosses is hurriedly arranged. Egos are soothed. Charles's responsibilities move to myself and the project carries on. Julie and I move into our villa in Sharm. I am thrilled but daunted. There is a long way to go before we have a functional research base.

Captain Wessam, the Centre's new manager, is a former soldier and Suez Canal shipping pilot. I had met him briefly in Ismailia and was left uncertain what kind of neighbour he would make. He had the bearing of one used to taking life very seriously indeed, his eyebrows wrought like rock strata. He spoke in a plodding monotone, leaning in close and fixing me with a rigid military gaze. Among his many accomplishments (most of them readily self-proclaimed) was expertise in scuba diving. He had promised Khodair, he explained, that he would take personal charge of training our new students.

A week after moving in, Julie and I meet Wessam by the dive store for our first dive together. I don't know whether the question of the particular nature of Wessam's diving qualification has ever been raised. He seems vague when I ask, but tells me he learned in the navy. 'Was that where you got your instructor's qualification?' 'Yes, yes, instructor...' He breaks off to receive a note from a student and then disappears for twenty-five minutes, leaving the conversation unfinished.

That Wessam might be past his prime is not a possibility he has ever considered. But two decades have slipped by since he saw active service, and the struggle into his wetsuit – now much tighter than it once was – leaves him red-faced and breathless. He straps on a hugely weighted belt, tightens it beneath the overhang of his belly, heaves a tank over one shoulder and strides off in the direction of the beach. Julie and I gather our own gear and join him at the water's edge where we find him leaning on his tank panting heavily, sweat beading his forehead.

'Are you alright?' I ask.

'Yes, yes. Just checking my tank pressure,' he says, quickly picking up the contents gauge. We get ourselves ready while he regains composure. Fixing us with one of his most serious looks, the captain in him reasserts control.

'We will enter the water here, swim out thirty metres, and on my signal, descend.' He inflates his buoyancy vest until it rises around his face like an Elizabethan collar and sets forth, trailing us in his considerable wake as he swims offshore, blowing noisily like a seal.

Below us the sandy bottom deepens gradually, punctuated by coral patches several metres across. Some rise all the way to the surface like columns, festooned with fish. Wessam pulls up abruptly and waves us to a halt. Despite his buoyancy vest he is kicking hard to stay afloat. 'Ready? Then let's go,' he gasps, thrusting the regulator into his mouth and hitting the deflate button on the vest, triggering an eruption of bubbles. With a look of surprise, he drops like a stone. We watch as he grows smaller, legs peddling furiously until he crumples onto the bottom ten metres down, scattering fish and disappearing briefly in a cloud of sand. By the time we reach him he is sitting upright, huffing a cumulus of bubbles, mask half-full of water as he struggles to find the inflate button on his jacket. I place the hose into his hand and watch him rise to a sixty-degree angle as the collar expands around his cheeks. Assuming the lead once again, he jabs his hand in the direction of travel and begins to pedal, raising more sand and shattering a clump of coral. But a startled look has replaced the frown of command. We follow uneasily as Wessam wends a trail of destruction across the seabed, wincing at each casualty. But the ordeal is brief. Twenty minutes into the dive, Wessam stabs a finger in the direction of his contents gauge, whose pointer is now in the red, and orders our ascent.

With a fully inflated vest and more urgent pedalling, he regains the surface. Without waiting to see if we have followed, he rolls on his back, spits his regulator and heads for the beach. Julie and I follow at a leisurely distance, stretching our time with the fish as long as politeness permits. Wessam is waiting for us, hands on hips, his frown reset to its familiar intensity. Ignoring Julie, he looks me in the eye: 'Well, Roberts. That was not bad, but next time stay closer. You took too long to get to the bottom.'

My first batch of budding marine scientists is small: three women and three men. There are no textbooks on coral reef biology, so I have spent months constructing highly detailed lectures from a box of books and research papers brought from England. The students are enthusiastic and soon longing to get in the water to see the reef for themselves, but Wessam is too busy to teach them to dive. At last, after our Centre has been open for six months and the stream of contractors and labourers visiting his office has thinned to a trickle, he announces one morning that he will begin dive training. Despite my misgivings, which I haven't found a tactful way of expressing, Wessam arranges to meet our three male students by the dive store next morning. I come along with an offer of help but am really there to make sure nothing dangerous happens. He arrives fifteen minutes late, already dressed in his full wetsuit zipped to the neck, sweat streaming from his face in the June heat. The students are immediately ordered into their wetsuits and the lesson begins. Seeing them swelter through the basics of diving equipment for the next hour, I begin to feel this is more an endurance test than dive training.

At last, by now half-dead from heatstroke, they make their way to the water's edge. Wessam hasn't finished though, and for another half hour recaps much of what he has just said. Dehydrated and exhausted, the students step into the water. I pull on my tank and follow at a distance. Wessam is still lecturing them at the surface so I descend to the seabed five metres down, glad of respite from the heat. Four pairs of legs pedal for what seems like an age before the lesson finally moves underwater. Wessam hits the bottom with a thump and gestures for the students to gather round. He looks like a Native American chief sitting there, snorting bubbles like smoke signals as he runs through the rest of the lesson.

Later that afternoon, Wessam seeks me out. He glows with satisfaction as he recounts the lesson at length. I have to admit it is a success of sorts: no one died, no one was injured, and somewhere three students will be excitedly recounting to friends the story of their first dive.

Lessons continue, but not everyone is happy. Two students, Amany and Azza, come to see me one morning. Wessam refuses to teach them to dive because they are girls, they tell me. I promise to have a chat. To begin with, Wessam is uncompromising. It would be shameful, he says. I leave it there for now, but over the following weeks both Julie and I try to persuade him, as do Amany and Azza, who will not be fobbed off.

The pressure pays off. One day, Wessam announces to me that he has found a way. The girls will wear loose-fitting tracksuits over their wetsuits and keep their headscarves on underwater. We assemble the next morning and I watch as he puts Amany and Azza through the same heat endurance test before leading them to the sea. Seen from below, the girls look like exotic fish, their coloured headscarves trailing like fins. Wessam skips underwater mask removal for fear the headscarves will drift away.

For some time, Julie has wondered what to do with her life. With options rather limited, we hatch a plan for her to begin research for a Masters degree with Liverpool University. We have caught wind of proposals to develop Sharm-el-Sheikh as a resort. Even with the limited tourism here, it is evident that coral can be badly knocked about by divers and snorkelers. Julie picks up this problem to study, embarking on her own career as a marine scientist with me as field assistant.

It should have been simple. I had planned so carefully at the surface, spent hours laying out the matrix of electrical cable on the ground, tying corners and splicing wires. At the end, I had a three-by-three-metre square with nine one-metre squares within. This is to be the basic sampling unit for Julie's research. At each of three sites we will place two three-by-three squares in an area heavily used by tourists, and another two for comparison in a similar place nearby not used by tourists. This, Julie hopes, will tell her how much damage divers do in the course of their fun. And, by sampling the same spots three times over a year, she will find out whether damage is increasing. Today, we are trying it out for the first time.

We swim out through a narrow cleft at a popular site, 'The Tower'. On either side, the reef walls are deeply shadowed, while below us a tongue of sand darkens to obscurity as it slips offshore. The cable feels leaden in the water and I have a bag of metal stakes and a hammer to juggle as well. We descend in haste. Rounding the cliff, the reef broadens into sunlight, revealing a gentler slope covered in what looks like a forest of pink, purple and orange trees, shrunk to knee height. Their trunks and branches are translucent, veined with green and white, their canopies bushy, like sprouting broccoli. The water is clouded with fish whose orange, purple and maroon bodies echo the colours of the forest. With a broad sweep of her arm, Julie indicates a suitable spot and I swim for it, dumping the cable on a sand patch and pausing to catch my breath. Then I hand Julie two corners and point to where she should swim, taking the other two myself and setting off in the opposite direction. Within moments I am pulled up with a jerk. The cable, so carefully folded at the surface, looks like knotted spaghetti. Julie is still trying to swim away, pulling the ball into a Gordian tangle. I shout into my mouthpiece to get her attention.[1] With a quizzical look, she sees the knot and slowly comes back. Ten minutes of unravelling later we start again, but a loop catches a coral head, swiftly escalating into mess.

By now I am cross. Frowning into my mask and gesturing vigorously we unravel and start again. Same result. With half the dive gone and nothing achieved I am in a red fury. Julie gives me a withering look, so to get her full attention I grab her regulator and pull it out of her mouth. I certainly have it now! Her expression changes rapidly, first shock, then disappointment, then simmering rage. Her eyes follow me dangerously as we try once more. This time, it works, but my attempts at light-hearted underwater congratulation are rebuffed. I have pulled the pin from this grenade and am helpless to prevent the explosion that will come at the surface. I hammer in a marker stake at each corner, lingering as long as bottom time allows to delay the inevitable.

All marriages have rough patches, I console myself several days later, lines that should not be crossed. Removing my wife's regulator

---

1. You can't talk but you can make a loud noise underwater.

underwater is now firmly implanted in my mind as a line not to cross again. A couple more dives and we lay out the sample frame in minutes with the grace of aquatic ballet dancers; harmony restored.

By now the Research Centre has begun to deserve its prefix. Ashraf, one of our Masters students, is affable, humorous, tall and flabby. He speaks softly too, in precise, lightly accented English and moves with a languid, energy-saving shuffle, shoulders thrust backwards to counterbalance his wobbling stomach. Appropriately enough, his Egyptian supervisor Salah has decided that Ashraf should study a soft-bottomed habitat. So somewhat reluctantly, he arrives in Sharm-el-Sheikh one day and announces that he is here to investigate mangrove forest fishes for the next twelve months. It soon becomes clear that Ashraf and Sharm-el-Sheikh are not well matched. I am not sure what he might consider his natural habitat to be, but it isn't roughing it with the rest of the students in oven-hot concrete boxes with broken air conditioners.

Ashraf has a vague idea of what he is supposed to do, which, he tells me, is to catch fish in tidal mangrove creeks with a beach seine net. This is a long, narrow rectangle of net with floats at the top and weights at the bottom which is pulled at each end by one or more people, dragging fish with it until the water is shallow enough to stop them escaping. On a clear morning in September, I take Ashraf and a friend of his from Ismailia to Sharm's best-developed mangrove – a scruffy patch of only a few hectares – to try things out. Mangroves are not easy places to work, as I discovered in Saudi Arabia. Watching the mangrove team come back from the field exhausted, caked head to toe in mud and savaged by biting flies, I had many times congratulated myself that I worked underwater.

The morning is breathless and the sea looking-glass smooth. An egret traces tiny ripples along the water's edge, its body alabaster white against reflected sky. Two wagtails work the strandline for flies against a crystalline sparkle of salt. By the time we have unloaded Ashraf's net, we are slick with sweat, or at least two of us are. Ashraf has busied himself with notebook and specimen jars. We pick our way carefully through the dense stick-root palisades that surround the trees. Water trickles among the roots and creeps across the shallow mudflat, warming it in the sun. It has a pleasant bathtub feel now but by late afternoon it will sting like a salt poultice. At every step, I sink calf-deep into black, sucking mud. Carrying the net shoulder-high, we head into the trees, aiming for a creek that runs through the heart of the wood. The canopy closes over and for a moment there is welcome shade before a cloud of insects materialises and settles onto every patch of exposed skin, seeming to know that with hands full we are powerless to resist.

Just when I feel I can stand it no longer, the trees part and the bottom slopes into a channel four or five metres wide. Sunlight filters through gaps in the canopy, greening the water surface. Leaving Ashraf and his friend on the bank with one end of the net, I unfold the other across the creek. The water is opaque like milky tea and I imagine stingrays at every footstep. By mid-channel I am chest-deep and the net presses me into ankle-swallowing mud. But with a few more steps the bottom turns upward and I climb to the other side. We begin a laborious drag along the creek, the net snagging roots every few paces, the water heavy in its meshes. I wonder whether any fish can be sluggish or stupid enough to get caught. But by the time we reach the creek head, a mass of mud-tarnished silver writhes in the net.

'Run and get the sample bottles, Ashraf,' I say, 'before this lot escapes.' Ashraf turns to his friend and says something in Arabic, and the friend goes to get them. I raise a quizzical eyebrow. Washed clean of mud, the fish are mostly tiny, gleaming like coins. We make two more sweeps of different channels before lack of jars and fierce midday heat force us to leave. Ashraf will have to repeat these samples every month for the next year, so that evening I suggest he enlists another student to help with future sampling. He looks a little uncertain, as if he has other plans, but then seems to agree.

Where Ashraf is laid-back, one of my own students, Mohammed, buzzes with nervous energy. Every morning he exercises furiously in his room, beating out press-ups and squat thrusts with an enthusiasm he also applies to his prayers, five times a day. He rarely wears anything other than a pal-blue tracksuit, which by the time he nears the end of his two-week-long visits to Sharm, has acquired a ripe bouquet. One evening, shortly before he is to make a trip back home, I call on him with Julie to take him for dinner. 'Just a minute,' he says, grabbing a bottle from the shelf and spraying it all over his tracksuit. It is a fragrance I can never forget: 'One Man Show'.

As well as his research on groupers, a family of predatory fish abundant on Sharm's reefs, Professor Ghobashy has asked Mohammed and his friend, also called Mohammed, to make a museum for the benefit of visiting dignitaries. I had been shown a museum of sorts on my first visit, a shabby collection of varnished turtle shells, dugong bones, dried pufferfish and chipped corals. I have never understood the appeal of dead creatures when the living are so close at hand. Apart from dugongs, which had long ago been hunted to a few lonely individuals, a fifty-metre walk would be sufficient to find every one of the museum's species in hearty, full-blooded health. But my arguments were scoffed at. Surely I could see, they said, how undignified it would be for dignitaries to get in the water? So now that our Centre is up and running, a more elaborate museum is called for.

The two Mohammeds embrace the task with the passion of Victorian naturalists, but sadly without their skills. Corals are prised off the reef just in front of the Centre, to my dismay, and sun-dried with their tissues still present. Rather than bone-white skeletons, these corals are shiny browns and pinks, and reek fishy smells. Fish are speared, gutted and dried, distorting their bodies and turning brilliant colours a uniform grey. Mohammed appears fretful and confides one day that he is concerned Professor Ghobashy will be disappointed. But the next day I find him cheerful again. Another student has given him her paints. He can barely wait to see my reaction as he half drags me into the lab. Six butterflyfish lie on the bench, covered in gaudy daubs of acrylic that make patterns never before seen in nature. I stare at them for a long time, wondering how to suggest that it would have been better to stick to the original colour schemes. When I look up, Mohammed has his arms folded and a broad smile on his face, waiting for the expected praise. 'Professor Ghobashy will love them,' I tell him, which satisfies both of us.

Most of the time, three of our neighbouring villas lie empty and shuttered. But every now and then they are the focus of intense activity. There is little warning of President Mubarak's visits: a day at most. The first time it happens I am confronted by a sinister black car parked near my house as I mount the last few stairs up the cliff, still wet from a dive. A man sits in the driver's seat in mirrored aviator sunglasses and black suit with the engine running and air conditioner on. The driver's sunglasses, inscrutable as beetle eyes, follow me as I walk into my house.

I change quickly and head next door to ask Wessam what is going on. Two men are just leaving. They glower briefly on the way past, their black suits incongruous in the wilting sun. Wessam is seeing them out with obsequious little bows and honeyed platitudes.

'Who are they?' I ask after they are safely back in the car.

Wessam adopts his most solemn face, the one he saves for Khodair and other VIPs: 'President Mubarak is coming tomorrow for three days. They are his security men. We must all leave by tonight; you, Julie, everyone. Only one caretaker can stay. Now if you will excuse me, I must tell everyone. There is no time to waste.'

By late afternoon, Julie and I have the car loaded and are ready to leave for Ismailia. Although this is unplanned, trips north are always useful to restock and meet with administrators and teaching staff. I pull all the external window blinds down on my house and lock them shut before leaving, although I can't imagine any security risk with the compound full of Mubarak's men.

We return several days later, arriving a few hours after Wessam. He is frowning so severely that his eyebrows nearly touch. 'Well, Roberts! The caretaker tells me you caused a security incident by pulling down your shutters. The military wanted to break into your villa to make sure nobody was hiding inside. He begged them not to.'

'So what happened?' I ask, seeing that nothing has been disturbed.

'They stationed a man on your patio pointing a machine gun at your house.'

Egypt has been jittery since Sadat was assassinated by extremists from the Muslim Brotherhood seven years before. Next time, we leave the shutters open.

Most of the time Mubarak is an undemanding neighbour. There is another benefit too. His villa is the only one with a garden. The university has to truck water in daily, so it is far too precious to waste on plants. But Mubarak has his own water tank and the caretaker uses it to irrigate a sparse display of flowers. When the caretaker has his afternoon nap, I sometimes jump over the wall to gather an armful of basil for pesto. Despite the flowers, Mubarak's villa is far from presidential, just two tiny bedrooms and a living room no bigger than that of a small family home. Perhaps he enjoys escaping the opulence of power from time to time? Does he like the reefs, I wonder?

With my daytime routine now well established, Julie and I at last have time to explore the reefs by night. Tonight is dark and moonless, the sea glassy black. We feel our way down rusty iron steps that bridge a short drop from cliff to water's edge. Water laps the shore with a soft repeated hiss, the slumbering breaths of a night sea. There is a clammy whiff of sunbaked seaweed and brine. Tiny silver fish leap in the light of our torches as we cross the reef platform, while bigger fish, stunned from sleep, blunder into darkness and unseen corals. At the reef edge, there is a light current flowing towards the headland so we descend quickly, following our light beams.

Brick-red fish with goggling mirror eyes scud in and out of the pool of light cast by our torches while loose shoals of translucent fish pick plankton from the water. I spot a sleeping parrotfish beneath a ledge, its body cocooned in a mucous bubble it blew around itself at nightfall. Although nobody is sure, the bubble is thought to disguise its scent from predators. I can't help feeling that those predators are lurking in the darkness. I check in Julie's direction and she waves her torch at my eyes. Blinded, I brush against something hard as I swim over, scratching my knee painfully and making me curse into my regulator. She has found a snail the size of a rubber glove: a Spanish dancer. I lift it off the reef gently and release it above the coral. The snail begins a writhing dance, its fringes flapping like the crimson pleats of a flamenco dress.

We move on down the slope, threading our way between dark columns, watchful for half-seen movements at the edge of visibility. Coral heads appear starkly bright in the light. Close up, the spaces between their branches vibrate with huddled damselfish, startled from sleep and nervous at the attention. The slope is steeper here, which means the current has pushed us towards the point. Julie is waving her torch at me again but the beam seems less dazzling. I move towards her wondering what she has found, but instead she points at the torch. The beam is definitely weaker, which is puzzling since we put new batteries into both torches before the dive. In the next few minutes her light fades to a red glow. The first rule of night diving is to abort the dive if a torch fails. But we have only been in the water twenty minutes and I'm damned if we are leaving already. Julie looks nervous as I gesture for us to continue. We still have my torch at least.

I check my depth gauge: 15 m down. There is a cave somewhere around here, which I want to see. By day it contains a shape-shifting mass of mirror-sided glassfish, and wedge-shaped hatchet fish, their bulging eyes ringed in yellow. Moving deeper, I spot a familiar clump of soft coral that marks the ledge overhanging the cave. Its feathery tips glow blood red and orange in my light. Shapes fill the water beyond, scintillating like chandelier crystals; the glassfish have left the cave. Something is wrong though, the illuminated fish at the edge of visibility are fading and the scene contracting. My torch is failing too. Julie's face is pressed close to mine now and the eyes in her mask are wide with fear. Bloody Egyptian batteries. Yet another thing that doesn't work!

I have been reading Jonathan Raban's *Arabia Through the Looking Glass*, and a passage about Egypt comes to mind:

'It is broken.' It was a universal explanation. The telephone system was 'broken'; the Semiramis Hotel across the river was 'broken'; the meters on the taxis were 'broken'. It was like living in a house where the cups fell off handles when you pick them up, where every light bulb blows when you switch it on, where the vacuum cleaner coughs gobbets of dust over the carpets it is supposed to sweep, where legs fall of chairs, beds collapse, ceilings are not to be trusted and the plumbing is a maze of burst pipes and blocked drains...It requires a certain philosophy to accept breakage on such a massive and continual scale, but once one has adjusted to the idea that nothing is likely to work, and when you find something that does, it is an occasion for a modest little celebration, one can be happy enough.'

The filament of my torch bulb glows like an ember, then winks out. The darkness is so complete it is physical, stultifying. I have been in Egypt long enough to be philosophical most of the time, but torches failing on night dives strain my composure. Perhaps we should have told somebody we were going for a dive (is that the first rule of night diving and torches the second?). I hold Julie tight. Finding her hand, I give her the signal to wait while our eyes adjust. My hand ignites a stream of sparks in the inky black. I wave it in front of us weaving a sparkler trail. Julie tries it, then writes her name in bold letters of planktonic fire. The phosphorescence is incredible. With no torches to dim the show, it crackles with every movement. My night vision restored, I now see the vague outlines of fish as they throw flashes of their own. Tiny sparks suggest the shapes of corals and sea fans where plankton is washing onto them with the current.

With vigorous waving I create my own current, setting off a welder's cascade of sparks to light up the reef around me.

We forget to be worried in the childish joy of this newly acquired superpower. Then a brighter light catches my attention, about the size and shape of a cat's eye, and I grab Julie to stop her waving. The sparks fade to darkness and I point out the eye. There are two now, shining a cool, pure light in our direction. Swimming toward them gingerly, I see another light, then several more pairs, moving about and winking on and off. As we round a dark mass of reef suddenly there are dozens of lights in motion. They belong to fish – flashlight fish. We lose our flashlights only to replace them with their living namesake! These creatures normally live far below diving depths, but at this headland, where the reef sheers upward from the abyss, they come nearer to the surface. The eyes are not eyes at all, but cheek patches filled with luminescent bacteria. Only one patch is visible from the side, but both can be seen when the fish turns head-on, looking like the headlamps on Batman's car. If glimpsed by day, which they rarely are, these fish are like shadows among the shadowy interstices of the reef. Their bodies are smaller than the palm of a hand and are coloured charcoal touched with brown, like partially burnt logs. We watch for ten or fifteen minutes, hypnotised by the bobbing light show made by the feeding fish, undulating like fireflies. At last we tear ourselves away, ascending towards a surface only vaguely paler than the void around us, throwing off cascades of sparks. I take my regulator from my mouth and upend it to create a free-flowing fountain of sparks from the surging air.

We break the surface far from our entry point having been wafted around the headland. Above us the Milky Way pours a river of light across the night sky, a mirror to the planktonic constellations below.

Whenever we get the chance, Julie and I head for Ras Mohammed, an iconic finger of land that extends ten kilometres offshore at Sinai's southern extremity. In the 1970s, while under Israeli control, it became a mecca for shark-diving thrill seekers. To the east, cliffs rise vertically above a narrow reef, while the west coast slopes gently offshore into a sprawl of mudflats and seagrass beds. The most dramatic dives are beneath a fawn-coloured bluff, dubbed the 'Shark Observatory'. Here the reef plunges so steeply that a stone flung from the cliff edge wouldn't hit the bottom until it was 500 m down. For reasons much speculated about among our friends who run local dive centres, there are not many sharks here these days. The famed shoals of hammerheads, much talked of since Jacques Cousteau's visits, have gone.

Ras Mohammed was protected by the Israelis, and after they returned Sinai it was quickly designated a National Park by Egypt in 1983. Although activities like spearfishing and coral collecting are banned there has been nothing much in the way of management. Then in 1988, another European assistance project arrives in Sharm, and with it a young couple, Michael and Connie Pearson. Its aims are courageous, given what I have discovered about the intransigence of Egyptian officialdom. Not only do they want to write a management plan and put rangers on the ground and at sea, but they plan to expand the park inland and along the coast into the Gulf of Aqaba. Michael is some ten years older than me, which will be an advantage, and comes across as energetic, opinionated and belligerent. It remains to be seen whether the latter qualities will help or hinder. In an early conversation, he tells me to make the most of Sharm's rugged charm. Plans are being laid in Cairo to turn South Sinai into an international tourism hub, an Egyptian Gold Coast. Julie's choice of research topic was prescient, I think.

'My job,' Michael tells me firmly, 'is to make sure it doesn't become another Costa Brava. The environment makes this place special. I want it to stay that way.' I wish him well. Neither of us realise just how crucial his project will become.

CHAPTER EIGHT

Moving a research centre

Egypt, 1988–90

THE LIGHT HERE IS DIM AND ETHEREAL. Far above, the restless surface fragments the light into indigo and cobalt flakes, like the stained glass of cathedral windows. But this vaulted ocean nave is twice the height of any cathedral and the fairground kaleidoscope of the shallows has been supplanted in the deep by dark coral plates spread out to catch the meagre light. Feathery soft corals cover the bottom, their plush tentacle crowns mouthing the slight current. Further downslope, I spot a fish I have never seen, so I tilt and glide towards it, writing a hurried description. I feel a light-headed calm, as if I'm floating in a warm cocoon. The soft coral tentacles beat with mesmeric purposefulness and exhaled bubbles ring like church bells. The rapture of the deep has me in its embrace.

I check my depth gauge – 55m – then roll sideways to look up. Julie and Richard, one of my Liverpool bosses here for a visit, are ten metres above, silhouetted against the distant surface. Richard gestures anxiously for me to ascend but I pretend not to see. This place is too restful to leave so soon. The scene is rendered in a subdued and restricted palette from the cool end of the spectrum, like the subterranean bar of a chic hotel. The fish appear less gaudy, the light emphasising pattern over colour, picking out contrasting stripes and swirls. Below, an unusual coral catches my eye and I drop deeper. Its large, greenish polyps fluoresce in the half-light. Fifty-eight metres on the gauge. Two more and that will be sixty; in less than a minute sixty appears on the gauge as I drift downslope. I roll again to check Richard and Julie and am jolted from my thoughts by Richard's arm pumping up and down, thumb upwards in urgent recall. Wondering what can be the matter, I shift course and rise to join them. His eyes bulge madly in his mask while Julie looks oddly detached. We rise up the reef slope pulled by the expanding air inside our buoyancy vests, venting at intervals to keep to a safe speed.

The ascent feels like a passage from pre-dawn twilight to new day as colours bleed back into corals and fish. My bubbles stop jangling and my head clears, as though coming round from a sedative. Enticed by depth, I had strayed dangerously into the zone of nitrogen narcosis, as Richard had seen. Most reefs around Sharm tumble vertically from their seaward edge until, somewhere between ten and twenty metres down, they veer off at an angle, sliding into the blue belly of the sea. The continuity of that slope lures divers, whether out of a sense of adventure or the pursuit of unknown creatures. The sport-diving limit was thenforty metres,[1] close to the edge of nitrogen narcosis. Extra nitrogen dissolved in the blood at depth makes you light-headed and drains reason just when you most need it – this is what's known as the 'rapture of the deep'. Within a year of our arrival in Sharm, two Israelis lost their lives attempting to navigate a submerged arch sixty metres down.[2] Despite this omen, it has

1.   It is thirty metres now.

2.   This site, The Blue Hole, near Dahab, has since claimed more than 100 further
     victims and has been called the deadliest dive in the world.

become a habit for Julie and me to start any pleasure dive with a plunge to forty-five metres or so, just to see what is there, before working our way slowly up the reef. At ten metres or less, we decompress gently and drink the last of our tanks in the richest part of the reef.

Frustratingly, all the obvious fish – by that I mean the damselfish, butterflyfish or surgeonfish of my research – seem to have been named already. But there is always a chance of something new at the edges of the known world, in other words, beyond the limits of safe diving. I am in awe of Jack Randall, a globe-trotting ichthyologist from Hawaii who has described more new fish than anyone else alive.[1] Jack has dived all over the Red Sea and written the definitive guide to its fish. His latest papers are about fish taken from sixty, seventy, even eighty metres deep. A little angelfish from French Polynesia, caught far below the realm of common sense, he named *Centropyge narcosis*. Reading the description, I wonder how much longer it will be before Jack is feeding the fishes.[2]

I have been in Sharm-el-Sheikh for eighteen months, halfway into a three-year contract. Against the odds (it feels) we have a working Research Centre, a group of (mostly) happy and enthusiastic students. With a new generation in training, the hoped-for renaissance in Egyptian marine science is underway. At last I spend more time teaching and supervising student research than wrestling administrators and recalcitrant construction companies. The days are full and there is a buzz about the place that continues late into the night.

Not everything is harmonious, however. A few of the Egyptian lecturers, finding little to interest them in coral reefs, resent every trip south away from family and the comforts of Ismailia. One

---

1. At over 730 species and still counting, Jack has now described more new fish species than anyone in history.

2. At the time writing, Jack is alive and well and still describing new fishes. He celebrated his 90th birthday in 2014 with a scuba dive.

such is Said Farghaly, a long-standing staff member, and, by his own assessment, the only scientist of international standing on the faculty. He trained in France some fifteen years before and there picked up the mannerisms of the French academic elite, to the irritation of his colleagues. I soon find myself in bitter argument with him over his poor treatment of the students. He sets them menial tasks to further his work, denying them time for their own research. Egypt is intensely hierarchical, like some ancient European dukedom, each level seeming to wield absolute power over the one below. Careers prosper or wither depending on favour from above. Those lower in the hierarchy are squeezed ruthlessly by those above. No doubt Farghaly was once abused by his superiors. One day, I have it out with him with several students present, causing him to flounce off. Later, alone, he berates me for humiliating him. Underneath my expressed contrition, I am glad the point has hit its target. But I will come to regret making an enemy of Farghaly.

First impressions proved misleading. I quickly grew to love Sharm's harsh grandeur: the saffron cliffs that gild the dark sea's edge; the parched rivulets of pebbles that vein the plains; the gentle rise through scree to ragged volcanic mountains. Their weathered peaks etch the horizon, flaming at sunrise and sunset in marbled cinnamon and butterscotch. This inhospitable landscape feels ancient as time itself. It has played backdrop to classic scenes from the Bible, Talmud and Koran, while hieroglyphs cut into the cliffs speak of earlier civilisations. Walking through this desert is a journey through history.

Until now, excitement, crises and the humdrum routine of establishing a new institution have consumed me almost completely. My own research has been on hold and I am desperate to rekindle the search for the secret of coral reef mega-diversity. I have brought to Egypt a new enthusiasm for a very old method: listing species. Birdwatchers everywhere love to list the species they see. I used to see this as little more than a quaint habit, or obsession, until I met Sir Peter Scott. By good luck, Sir Peter gave me my first job fresh out of my PhD. He approached Rupert, wondering whether any use could be made of the meticulous lists of coral reef fish he had created in decades of world travel.

After several exchanges of letters, Rupert and I drove to meet him in November 1987 at his home at the Wildfowl and Wetlands Trust near Bristol. Then in his seventies, Sir Peter was a gentle, almost meek figure, a man of middling height with owlish glasses and golden corduroy trousers. Not at all what I expected for a man of his achievements. His house was mired in the heart of a wetland owned by one of several conservation bodies he had founded. In his living room, a floor to ceiling window opened directly to a lake where a boisterous crowd of waterbirds jostled in the glow of a late autumn afternoon. Several towering swans stood on a wooden deck beyond the glass, their bills vivid yellow and black. 'Those Bewick swans are just back from Siberia,' he told us. 'One of my favourites.' Reaching for a book on his desk, he showed us page after page of painted portraits of Bewicks just like them, each viewed from left, right and centre like police mug shots. Every beak had a different pattern, every swan a name, and this was the family album. I was struck by the delicacy and skill of these likenesses.

Sir Peter was a colossus in the world of conservation. He co-founded the World Wildlife Fund in the 1960s, designed its famous panda logo and started the Species Survival Commission. The latter body establishes conservation plans for endangered plants and animals and orchestrates the Red List of Threatened Species, the definitive accounting of the world's diminishing biota. Like many conservationists, he had as a young man preferred shooting, blasting his way through thousands of waterbirds. In one of those Karmic acts of reconciliation, he devoted his later years to saving nature, especially wildfowl.

Somehow, in this already extraordinary life, he also won a yachting medal at Hitler's 1936 Olympics, was decorated for gallantry in World War II, became a record-breaking glider pilot, and was a prolific author and respected television presenter. Perhaps life lived at such a frenzied pace was the inevitable outcome of being the only son of a famous polar explorer. No wonder I was taken aback by his modest charm.

It was Sir Peter's diaries that we went to see. Spread across a metre or so of shelf were more than twenty artists' notebooks, all about six by eight inches, and one-and-a-half inches thick. Most were stained and worn through heavy use and lengthy travel. He took one down and handed it to Rupert, who opened it reverently and began to leaf through. The pages crawled with glossy lizards and opalescent beetles, swam with coral reef fishes, took dramatic flight with parrots, and were redolent of the imagined scents of gorgeous blooms. All were rendered in the same beautiful hand that created the swan portraits. The text too was a work of art, interweaving in a precise script the stories of his travels with descriptions of plants and animals. There were long lists of coral reef fishes whenever the itinerary moved to tropical shores.[1]

Over two days with Sir Peter that would live forever in my memory, lake-bound amid a splashing cacophony of waterfowl, Rupert and I photocopied every reef fish list and sketch we could find. By the end, we had a sheaf of hundreds of pages, with lists from places scattered all the way around the tropics. Back in York, I cross-checked every identification, found the name of every species drawn and used the lists to plot their geographic ranges. Five months later I had an encyclopaedic knowledge of coral reef fish. But prolific as they were, Sir Peter's notes were too fragmentary to publish, leaving great holes in species' ranges in the places he had not visited. They did, however, lay the foundation for something more substantial, more thorough, something I could make a mark with myself. I would begin in the Red Sea.

---

1. Sir Peter's diaries have been published in extracted form as a series of books.

Many of the fish here are familiar from Saudi Arabia. Like those further south, the reefs plummet into deep, clear water, although the fringe that edges the shore is narrower. The narrowing continues north into the Gulf of Aqaba, the tentacle of sea that borders Sinai's eastern coast. Reef width is a quick way of telling how favourable conditions are for coral growth. Reefs grow upwards until they are stopped at the surface, but can extend offshore much farther, so the width of the reef reflects how fast it has grown seawards since the last Ice Age ended.

Coral reefs find their sweet spot in the central Red Sea, where the water is warm and clear. In the south, it is too turbid for vigorous growth, while the far northern Gulfs are at the edge of viability. The desert burns by summer but gets cold enough in winter for snow to sometimes frost the peaks of central Sinai. Winter winds from the mountains cool the sea to temperatures that only a thick wetsuit can make comfortable. The corals manage, just. At a minimum of 18°C, this is as cool as a reef can take and still flourish. To add further stress, no permanent rivers flow into the Red Sea, so intense evaporation drags a flow of water from the Indian Ocean, to set up a gradient of increasing saltiness going north.

On one of our early forays into the Gulf of Aqaba, I was fascinated by a fleeting glimpse of a fish. Slender and no bigger than a mouse, it slipped behind a coral almost before I had registered its presence. It had the sparse colours of a Japanese watercolour: pale grey with a dusky brushstroke along its back, a dab of blue on each cheek, and a flowing dorsal fin peppered with black. It wouldn't come out again, but I had seen enough: *Pseudochromis pesi*, the pale dottyback. According to Jack Randall, this is one of a handful of species only known to exist in the Gulf of Aqaba.[1] That makes it a great rarity as well as a conundrum. The conventional wisdom that I was taught has it that marine

---

1. More recently, it has been photographed just outside the Gulf of Aqaba too.

creatures are geographically widespread with large ranges. Most species either lay eggs on the seabed and tend them for a few days until they hatch into larvae and drift away in the plankton, or they release eggs directly into open water, never to see their young again. This rootless start, drifting who-knows-where at the whim of ocean currents, seems at odds with a small geographic range. How, I wonder, can a fish have a small geographic range if it surrenders itself to the wandering water masses that swash above these reefs? There are parallels here with the abrupt change in fish communities that I saw in Arabia between the central and southern Red Sea. The patterns point to some force preventing larvae from dispersing freely with currents, or preventing their survival when they do.

This puzzle begins to resolve into a working hypothesis (I like that word) when Julie and I take several of our students on a foray into the Gulf of Suez. We charter an old Baltic icebreaker that is seeing out its rusty years here. The Gulf of Suez is very different from the Gulf of Aqaba and the Red Sea. Where they plunge into a thousand-metre abyss, here depths are measured in tens of metres. The bottom is sandy and the water clouded with silt, much like the southern reaches of Arabia. As we cruise north into the Gulf, the character of the reefs shifts rapidly. Fish I haven't seen since southern Saudi Arabia reappear, such as hooded butterflyfish with their chocolate cowls, and powder-blue Arabian angelfish, whose yellow-flag tails and crescented flanks glow in the murk.

What I need to make sense of, I ponder one evening while resting at anchor, is why there aren't more fish here typical of the reefs around Sharm. Water streams north more or less continuously to replace evaporative losses. It must carry legions of tiny larvae with it just as currents should mix larvae between the very different central and southern Red Sea reefs. That same thought from southern Arabia comes back to me now. Even if the habitat here isn't ideal, it would surely be better for a larva to parachute onto a sub-optimal reef and try its luck, rather than face certain death in the plankton. But I see no tiny juveniles of these species here, which gets me wondering: what if none survive the planktonic journey?

Up to now the action in coral reef science has concentrated on creatures living on the reef or newly arrived. When the planktonic life stage is considered, it is only as a supply of new arrivals. Those arrivals are obvious enough on the reefs. Earlier in the day, I found a halo of glassy fish, each no bigger than a fingernail, hovering above a rounded yellow coral head. Having survived the perils of their planktonic odyssey, they now had to take their chances on the reef. Many would not last a single day and night. An old ichthyological adage says that the average fish lives ten minutes, given the billions of eggs spawned and the minuscule number that make it to adulthood. It's not quite that bad, but eggs, larvae and juvenile fish are on the menu for a terrifying number of other reef creatures. No reef scientists, so far as I know, have thought about the open sea as a habitat for larvae. What if the creatures typical of deep, clear-water reefs have larvae that require clear oceanic water to survive? This could work the other way around. If the ones that thrive on silty reefs need cloudy water as larvae, then differences in survival rates in different water bodies might keep the communities separate. I do a few back-of-the-envelope calculations and discover that it would only take a difference in daily survival rates of a few percentage points to keep the communities of these different water masses distinct.

There is no better feeling in science than coming up with an original idea. At last I am thinking for myself. Scientists have long apprenticeships. To begin with you follow in others' footsteps, weighing their ideas, challenging their interpretations, like young elephant seals testing themselves against grizzled beachmasters who have seized the best spots. It is a combative process played out over years. Successful, established scientists are those who overthrew the beachmasters of their day. However, instead of keeping truly open minds, as we are taught good scientists must, many hunker down and expend their energies in later life shoring up their own ideas.

If scientific ideas are sound, they should remain impregnable. But most eventually are overwhelmed by fresh thinking, better methods or even new fashions. Thomas Kuhn, a philosopher of science whose ideas I have just then come across, reckons that science proceeds as a series of revolutions in which new ways of thinking depose the old in sudden waves of acceptance. Some wits point out that these revolutions only occur when the strongest proponents of particular paradigms retire, or die.

Halfway through our project, we gain a jetty across the reef in front of the Centre. It's not the kind I wanted. Instead of the neat wooden boardwalk I had in mind, Wessam brought in friends from the Suez Canal Authority to advise. What we needed, they said, was a series of floating steel pontoons bolted together and anchored at the beach end. I pleaded with Wessam not to waste money. Such a jetty might work in the calm of a canal, but this is the open sea. A southerly blow could take out a clunking jetty such as this.

By this stage, I was used to being ignored. Egyptians have a great respect for expertise. In the matter of fish names I might be peerless, but without an engineering qualification I have nothing worthwhile to say on jetties. It was this same respect for expert advice that led them to accept the foreman's recommendation that the water pipe from the sea to the wet lab need only be buried ten centimetres deep rather than the minimum of fifty I advised. In mid-summer, the water reached the aquaria at over 40°C, broiling their inhabitants. It was the same with rewiring the wet lab. The electrician brought two-core sockets instead of three, bending the earth wires out of the way. My protests were met with a condescending look and an implicit 'are you an electrician?'

From my clifftop vantage, the jetty I am looking at with mounting concern on this blustery morning is a steel behemoth. In the few weeks since installation, the three one-tonne sections have already pounded underlying corals to stone chips. Today the wind has set up a sharp chop. It wouldn't trouble a swimmer, but the jetty is making heavy weather, lurching from side to side and whiplashing the steel cables that fix it to the beach. I hurry to Wessam's house, finding that he is already on his way to muster help. Running to the beach I am brought up short by an agonising pain in the toe. Some damn fool has driven a steel spike into the ground right in the middle of the path. I stop and look at the blood trickling from my foot, but there is no time to linger so I pull out the spike and half run, half hop the rest of the way.

The beach is chaotic. Wessam has mustered the labourers to help. Several have hold of the cables but are being jerked about like dolls by the lurching jetty. The anchor points have been bent flat and their concrete foundations are cracking. I grab a cable only to be flung clear. Wessam bellows orders, his voice booming above the crash of waves. A few minutes later, the first cable wrenches from the ground, quickly followed by the second. Freed from restraint, the jetty begins a brief and highly destructive passage from reef to beach, steel shrieking on rock. The labourers flop onto the sand, soaked by sea and sweat. His face drawn, the lines at the edges of his mouth taut, Wessam surveys the ruin of our jetty, for once speechless.

With the labourers left to secure the wreck, I hobble back to the Centre to look for the obstruction that cut my toe. The steel pin lies where I had thrown it. I didn't notice in my haste, but there is plastic flagging tape tied to one end. Looking around, there is another spike about ten metres away and two more by the side of the road. I pull them out and put them in the lab. I'll have it out with the culprit later, whoever that might be.

I ask around the students, but all deny any knowledge until I speak to Amany, who tells me that she saw some men with surveying equipment taking measurements early that morning. It is typical, I brood, my toe still throbbing, that the university would have plans for the Centre that nobody has thought to tell me about. I confront Wessam later, but he has no idea either and demands to see the spikes. I bring them to his office but they offer up no further clues. As I turn to leave, he says, looking severe, 'Wait a moment, there is something else. The librarians have been complaining that Ashraf kept them in the water at the mangrove for three hours this morning catching fish.'

'The librarians?' I ask, puzzled. 'Do you mean the labourers?'

'Yes, that is what I said. They are very unhappy.'

The so-and-so! That's why Ashraf looked shifty when I asked him to find another student to help. Poor labourers. They have enough to do without freezing on Ashraf's behalf.

Next morning I rise early, hoping to intercept the mystery surveyors. The wind has turned overnight and blows hard from the desert, bringing a winter nip. The air is gritty and the sun glows weakly behind an ochre dust pall that blurs distant mountains. There is a truck parked down below, from which three men are unloading survey equipment. I am in luck. I hurry down and stride over to the one who looks like he is in charge.

'What are you doing?' I ask, hoping his English is better than my Arabic.

He replies in halting but perplexing English. Instead of Suez Canal University, he tells me they are here to survey the site for the Abu Dhabi Investment Company.

There must be some mistake, I explain, this is the Madrassat el Bea, the Marine Research Centre of Suez Canal University. He is adamant though. I ask him to follow me. Wessam will sort it out.

Wessam is eating breakfast in striped pyjamas. He greets the surveyor cordially and after a brief explanation from me, asks to see his papers. Everyone in Egypt has papers. Nothing can be done without a clutch of permits battered with official stamps and signatures. Wiping butter from his fingers, Wessam takes the papers and begins to read slowly. His expression stiffens as he turns the pages. One is from the Ministry of Reconstruction and one from the governor of South Sinai. They grant permission to the Abu Dhabi Investment Company to survey the site in preparation for the construction of a luxury hotel. There is nothing from Suez Canal University. Wessam is as confused as I am now and interrogates them at length in Arabic while I struggle to catch the gist. An hour later, the surveyor leaves having been told his team cannot work here until they bring permission from the University.

Wessam wastes no time. Khodair is away, but at length he reaches the university vice president. On hearing Wessam's news he is angry that Khodair has not told him about a matter of such importance. Calls will be made, he promises. Wessam stays close to the phone all day but it doesn't ring. Finally, at eight o'clock, the call comes but it is not the news we expect. When Wessam puts the phone down his face is grave: 'President Mubarak has given this place to Sheikh Zayed of Abu Dhabi to build a hotel. We have been told to cooperate with the surveyors.' I hear the words but can't believe them.

'Surely there is a mistake?'

Wessam shakes his head. 'Even Khodair didn't know,' he says.

Suddenly I feel an urgent need for fresh air. Several dozen cockroaches streak away from the light as I open the door. There is a smell of drain on the night air.

Julie is appalled, but after her initial shock suggests that having only seen this place empty on his visits, Mubarak probably thought it was derelict. If we tell him there is a Research Centre, surely the mistake can be corrected? I begin a letter writing campaign, firing off one to Mubarak, another to Sheikh Zayed, to his investment company, to the governor of Sinai, the mayor of Sharm-el-Sheikh, everyone I can think of. Under cover of darkness I also begin a clandestine campaign of sabotage, pulling out survey pins and moving others. A few days later, the mayor makes an unexpected visit, his first call since my arrival two years ago. He has the bearing of a former general and the gravel voice of one who spends his days giving orders. Wessam gets the brunt of his ire for my disruptive behaviour, which has evidently been communicated up some chain of command and back down again to land with the mayor. He accepts the reprimand with meek nods and murmured compliance. He is less meek with me later, ordering me not to interfere with the contractors. But I can't resist – the stakes are too high. After several weeks, I am summoned to Ismailia by Khodair.

Khodair's skin is shiny in the late morning heat, giving him a reptilian look. Thick forearms flex as he cracks his knuckles one by one. He reminds me of Sobek, the crocodile god of ancient Egypt, calculating and ruthless. I expect to be brow-beaten, but his voice is low and syrupy: 'You have been making trouble in Sharm-el-Sheikh.'

I have had plenty of time to prepare a little speech, but faced with his narrow eyes and yellowed teeth, the words flee.

'Well, what have you to say?'

I explain, somewhat untruthfully, that I only removed survey stakes where they were in the way. Then all my pent-up frustration spills out. We are on the cusp of achieving something at last, I tell him, only to have it snatched away. Khodair is unexpectedly sympathetic and tells me he hopes to have good news soon. He is negotiating with the government to move the Centre to a new site.

'Go back to Sharm-el-Sheikh and prepare. But don't get in the way of the Abu Dhabi Investment Company again,' he warns. 'You will upset powerful people.'

His stony look leaves me in no doubt that our next meeting will be less amicable if I disobey.

Months of wrangling ensue, most of it behind the scenes. Eventually agreement is reached to move the station to a site by the port, ten kilometres away. After all the hope, effort and money poured into this place, a move is better than nothing. Although I am mightily relieved, it is a Pyrrhic victory; ahead is another succession of tenders, contractors' meetings, laboratory fitting-out committees, just when I thought they were over. It feels like cresting a ridge to find a greater mountain ahead.

We return to our previous routine, but with a new intensity, like the condemned counting the days to execution. For weeks, then months, little happens bar more visits by surveyors and engineers; new pins to trip over and curse, trenches to fall into. I get a chance to question Khodair again about the future one evening in Ismailia at a gala dinner to celebrate two years of our project. With the Sharm Centre's future now 'secure' there is little sense of irony in the event. We gather at Ismailia's grandest hotel, the crowd milling about until Khodair makes an entrance and is seated at a central table. Out of politeness I join him, as his table is nearest to me. To my horror, when everyone else has sat down, the two of us are marooned together, alone.

Khodair eats as he talks, with brute efficiency. A steak is sawn up and despatched in minutes, peas mustered, fondant potatoes hardly noticed on the way down. The approach leaves plenty of time for monologues, gauche questions from me and awkward silences. Khodair assures me that one million Egyptian pounds (£200,000 sterling) has been allocated to Suez Canal University by the government. The move will take two weeks, a month at the outside. His expression seems genuine, but I wonder whether the greater skill here is in acting or self-delusion. Nothing in Egypt happens fast, and without constant pestering, nothing happens at all. I am reminded of a quotation by William Golding that I used as an epigraph in my first Egyptian diary: 'Expect nothing to be done, but when it is take refuge in incredulity.'

I quiz Khodair further: 'It would really help to have a date for the move, so we can plan ahead.'

'Dates, yes. I am in close contact with authorities, very close, yes.' He pauses to scoop half a jelly into his mouth and swallows hard. 'You will have a date.'

'Will it be weeks or months?'

He frowns at my persistence, or impudence. 'You will know in good time,' is the enigmatic reply.

I am woken in my villa in Sharm-el-Sheikh by a deep engine roar. Scrambling up, bleary-eyed, I see from my kitchen window an enormous flat-bed truck. Wessam is banging on the door before I finish brushing my teeth. He is dishevelled, unshaved and slightly breathless. 'The move is beginning. You and Julie must move into the villa next door so they can take yours to the new site. You have twenty-four hours. Here is the key.' The villa belongs to the Ministry of Reconstruction (or Decay and Dilapidation perhaps?). A look inside confirms the worst: it is squalid. All moves in Egypt begin with soap and scouring powder but Julie has had enough. We have already scoped alternatives and begin preparations for a move to a bedsit by the sea in the old town.

By midday the truck has been joined by a huge crane. They waste no time, beginning with one of the labs. Everything here was trucked in from Israel and each concrete unit still has lifting hooks at the corners. I watch with trepidation: will the hooks hold after two decades in the sun? The hook man stays on the roof holding a chain as the hoist begins and I imagine his head flying off as the chain gives way, but the unit is landed on the truck without incident. Over five days of unprecedented efficiency, twenty-three buildings are moved to the new site. Only one hook fails, breaking loose with rifle crack whiplash, just missing the lift man.

Inevitably, activity at the new site is limited to plonking the buildings down in neat rows to fit the space available. There was no preparation and there is no plan. A truck arrives from Ismailia to take away fish tanks, lab equipment, generators, compressors, and a hundred other things that form the lifeblood of research. The days are a blur of hard labour, but from time to time I stop and watch the contractors flock over the site, carting it off piece by piece like a carcass dismembered by vultures. Then all of a sudden the end comes. Nothing is left but dust and dashed dreams.

Before he leaves in the last vehicle for Ismailia, Wessam assures me that we will move into the new Centre in ten days. I have to admire such brazen optimism from a man who has accumulated a lifetime of setbacks and delays. Left to contemplate the future, Julie and I stroll along the cliff tops to a favourite bay. Tiran Island looms over the sea like a sentinel, ageless and enduring. There will be other opportunities, it seems to say; this is not the end. Below, the reef beckons, a turquoise streak alive with possibilities. I have instructions from my Liverpool bosses to stay in Sharm and fit out the new Research Centre as it is rebuilt. Experience suggests it will be a long time before there is anything to fit out. In the meantime, freed from all but minor responsibilities, the reefs are ours.

We begin by finishing Julie's Master's research on the impacts of tourism. In two and a half years, several new hotels and dive centres have sprung up and visitor numbers have doubled. Even before doing the statistical tests that science requires, it is obvious there is more damage in popular dive sites than in places where no-one goes but us: corals missing branches, torn sea fans, scratched coral heads. In several places, we struggle to relocate the pins we used to mark the corners of Julie's quadrats, despite detailed sketches. Some wear soft corals like fur coats, others have been pulled out by inquisitive divers. Luckily, enough remain to complete the work.

From time to time we check progress at the new site. Several caretakers have occupied what remains of our old villa and always greet us with gap-toothed smiles. Weeks after the move our hopes rise when a wall is built. It looks sturdy to me, but not to some unknown foreman, who sees to it that a section is knocked down again. Water pipes, sewage and electricity would be more helpful, I feel. They will be here soon, I am assured on a visit to Ismailia to teach my classes. But more weeks pass with no activity, then suddenly four deep holes appear, for the septic tanks I am told. Two sandstorms later they have filled up again. Promises that we would move into the new Centre in ten days were always fantasy; after four months of inactivity, ten months would now be recklessly hopeful and ten years not unreasonably pessimistic.

Ah well, all the more time with the fish. As a PhD student, I spent long hours plotting fish territories in Saudi Arabia in order to better understand how they sub-divide precious resources of food and space. Surgeonfish and damselfish constantly whizz about their territories, driving out interlopers, scrapping with neighbours and taking hurried bites of seaweed. I have long been fascinated by butterflyfish though, several of which I know to be territorial. They eat corals and other invertebrates and it should be easy to estimate the overlap in their diets just by recording what they nibble. Do species partition available food, each specialising on different fare, or is there lots of dietary overlap, which would require a different explanation for coexistence?

Butterflyfish are sluggards compared with surgeonfish and damselfish, ambling around their patches of reef. It will take patience to plot their territories. With my diary all but clear, I have the time at last to begin.

I choose a bay near the old Centre, too remote for tourists, and go there every day for a month. Floating almost motionless seven hours a day, I plot every movement onto a sketch map of a hundred-metre section of reef, record every nibble, note every churlish encounter. Some species, like the chevron butterflyfish, are cooperative. They buzz about territories whose centre of gravity is always a large table coral and never overlook the opportunity to remind neighbouring chevrons of the limits of their patches. Others are subtler, like the Crown butterflyfish, male-female pairs of which merely promenade along mutual boundaries. Some are confusing, like the raccoon butterflyfish which live in monogamous pairs most of the time, marking borders with heads-down, fin-raised displays. But then, without warning, neighbours form milling groups of eight or ten fish. Blue-cheek butterflyfish are exasperating. Pairs remain motionless for hours underneath coral heads, making me wonder if they have territories at all. But then, staying late one evening, I discover that they come to life in the hour before sunset. For the next two weeks, I crawl out of the sea exhausted long after the first stars appear.

By the end of the month I have discovered that butterflyfish societies are a miracle of organisation. Each species defends territories only against its own kind. This seems to be because there is limited overlap with other species in their diets, according to my notes. Within species, the borders of every territory interlock perfectly: there is virtually no overlap, no disputed ground, no space unused. Most species maintain their territories with little apparent effort, a nod here, a fin raise there, almost as though separated by unseen fences they are too polite to cross. Between species, there is almost complete indifference.

Observations are one thing in science, but experiments have more strength to discriminate between different ideas. I decide to become a disruptive influence in the lives of my subjects. One species in particular interests me, the Red Sea bannerfish. They almost always live in male-female pairs, although where gelatinous plankton food is abundant, they sometimes form schools hundreds strong. The ones that live in pairs feed on bottom-living invertebrates like soft-corals and sponges. I have already worked this out the old-fashioned way, by spearing fish and examining their stomach contents. At the same time, I inadvertently stumble across a feature that is unique among butterflyfish: you can tell the sexes apart visually.

In most butterflyfish pairs the mates look identical and at first glance so do Red Sea bannerfish. But these fish have two tiny horns on their foreheads and the male in a pair always has the bigger horns. I have the key for an experiment. I want to see if lone pair members can defend territories on their own, or if they will be ousted by neighbours and their lands usurped. So for several more weeks, I wreak havoc in the orderly world of bannerfish, taking out one or other sex from a pair to see what happens. The result is completely unexpected. Every time I remove a pair member, whether male or female, they are replaced overnight by a new fish. Almost immediately, the newly arrived pair member assumes the role of the deceased,[1] patrolling alongside their new mate. So much for true love and monogamy!

Like much research, it raises more questions. Where do the replacement mates come from? Were they non-territorial fish from schools (I know of none nearby), or were they members of other pairs on the lookout for vacancies, trading up to a better territory when the opportunity arose. As far as I can tell, none of the new fish come from territories nearby so I am left to wonder.

I drink up the long days and months of research, quenching a thirst for discovery that has been set aside too long. My mind swims with questions, possible answers and fresh ideas for

---

1. Like most people who begin their career as killers, even in the name of science, my appetite for 'removals' soon waned. In the end, looking into the curious, trusting eyes of a grouper at the end of my speargun, I couldn't bear to pull the trigger.

experiments. I wish I had three more years, but it is August 1990 and time to move on.

✺ ✺ ✺ ✺

My contract at an end, I wait with Julie in the check-in queue at Cairo airport. I have a job interview in two days for a lectureship in animal behaviour at Liverpool University. It seems like a dream job and I am anxious to get back and prepare. With my books long since sent for shipment I need time in a UK library to refresh myself on academic theory. A day isn't much, but it should be enough to sharpen up for the interview.

As we shuffle forward, I am a muddle of emotions. Our bags are full of data notebooks too precious to trust to our shipment back to Britain. Most has been collected in our last year, the booby prize from time freed up by loss of the Research Centre. The years here have been a rollercoaster of successes, frustrations, disappointments. In the end, our project was defeated by Egypt's bottomless ability to thwart itself. What should have been easy – for what could be easier than spending a large bag of money or teaching enthusiastic and motivated students – frequently verged on impossible. I had done my best, but the clashing of cultures had often been voluble. And Charles's suspicions of malicious intent could not be fully laid to rest. Suez Canal University had its dark corners and its scheming.

What had I achieved in three years? Our Centre had gone from dereliction to prosperity and back: dust to dust. Was it all for nought? In bleaker moments I am doubtful, but then I take comfort from the thought of my students' new-found love of the sea and enthusiasm for marine science. I step back to let two stern-looking men in dark suits through the queue, but they stop in front of us. 'Callum Roberts? Julie Hawkins? Come this way.' They have a sheaf of papers in their hands and our photographs are on the top page. My stomach lurches and Julie looks confused. These men are not wearing police or army uniforms, so who are they?

They take us to some nearby tables. 'Put your bags down and take everything out,' one of them says. There is nothing to do but comply. Before long, the table is strewn with our possessions. Other passengers give us suspicious, sidelong looks, no doubt thinking we are carrying drugs. The check-in queues dwindle as the men plod their way through our belongings, looking everything over thoroughly and placing various items in a separate pile. When the first coral specimen is pulled from a bag, carefully wrapped in newspaper, a part of Julie's reference collection, the men's faces light up: gotcha![1] I try to reason with them, then to hurry them, insisting that we will miss the plane. But they won't talk. The airline staff disappear and we are left in the empty thoroughfare watching our lives being picked apart. I begin to understand from snatches of conversation that they have instructions to confiscate all our data, photographs and scientific specimens. The name 'Farghaly' comes up more than once. Him! I feel the blood drain from my face as the gravity of our situation becomes clear. The data in our bags is the raw material from which we hope to forge our careers – computer disks, notebooks, photographs – everything from three years of fieldwork. There is no back-up!

One bag is brim-full with boxes of photographic slides and dozens of rolls of undeveloped film. All our underwater pictures are here, countless hours of painstaking effort, especially by Julie. We have a book planned on the natural history of coral reef fish and a publisher lined up. The men set the bag aside. I plead with

---

1.   The officials were within their rights to confiscate the coral. All hard (scleractinian) corals were listed under CITES, the Convention on International Trade in Endangered Species, in 1985. Transporting corals without a permit was therefore illegal, but, in a Catch-22 situation, there was no permit-issuing body in Egypt to apply to at the time.

them to give it back and grab the handle. But they threaten me with arrest and I let go.

After two harrowing hours, a heap of corals and all our photographs sit at one end of the table, the rest of our things at the other. But fortune smiles even at this dark moment. These plain-clothes police have missed the real gold: they don't know what data looks like. They confiscate our coral specimens and photographs but let us keep our notebooks and computer disks. On such twists of fate whole careers turn.

CHAPTER NINE

Sharm-el-Sheikh revisited

Egypt, 2012

IT IS 2012 AND I AM IN THE COURTYARD of the Sofitel Beach Resort looking across Sharm-el-Sheikh's Na'ama Bay. Before me lies the same supple curve of beach and cliff that, over twenty years ago, I spent countless hours admiring from my house. Mubarak and Sheikh Zayed had had their way and the hotel constructed from their alliance is luxurious and its grounds unexpectedly verdant. Lofty palms sprout from a thick bed of grass that covers the naked rock like a bad wig, lifting slightly at the edges. Bougainvillea cascades over elegant white arches in drifts of purple, pink and orange. Below me, a vast turquoise pool is the centrepiece of the lower level, occupying the space where our classrooms and labs were. As a hotel it's hard to fault, but somehow it diminishes this place.

The sea is as vivid and enticing as ever, but the land before me is utterly different. Gone are the khaki hues of desert sand and rock, replaced by the glint of whitewashed concrete, steel, tinted glass and manicured gardens. As far as the eye can see in both directions, a continuous belt of development extends inland a kilometre or two from the water's edge.

Driving from the airport, it was hard to get my bearings. Familiar dry riverbeds and rock bluffs have been remodelled, removed or submerged by construction. Blank walls run for kilometres beside the road, shielding the resort inhabitants from barren desert and blocking once heavenly vistas of mountain and sea. That desert, which seemed so pristine and eternal when I lived here, is scarred all over by random pockmarks where builders have carted away fill material or dumped their waste. Plastic bags and discarded packaging blow across the plain and flap from twisted rebar and dead acacias. The metamorphosis seems even more discordant when night falls and the bay ignites into an electrified frenzy, broadcasting garish entreaties to the darkness. Signs for casinos, restaurants, hotels, car hire and floor shows clamour for business, pushing back the stillness.

This is my first time in Sharm-el-Sheikh for sixteen years, an odd omission given that these are the closest coral reefs to my home in Britain. In truth, I have actively avoided the place. To return somewhere you once loved deeply in the certain knowledge that it has been so altered is to court disappointment. Sure enough, the timeless majesty of desert has been sacrificed to progress. Yet it is easy to see why a country like Egypt, struggling to make its way in the world, would make this choice.

Julie and I are here to introduce our Masters students to coral reefs. Rupert, my old friend and PhD advisor, is back with us to run the course along with his wife Mauvis Gore, also a marine biologist. We have two daughters in tow, aged twelve and thirteen, both already qualified scuba divers. Our students chatter excitedly as we head for our first dive, but Julie and I have grave doubts.

When we published our predictions in the early 1990s about the damage that mass tourism might do to Egyptian reefs, people from the Ras Mohammed Marine Park and Environment Ministry scoffed. We were alarmist, they said. Development would stop far short of the 1.2 million tourist nights per year that we forecast. But we had seen Mubarak's ruthlessness in his disposal of our Research Centre and how environmental concerns were brushed aside by his money men. In reality, we were much too cautious. By 2015 there was hotel capacity in South Sinai for over 25 million tourist nights per year. We saw in the 1980s how much damage a small fraction of these tourists could do.

'What do you think it will look like?' Julie asks uncertainly as we drive to the dive site.

'I dread to think.' We are silent the rest of the way.

It isn't just the mass tourism. There have been more sinister developments for reefs worldwide. From late 1997 to early 1998 tropical oceans sweltered in unusual warmth as a vast pool of overheated water spread across the Pacific and Indian oOceans, linked to the El Niño–Southern Oscillation, the same climatic disturbance that destroyed Galápagos's coral reefs in the 1980s. Reports soon began to come in of mass coral bleaching.

As New Year 1998 came and went, the internet began to crackle with stories of overwhelming coral death and it became clear a major calamity was underway. All over the world, immense banks of coral lay in ruins, which only a few months previously had pulsed with life, stifled to death by hot water. It felt like one of those disaster movies in which the first reports of the unusual soon coalesce into a deluge of terror as aliens mount their invasion or a virus spreads. By year's end, a rough accounting suggested that something like 70 per cent to 95 per cent of all corals had perished across a vast swathe of the Indian Ocean from the Seychelles to Sri Lanka, Kenya to the Maldives. Pacific and Caribbean reefs racked up additional losses of 30 per cent to 50 per cent. This catastrophe had no historical precedent.

Although mass coral death also reached the southern Red Sea, taking out mountainous coral heads hundreds of years old, here in the north it remained cool enough to spare the reefs. Still, I reasoned as Julie and I pulled on wetsuits, even with more favourable conditions there is sure to be a lot of damage here, being under such stress from tourism. I must have been frowning because Mauvis asks what the matter is. Julie laughs, and, lowering her voice so the students won't overhear, replies for both of us, 'We're hoping this won't be a disappointment! So much has changed.'

'Don't worry. I think you'll be pleasantly surprised.'

Mauvis is Jamaican and in her late fifties, her dark wavy hair streaked with grey. I should trust her opinion as she has seen a lot of reefs in a long career, and she and Rupert have taught field courses here for several years. But I can't quite shake off my anxiety.

We cross the reef on a walkway made of floating plastic pontoons installed by the hotel whose dive centre we are using. The students go in first, then we jump. When the bubbles clear, it feels like I have been whisked backward in time. Corals bristle at the reef edge, some smooth and rounded, others folded like brains, or extending like shelves, all hemmed in by stubby-fingered branching colonies and the ochre plates of fire coral. Splashes of purple and the gently rounded waves of coral bushes remind me of moorland heather in bloom, but here with alien smudges of blue, hot pink and apricot. A shoal of *Abudefduf* damselfish gravitates towards us, milling about like huge butterflies, their black-and-white barred bodies briefly rendering the scene in monochrome. Fish storm above the drop-off, their polychrome clouds effervescing in the sunshine. Below us the reef plunges vertically, losing itself in shadows that darken into a blue-grey abyss. It feels so natural and familiar, in sharp contrast to the foreign world above water.

It isn't the same of course. Some of the larger stony corals are dead and overgrown by ephemeral soft corals. There is more tourist damage too – shattered clumps of coral, severed branches, trampled sponges – but it has the feel of a place that is coping, not a reef struggling to survive. It remains vibrant, beautiful and uplifting, like a favourite country walk.

Our students bombard us with questions from the moment our heads break the surface. Most have never seen so many different creatures in one place or felt so accepted by wild animals. I never did solve the enigma of this extraordinary richness, nor, so far, has anyone else. Many ideas attempt to explain the eruption of life. One holds that because coral reefs are tropical, they haven't suffered the Ice Age extinctions of higher latitudes, so they have accumulated species from long, uninterrupted stretches of evolution. The tropics are also highly productive and relatively stable, so they can support specialist species that more finely divide available resources than is possible in seasonal temperate and polar seas. An example from land makes the point well. It would be impossible for a species to eat nothing but fruit in temperate latitudes because fruit is seasonal. But it is a simple matter in the rainforest where there is always fruit to be had from some plant or other.

These explanations of high diversity all involve biology, by which I mean that the interactions among species and with their environments are important. However, in the last decade some theorists have pursued a different line, suggesting that the greater richness of the tropics is an effect of chance. If you were to drop a bunch of species with different geographic range sizes onto the surface of the planet at random, they argue, more of their ranges will overlap in the middle than at the polar edges of the habitable world. This happens because while small ranges can fit anywhere, big ranges would be constrained by barriers at the edges so lots of them overlap in the middle. Middle regions therefore have lots of species and the margins fewer. In other words, richness would be high on coral reefs for purely prosaic reasons of geometry. The same thing works longitudinally. The boundaries here are supplied by Africa and the Americas bracketing the Indian and Pacific oceans, so South East Asia, which is midway between them, has the most species. I recoil instinctively from this idea, as do many colleagues. Such an explanation feels like someone pulling a well-loved rug from underneath our feet. How can it be possible for nature in all its splendour to be explained by mere mechanical assembly rules? Fortunately, recent thinking has shifted again to the idea that biology plays a role and that patterns seen in nature do not conform exactly to this joyless prediction; nonetheless, the match is close.

In 1994, four years after I left Egypt, my pursuit of an answer to the secret of reef diversity took me to Palau. This tiny archipelagic nation lies at the edge of the global epicentre of coral reef diversity, 900 km east of the Philippines. So rich are the reefs of South East Asia that the region is dubbed the 'Coral Triangle'. While the Red Sea hosts about a thousand species of fish, Indonesia and the Philippines have over three thousand. More than five hundred of the world's eight-hundred-plus shallow-water coral species occur in the Coral Triangle. Compared to Egypt, Palau's reefs support a mind-corrupting turmoil of species. By the time I went there I had begun using a different method to count fish. Instead of swimming for a set distance or time and counting all the fish in a belt several metres wide, I now counted them for fifteen minutes in a ten-metre diameter circle. This was better in the Caribbean, where I then worked, because reef habitat there is patchy and long-distance counts aren't practical. But when I tried it in Palau, my brain nearly jammed.

For those who love coral reefs, Palau is close to heaven on Earth. Like Egypt, this country has reefs above and below water, although rather than the rufous layers of the Red Sea's fossil cliffs, Palau's fossil reefs are gleaming pinnacles of limestone, shaggy with tree ferns, elephant ears, lianas and dripping moss. Over tens of thousands of years, rainwater has etched these raised reefs into a labyrinth of islets, passages and cul-de-sacs. We approached the dive site through this maze, following winding water trails between soaring cliffs and along shadowed gorges, emerging at last into hard sun-glare and the borderless immensity of mid-ocean. The boat driver steered towards a serpentine ridge of reef visible only as a malachite smear on the dark sea, crossing it through a channel. A swift current slapped the gunnels as he threaded the narrows to a small bay that opened on the ocean side where we would dive. Below the surface, in the sharp-edged clarity of pure oceanic water, the reef fell away in an amphitheatre of breathtaking scope. Rounded corals looked like velvet pillows heaped on the terraces, while sea fans rusted on the slopes, bent and quivering in the current. Descending to fifteen metres, I picked a spot directly beneath the boat, started my stopwatch and wrote down the first fish: '*Monotaxis grandoculis*, the bigeye emperor, seven individuals at 50 to 70 cm long.' Broad-finned, with large forked tails and three dark squares on their leaden flanks, these fish are almost always the first counted because by day they hang above the reef in full view, nearly motionless. Glancing up, I spotted ten other species, at least, milling about within the space of a metre or two. Before I could decide which to record next, several others took their places: parrotfish green and maroon as their jungle namesakes, barracuda like silver ingots, gobies with red-striped faces glimpsed in their burrows. I scribbled them down, freezing the moment in my mind's eye, before looking up for more. The minutes ticked by in a feverish ordeal of species identification and counting. By the end of fifteen minutes, my board crammed with coded-names, strings of numbers and cryptic sketches, I had recorded ninety-five species of fish in my ten-metre cylinder of reef.

Within a handful of dives, I discovered that the leisurely simplicity of Caribbean fish counting was supplanted by a head-spinning, pencil-busting burst of speed writing. To make things tougher, currents poured across the Palauan reef slopes like a liquid treadmill. I had to swim hard just to stay put. It felt like one of those mad endurance tests a television game show might devise.

I had already amassed similar counts from reefs all over the Red Sea and Caribbean. When I plotted the number of fish species counted against the total number reported from a region, there was a straight-line relationship, angled at roughly 45 degrees: the more fish present in a region, the more there were in the snapshots of my counts. Put simply, in richer regions, the species packed more tightly into the available space. When I added the Palau data to the plot, the straight line just sailed on upwards. I had been expecting it to bend and level off, like the rise to a hilltop, as a limit was reached on the number of species that could share a given amount of space. There must come a saturation point, I reasoned, when the available resources can no longer be subdivided further. But the straight line of my graph said that there was no ecological limit to coexistence at this scale. What limited the number of species in my counts was the number available from the regional pool.

All this time I had been looking for the secrets of coexistence at small scales, but this panoramic view said that the processes that set the number of species present operate at far larger scales and over very long periods. It is the balance between evolution and extinction that fixes the variety of fish in a region and this in turn dictates diversity on the reef. The sheer wonder of this idea was thrilling. Left alone for enough time, coral reefs might just carry on getting richer and richer as evolution adds more species. In fact, palaeontologists already had this figured out. Plotting the number of species on Earth over time shows that life has been getting more varied for the last 200 million years. Over the long creep of geological time, the world has been filling up with new species in a slow-motion evolutionary explosion. There was a brief setback 66 million years ago when there was trouble with an asteroid that dinosaurs and many others didn't enjoy. But this mass extinction aside, for a very long time, the rate at which new species have been added to Earth has been greater than that at which they have been erased. The struggle for life has propelled nature to ever greater creativity. What could be more wonderful!

Looking back, I am glad that coral reefs have guarded their mysteries. The structure of DNA can only be solved once. The complexity of the living world will keep us probing, guessing and arguing for centuries to come.

In 1991, I published my ideas about how differential survival of larval fish during dispersal on ocean currents might help determine the make-up of reef communities. To me it felt like a major achievement on the road to becoming an independent scientist. I was delighted then just to have had an original idea. But better than having ideas is having them accepted by the rest of the scientific community. Since my study was completed, reef science has acknowledged the importance of larvae. Rather than drifting passively from place to place, we now know that many of them have some control over their dispersal. But my idea about larvae being adapted to different open water habitats has sat on the shelf. Google Scholar, a tool that keeps track of scientific publications, says it has only been mentioned in other studies twenty-three times in thirty-seven years, and four of those mentions were by me!

Meanwhile, in Sharm-el-Sheikh, Julie and I revisit old haunts over the next two weeks, experiencing alternating anguish and elation. The most congested parts of the coast have been badly bashed about. Some of our favourite places, once hard to reach but now with huge hotels parked onshore, have lost their enchantment. It is hard to experience serenity when forty divers elbow one another and a hundred swimming legs pump overhead. But the reefs still crackle with life, and unlike many I have dived in the last twenty years, there are lots of big fish about because they are protected from fishing. These reefs are like boxers, struggling on, bruised and bleeding but still on their feet. Their mistreatment is not deliberate. They are simply loved too much. Our hopes are kindled by places as yet undeveloped, some off the beaten track, others successfully protected by national parks. Here corals and fish live on undisturbed.

The truth is that protected areas have saved the Sinai coast from complete ruin. Michael Pearson, the man hired to set up the park in the late 1980s, got his way, to my surprise and pleasure.

Ras Mohammed National Park covers 850 square kilometres, extending far inland from the wet tip of the southern peninsula to the arid folds of the mountainous massif. Sister parks cover long sections of the Gulf of Aqaba coast. With Michael at the helm in its early years, followed by a French couple, the park introduced protection measures that placed it at the forefront of global conservation. Sewage discharge to the sea is forbidden here. Instead it is directed inland to treatment plants that render the water fit for irrigation of all the greenery that now softens the desert. Hotels are not allowed to damage the reef or build within thirty metres of the shore. The benefits of this policy can be readily appreciated in Hurghada on the other side of the Gulf of Suez. There they have carved up reefs for marinas and built on top of them as the Saudi Arabians did, killing the golden goose. Where tourists trampled corals when we lived in Sharm, today they walk to the edge of the reef on floating pontoon jetties (fortunately, a great deal more lightweight and durable than the steel one blown away at our research centre). Men with whistles enforce this rule whenever someone steps onto the reef.

A few days into the trip, Julie and I catch up with an old friend, Mohammed Salem. Mohammed had been an Egyptian PhD student of Rupert's when I was appointed lecturer in York in 1995. He now manages the South Sinai Protectorates, which includes not just the Ras Mohammed park but thousands of square kilometres of land too, including the mountains and valleys around St Catherine's Monastery in central Sinai, one of the earliest in Christendom. He greets us enthusiastically, but it is impossible not to notice a weary, drawn look that has been acquired since his student days. Although the laws that safeguard his parks are strong, enforcing them takes nerves of steel. As we talk over the following days, he explains in a calm and quiet voice how the park is underfunded while the money and political power behind the developers feels boundless. The parks are sustained by a levy on tourism, but not enough money reaches the places where it is needed. Mohammed is short of rangers, boats and fuel, and it is hard to attract good staff on government salaries when better paid options are available in the dive centres. Nonetheless, thanks to dedication and moral courage – for, to Mohammed, protecting nature is a battle on behalf of future generations – the parks are working. Development stops where the park begins. May it always be so.

Ras Mohammed itself is much harder to visit by land than it was when Julie and I were here[1]. You need special permits and must pass through military and park checkpoints. Even when you have the personal authority of the park manager, we discover, there is still great difficulty. Our bus is stopped, permits pored over by officials startled from sleep, phone calls made, the guards argue among themselves, more phone calls are made, and when our permits are finally declared genuine, humour is restored and access granted. The peninsula is virtually unchanged since we were last here apart from the imposition of an absurd entrance gate. In a blemish visible for miles, nine gargantuan concrete slabs rise from the plain, several leaning together at a jaunty angle. They resemble Stonehenge monoliths more than anything from ancient Egypt.

Our permit allows us to pass yet another military checkpoint and more guards unused to being disturbed. After several kilometres bouncing along a rutted track, we reach a little-visited bay on the shores of a deep inlet. Dunes tilt gracefully from the shore into the sea, creating a pale margin to its ultramarine intensity. Underwater, garden eel 'meadows' sprout from the banking sand, the eels' heads waving in the current as they catch passing plankton. Held by tail tips lodged in burrows, each eel extends a half metre or so above the sand. They look like thousands of snakes swaying to the notes of an invisible charmer. Watching their sensuous movements, I begin to feel it is they who are the charmers, and me the captive of their mesmeric dance. In a strange act of underwater trickery,

---

1.   Access by sea is very easy in one of the dozens of tourist boats that go there every day.

the meadow shrinks ahead as we approach, first to a short turf and then disappearing altogether as the eels withdraw under the sand. How they swim backwards into their burrows is a mystery. But after they have slipped away, all that is visible on the seabed are dark holes, each the size of a penny.

After the dive, I clamber across a gravel-covered hill behind the beach in search of a quiet spot to pee. There is a scatter of coloured stones among a background of dark pebbles washed here long ago from the mountains. I pick one up and turn it over. It is chert, a flint-like rock that flakes when struck, and by the look of it, this one was shaped by a human hand. Three flakes have been expertly removed so that the stone narrows to a point at one end. It has been burnished to a warm sheen by numberless millennia of blown dust, highlighting streaks of red and umber. I stroke it, then hold it as it was meant to be used, point down, finger and thumb slotted comfortably into grooves made where flakes were knapped off. I could be the first human to pick this stone up since it was tossed aside by its maker thousands, maybe tens of thousands of years ago.

Dozens more worked stones surround this one and over the rest of the trip I search the ground whenever I can. There are stone tools all over the place, one a round hammer stone discarded where it lay after it split millennia before. I stumble upon an ancient Egyptian faience figure, lost in the desert an age ago. It fits the palm of my hand and looks like a stiff hieroglyphic figure from a temple wall. The turquoise glaze is cracked and worn, exposing patches of pale ceramic underneath. Near Ras Mohammed's Shark Observatory there are time-worn signs of habitation that I completely missed when I lived here. Baked into the cliff tops are the charred scars of prehistoric hearths. It takes little effort, in this wild setting, to imagine a group of early humans sweaty and dusty from the hunt, gathered about a fire. I wonder whether they got as much pleasure as I do watching the sun set over this warm, embracing sea. The hearths and scattered relicts serve as reminders that Sinai was always the most important route out of Africa for the ancestors of modern humans.

When we lived here I was oblivious to stone tools; they were unnoticed chips in a desert of rocks. But I have become fascinated by them in recent years. The experience reminds me of when Julie and I read a magazine article about bedbugs when we lived in Sharm and promptly found one in our bed. That same year I read about how deserts and ice fields were the best places to find meteorites and quickly spotted a fist-sized meteorite on a regular walk. It had been there all along. How much of the world around us goes unnoticed because we are unable to read the signs? One of the greatest gifts of education and a curious mind is to bring that world to life.

Similarly, underwater life is a startling example of our selective blindness. The old books that crowd my study shelves show that sea creatures were overlooked by the great majority of travellers to Egypt and Arabia. Take Arthur Penrhyn Stanley, an English theologian who became Dean of Westminster in the mid-nineteenth Century. He wrote of his Near Eastern travels in an 1866 book called *Sinai and Palestine*. In 550 exhaustive pages, he described their history, scenery and people but mentions marine life on just one, and that was only to say how sea shells were smashed to pieces under his plodding dromedary's feet. How could he miss something that so defines Arabia? When it comes to Sinai at least, today the position is reversed: tourists look to the sea; the desert is backdrop.

On our trips back and forth to Ras Mohammed, we pass the bay to which our Research Centre was moved after Mubarak's calamitous gift. Julie and I stop there one day after a dive. There is an impressive wall. That at least was finished. A notice on it declares ownership by the Faculty of Tourism from Suez Canal University. It is fitting, I suppose, to train students here for the industry that has swallowed this coast. But they evidently use only a small fraction of the buildings because drifts of dust are heaped about the remainder, rounding edges and entering unbidden through doorless frames. An imposing gate bars access. I can't help but wonder whether behind it lurk the same toothless caretakers we said goodbye to twenty-two years before.

'Expect nothing to be done, but when it is take refuge in incredulity.' My William Golding quote captures how I felt much of the time about Egypt. In reality, I came from a parallel world. The gap in understanding was a gulf, the Egyptians' frustration with me at least as great as mine with them. As a fresh-faced twenty-five-year-old I must have been intolerable to many of the senior Egyptian university staff, and probably to the juniors too. Rereading today the letters I wrote to Khodair, president of Suez Canal University, I wince at shoutily underlined sections. No wonder our relationship was prickly. My demands must have seemed rude and unreasonable. I just wanted to work quickly and see jobs done well. I wasn't carrying a lifetime of minor disappointments so I had not developed the appropriate sang -froid when it came to setbacks and delays. *Mumkin bukra, inshallah* – maybe tomorrow, God willing. These phrases were a mantra for survival, talisman against insanity. But nothing ever changes unless you throw new people into the mix which was, I suppose, one reason that Europe funded our cooperation. I was a young man in a hurry, determined not to be overwhelmed. I knew that I couldn't change Egypt, but I so wanted to plant new ideas.

As I write, a glance at Google Earth shows that the last remains of our Centre, the buildings we revisited in 2012, have finally been obliterated. The site in the photograph is bare, and earth has been pushed into the sea to create an uncompromising square edge that interrupts the crescent of beach and entombs a luxuriant seagrass bed. I remember the thrill of discovery when I took a student there for the first time in 1988. Diving under the nose of the neighbouring military port could attract unwelcome attention, and to dive centres and tourists, seagrass beds couldn't hold a candle to coral reefs, so nobody went there. But to Osama, my student, and me it was paradise. A meadow of the lushest, thickest bladed seagrass I had ever seen sloped offshore. Light rippled in green waves across the swaying field, while shoals of olive fish melted into thickets at our approach. Moving deeper, the outline of something dark and alien coalesced at the edge of visibility: a sunken ship. The boat lay on its keel at a slight angle and was nearly intact apart from a gaping hole in the deck. Corals crenellated the superstructure and encrusted its plates, all perfectly intact, unseen and untouched by any human. Judging by the rate of coral growth and the size of the colonies, the boat had been here since the Israeli occupation. Fire hoses lay in thick coils on deck, still attached to the pumps. Seventeen lionfish the size of hawks hovered above the entrance to the hole, like tomb guardians. Their spread fins were like patterned Chinese fans, their bodies tigered with crimson bars. Fish flowed in lustrous rivers around the rusted hulk, streaming from portholes and pouring through twisted rails. I've never been a big fan of wreck dives, but this was ravishing. It couldn't last, of course. As soon as I told friends in the dive centres, the draw of the wreck overwhelmed caution about the military. In only a few months the corals were shattered by clumsy divers and the magic had fled.

We never did get back our photographs or corals, confiscated in 1990. Robbed of time for final preparation by our airport delay, my lectureship interview in Liverpool was a disaster. I can still see that row of earnest and expectant faces on the other side of the table after the killer question had been loosed. 'How would you teach Fisher's sex-ratio theory to a class of seventy undergraduates?' My mouth dried to a rictus; I was done for. For the life of me I couldn't remember what Professor Fisher had said about sex-ratios; I couldn't think whether I had ever known. My interrogators began to shift restlessly. 'First of all, I would remind myself what Fisher's sex-ratio says…' I began, knowing my canoe had just passed over the edge of the waterfall.

I rue the loss of our photographs, but we were so fortunate to keep our data. It seems an extraordinary oversight for the police to have made. But in 1990, few people in Egypt had personal computers, so computer disks were a novelty. And perhaps our notebooks didn't count because they were written in English. I don't know. Sometimes luck doesn't need explanation. A few months after leaving Egypt, one of my former students wrote to say that Said Farghaly, my nemesis from Suez Canal University, had begun to include some lovely photographs in his lectures. He claimed to have taken them himself, which was peculiar for a man who couldn't swim. There was also now a bag in his office labelled 'Callum Roberts'. For years I indulged in elaborate fantasies about what I might do if I came across Farghaly again at some scientific conference – push him in the hotel swimming pool was a favourite option. But I never saw him again. Decades on, there is no enmity any more, just a lingering sadness that marine science in Egypt was stalled by a mere hotel, one among hundreds that now line the coast. I wonder if Mubarak, while he languished in jail after the Arab Spring, ever thought fondly of his trips to Sharm-el-Sheikh.

But the students I taught have prospered, many gaining positions at Egyptian universities, in the National Parks or abroad. One of the Mohammeds is still at Suez Canal University and his website shows him with an enthusiastic class on a field trip to learn about coral reefs. Three quarters of the students in the photo are women, and all are in the sea studying their subjects at first hand. It brings a tear to my eye.

Julie and I leave Egypt from our field course feeling better than expected. The reefs have been spared most of the grief meted out in other parts of the world. I wish that all had done so well. Fifteen years on from the 1997–98 warming episode, the case was beyond reasonable doubt: coral reefs were dealt a body blow worldwide. A few had bounced back but mostly in remote places where there was little else to trouble them. The majority had lost their vigour. In some ways, what has happened to coral reefs feels like my own journey from youth to middle age. Those days seem so close, but how different everything looks now. My first discovery of the coral world, aged twenty, was such an adventure, whereas it is commonplace today. Remote regions that once took days to reach are within a few hours of major cities by air. It is a tragic irony that just as people have come to know and love them, coral reefs have become deeply imperilled.

CHAPTER TEN

The aftermath of war

Arabian Gulf, 1992

SOON AFTER THE FIRST GULF WAR, in late 1992, I get a call from Andrew Price, 'Captain Haddock' from our Red Sea sailing adventure. Now marine advisor to the World Conservation Union in Switzerland, he is leading an effort to assess war damages to coral reefs and other habitats in the Arabian Gulf and wants my help. Saddam Hussein annexed Kuwait in August 1990, not expecting more than local opposition. He could surely not have imagined that within six months the fury of a thirty-four-nation international coalition would be hurled upon his forces.

Saddam's disregard for nature was already notorious; he drained his country's magnificent southern marshes in order to destroy the Marsh Arabs. And his appetite for revenge did not stop at the coast. When his retreating soldiers sabotaged Kuwait's coastal refineries, they bled over a million barrels of crude oil into the Gulf. I had watched aghast as satellite images showed vast slicks creep south, pushed by powerful desert winds. One by one they surrounded and swallowed up islands that I knew to support the Gulf's richest and most beautiful coral reefs.

I fly from the UK to Saudi Arabia via Bahrain, an island off Saudi Arabia's Gulf coast, taking a taxi over the sea to mainland Arabia.

The connection, part bridge, part causeway, is a major engineering feat. For twenty-five kilometres it affords broad vistas of Persian blue sea, traced with the pale meanderings of sandbanks and blue-green smudges where seagrass meadows grow. Andrew Price had spent several years assessing the likely damage to marine life that this road would cause, but his reports had little influence. I ask the driver about the queue of traffic coming the other way. What could draw all these people to a tiny island like Bahrain? He scowls. 'They are very bad people. Go to nightclubs, drink beer.'

The Gulf coast is largely flat and featureless on the drive north the following day, save for the towering columns and chimneys of refineries, desalination plants and power stations that here and there rise from the shore. There is a whiff of hydrocarbons on the wind, especially nearing Jubail, whose industrial outline is a tangle of pipes, tank farms and gas flares. This will be my base for the coming week, where I will be headquartered with the 'Marine Habitat and Wildlife Sanctuary for the Gulf Region Project'. As its name suggests, it aims to create a marine protected area hereabouts, but the war has been a serious setback. Some of the prime candidate sites have been oiled.

The project team is based in one of the many walled compounds favoured by the expatriate workforce. Like little international islands in an Arabian sea, the compounds separate infidels from believers, allowing a slightly greater laxity of dress and expression than is permitted outside. Although alcohol is strictly banned, yeast and grape juice often find themselves in the same bottles in places like this. Iain Watt and Thomas Müller welcome me warmly. Iain is English and runs project logistics. He has the thick-set, muscular build of a beer-loving scuba instructor and gives my hand a fierce squeeze. Thomas, who is German, is tall and slim and has the look of an academic. Like me, he specialises in fish, giving us plenty to talk about.

We are up early the next day, the sky flushed with dawn. I grab a hurried breakfast of flatbread, fig jam and sweet tea. Our destination is twenty kilometres north where the coast was badly oiled. There a sickle-shaped island called Abu Ali curves offshore, enclosing a sprawling complex of sandbanks and channels, rimmed in places by mangrove. This region is a powerhouse of marine productivity, supporting immense nurseries for the fish and shrimp that sustain fisheries further offshore. Twice a year, tens of thousands of birds swoop down and pause their long migrations to and from Europe and Asia, refuelling on the overflowing platter of mud-loving invertebrates. But the shape of the coast made this bay a trap for oil drifting south from Kuwait. Thomas tells me that the number of grebes and cormorants stopping over here plummeted last year. More than thirty thousand were killed by the oil.

I am eager to be underway, but an hour later we are still hanging about the vehicles. Several senior staff from the Environmental Protection Administration have yet to arrive. Waiting again. A group of young Saudis in snow-white, iron-creased dishdashas are smoking beside a luxurious 4 x 4 with windows so black it must be hard to see the road. They drop their butts where they stand, barely pausing before lighting up again. One has mirrored sunglasses perched on top of his red-checked gutra, another a gold watch that dangles loose, like a bracelet. It doesn't look much like field attire. I walk over to introduce myself and get chatting to one, whose name is Aziz. He and his colleagues from the Environmental Protection Administration are taking advantage of my visit to see the oil damage at first hand.

Another hour passes. Eventually two older men arrive accompanied by army officers. After ten more minutes and many salaams, the signal is given to leave. Iain, Thomas, Aziz and I get into the Land Rover, while the others get into the executive 4 x 4s.

We pull up near a stunted group of trees that cast a slight green shadow on the lagoon at the head of a long coastal indent. Anywhere else, this clump would elicit no more than fleeting acknowledgement, but here they are the only trees in miles of level, empty, sand-blown coast. In nature conservation as in other walks of life, rarity begets value. This shabby mangrove patch is the most northerly in the world, according to Aziz, who explained it to me on our journey from Jubail in carefully imprecise English. Even with the sun up, the air is chill on this late November morning. It is not the searing mid-summer furnace that holds back the northward march of mangrove here, but winter frost. A slight breeze from the sea ruffles leaves so caked in dust, they wear a dun mantle of desert. Instead of the freshness of open sea, it wraps us in a choking, alien stench, like the interior of a stuffy garage: oil.

I am puzzled at first as there is little sign of oil. But moments later my shoe sinks into a morass hidden under concealing wind-blown dust. The executive 4 x 4s are just arriving, having lagged when we went off-road. We parked well back from the mangrove, but the cars come to the edge of the trees, their tyres squeezing glossy tar from beneath the mud, wrapping them in a black, shining crust. A door on the first vehicle swings open to reveal an interior of spotless tan leather. One of the Saudi chiefs looks at us uncertainly, but then steps out, lifting the hem of his dishdasha to keep it from the mud. Following his lead, the party disembarks, delicately stepping through the mud with dishdashas gathered like eighteenth-century ladies in a filthy street.

Wading offshore, we find the water clear and the bottom looks normal. I push a spade into the mud to find that the oil has seeped deep down, poisoning the seabed. Each mangrove tree sits within a corona of aerial roots that sprouts vertically from the mud. They use the roots to breathe in the oxygen-starved sediments, but here every root is sealed in black. The trees are dying. Even vigorous mangroves would struggle in such pollution, but here at the margins of existence, there seems little chance. The most northerly mangrove in the world may soon be somewhere else.

After poking about for a while, I head back. The Saudis are back in their 4 x 4s, but one of their drivers is by our Land Rover rubbing down a pile of shoes with a cloth soaked in fuel from a jerrycan. The oil is viscous and resistant and he seems only to be redistributing it across the fine patterned leather of the shoe in his hand. I wonder if they will charge them to expenses.

The next stop on our tour is where the crescent curve of Abu Ali stretches offshore. Although once an island, Abu Ali is attached to the mainland by a causeway. 'There's a reef of sorts here,' Thomas tells me on the way, 'but it is very poorly developed'. Unlike the Red Sea, the Gulf has little in the way of reef fringing its coasts. Most coral development lies further offshore, around islands. 'Floating oil covered these reefs for weeks during the peak of the spill,' Thomas says.

'That wasn't the first spill though,' Iain adds, 'There have been lots of smaller spills here over the years.'

The breeze is fresher here, bringing relief from the cloying reek of oil. A pavement of brown tar covers much of the beach. Iain pokes a stick into it, creating a wound that seeps a trickle of black. Fifty metres offshore, low wave crests steepen slightly above a greenish line in the sea. The tar continues underwater as I swim out, and in places is at least half a metre thick. I expect a coral graveyard. The back of the reef is mainly scalloped rock but at the seaward edge the bottom is covered by grey domes of densely branched coral. Many are one or two metres across, which with growth rates of a few centimetres a year at most, mean they must have survived the spill. They look healthy too. It's a minor miracle.

There are plenty of fish, but all are juveniles. Some juveniles are miniatures of the adults, but many are distinctive enough to seem like other species altogether. The powder-blue Arabian angelfish with their daffodil tails and crescented flanks are here represented by juveniles of dark indigo, marked with swirls of white that look like the isobars on a stormy weather map. As adults, spotted drum fish have wedge-shaped bodies marked by diagonal black bars that narrow towards the tail across white face and flanks. On the dorsal and tail fins there is a constellation of black stars. Their tiny versions, by contrast, have extravagant extensions to dorsal and ventral fins making the fish look like a piece of black and white ribbon blowing in the current.

Back on the beach, Thomas tells me why there are no adult fish. 'At the end of last year,' he says, 'the water cooled sharply when strong winter winds blew from the desert. The fish all disappeared. Most likely they died as there are no other reefs near here they could escape to.' We head back as darkness falls, Jubail's skyline lurid with dancing gas flares.

We are on the waterfront before dawn to load a boat with scuba tanks and kit for a three-day trip. Saudi Arabia has six islands between forty and a hundred kilometres offshore. They have the best coral reefs in the Gulf, although reefs are rare in this muddy sea, covering just one per cent of Saudi waters. We are to visit three: Jurayd, Jana and Karan. Soon after the sun crests the horizon, Iain guns up the two big outboards, lifting the boat into a bouncing plane across smooth water. Two hours later, we sight Jurayd, the closest island. Above water it is little more than a low bank of sand half a kilometre long. Sand is not its most obvious feature though. The first you see of the island is a dense clutter of dhows anchored in the lee, their graceful prows curving skywards like a fleet of Roman triremes.

As we near the island I make out figures on board, washing faces, hanging clothes, emptying slop buckets. 'Fishing boats,' Iain shouts above the engine roar. He slows to thread a path among them, peering over the side at times to avoid submerged anchor ropes. We cast our own anchor over a patch of sand near Jurayd's eastern tip. I have two sets of fish counts to do, repeating pre-war surveys by other scientists. Thomas advises me to swim around the exposed face of the island and start there. Having waited so long for a glimpse of these reefs, I wrestle a tank on and am quickly over the side. Plunging into the sea normally brings relief from the bustle and noise above water, but here the opposite is true. I'm surrounded by the raucous growl of generators throbbing from within the dhows' wooden hulls.

Below me a tongue of sand slopes offshore. But as I round the corner the noise subsides and corals blossom from the reef slope in spreading tables, bushes and pillowing mounds. Chrome yellow corals form upright plates that look like the coiled peels of metre-wide apples. Others form cones open at the top like a horn of plenty, their insides warted by polyps rough with spikes like tiny hedgehogs. Striped *Abudefduf* damselfish, Arabian angelfish, and the same feisty, scudding surgeonfish I studied for my PhD lend the scene a Red Sea feel. But there are differences, variations on Red Sea colour schemes, like the Arabian butterflyfish, a slender yellow oval rimmed in black, like a lemon slice edged with molasses. Apart from the black dorsal fin, it's a dead ringer for a Red Sea species. The reefs are much less well developed here too, petering out into sand and rubble in fifteen to twenty metres of water, but there is plenty of coral. I head through a shoal of tiny fish that flicker beneath the surface like a summer shower. Given the high density of heavy-bellied snappers, sweetlips and bream, it is clear the men on the boats do not fish here. In fact, they fish far offshore over vast plains of sand and mud using wire traps of surprising size, large enough to host a dinner party inside.

My counts complete, I follow the reef around the island, hugely relieved to find it intact and unsullied by oil. But when I round the western tip, there is more rubble. As I head in the direction of our boat, there are upturned coral tables, toppled bommies, brains split open and bushes pummelled to fragments. It looks like the aftermath of an earthquake, but the cause here is unnatural. Jurayd's reefs survived the Gulf War only to be pounded to bits by the anchors of Saudi Arabia's own fishing fleet. Discarded nets are caught in the corals and ropes knot their branches. It's the worst damage I've seen.

After the dive I swim to the island to check for oil. Terns lift off in a shrieking blizzard of wings. The sand is clean and firm at the waterline. I dig a pit with my hands, scooping wet sand until coral fragments prevent further progress, but find no oil. The strandline is cluttered with twigs, pieces of rope, plastic bottles, Styrofoam cups and a hundred other reminders of 'civilisation'. But aside from a few tar balls, their sticky surfaces disguised by beach sand, there is no oil. Perhaps it never reached this island, I wonder? If the oil hugged the mainland coast it could all have been trapped behind the island of Abu Ali and ended up in the bay we saw the day before. Back on the boat, I ask Thomas. 'I'm not sure,' he says. 'I think that oil passed this way but we weren't allowed on the islands for several months after the war. Most of the oil had either beached somewhere or evaporated by then.'

We overnight with the dhows, the creak of timbers and drifted strains of Arabic song adding to the music of the sea. The night is moonless and the stars so bright overhead it feels as if you could reach up and touch them. We wake early, dew-soaked from sleeping on the open deck. The glow of approaching sunrise is building in the east, deep red above the dark line of sea. The sound of a hacking cough followed by that of a throat-gargling spit drifts across from one of the dhows. We breakfast on custard creams and sweet mint tea, keen to be off. Our next stop, Jana Island, lies twenty-five kilometres to the north, taking us closer to the source of the oil, still 250 km away in Kuwait.

We reach Jana two hours later, windblown and ears ringing. The relief is palpable when the engines are finally cut. There are only two dhows here and we anchor well apart. Jana looks much like Jurayd, a slender oval of sand no more than a couple of metres high. Low shrubs cover its interior, their branches speckled with resting seabirds. We are soon in the water. Skirting the island, corals cover a third to a half of the seabed. In places, carpets of grey polyps form an almost continuous blanket over the underlying rocks, their pulsing tentacles wafting food into millions of mouths. Columns rise through them, their surfaces knobbed and bushed with purple and maroon branching corals and furred by hydroids. Mounds covered with a slippery layer of green weed indicate dead corals, but a close look reveals tiny warts where fresh coral settlers pock the surfaces. There are tumbled colonies and patches broken by anchors here and there, but nothing like the carnage at Jurayd. On land, the only evidence of oil I can find is in tarred patches of beach rock on the north coast, which faces Kuwait.

The disappearance of some of the spilled oil can be put down to microbes. Oil is organic, and as well as being a source of power for us, it is a source of energy for microbes. The Arabian Gulf seafloor naturally seeps oil, just as there are hundreds of natural seeps on land. Tar was used to pave the streets in eighth-century Baghdad, and bitumen seeps were mined to waterproof ships and houses. Recent studies reveal Gulf waters to be rich in microbial gas guzzlers, but how fast they can clear up spilled oil remains unknown.

The following day, we motor north to Karan Island, edging another thirty-five kilometres nearer Kuwait. This place was definitely not spared. Fourteen thousand cubic metres of Saddam's oil were scraped from its beaches after the war, Aziz told me. But the island we approach now, another low-lying berm of sand, looks clean. Below water, encrusting corals drape the bottom like chain mail, the corallites' brown ridges contrasting with mint-green centres. Some are several metres across and must be at least a century old. In other places, moss-green and pale-tipped branching corals overlap one another like spread Japanese fans. Domes rise through them, their slopes the colour of dark earth scored with meandering ridges and valleys like a field ploughed by a drunken farmer. Slate-grey damselfish the size of playing cards fill the water while the green bullet bodies of wrasse slip in and out of clefts and crevices. I search closely but there is no sign of oil, no bleaching, no evidence of disease, no mass grave of war dead. Can oil really be this benign?

Our survey complete, we head back to Jubail, arriving after nightfall. Iain steers a tentative course between winking green and red channel markers. Just as in Qatar, the city here marches seaward on angular slabs of man-made land, sucked and scraped from the seabed and dumped upon habitats whose value was underestimated and unappreciated. Flood-lit refineries, gas flares and street lamps flicker on the inky water. I am at the end of the Saudi leg of my trip and have seen the place where Saddam's oil ended up – in the dying mangroves and contaminated sediments of Abu Ali bay. The offshore reefs have had more luck, escaping all but minor injury. But the terrible destruction inflicted by the fishing fleet shows how fragile their existence is in this fast-developing region, hemmed in by the industrial maze. As we approach the dock, I worry for the future. Will our capacity for harm outpace the desire to protect?

The Gulf Marine Sanctuary Project, whose staff I've been travelling with, feels a slender response to the need. To industrialists, the Gulf seems no more than a convenient resource from which useful things can be taken and into which the unwanted can be disposed. On the flight from England I read some horrifying statistics about the industrial complexes that surround us. A single Saudi fertiliser plant flushes 5.8 million cubic metres of water contaminated with ammonia and heavy metals into the sea every year. Every refinery discharges water laden with thousands of tonnes of hydrocarbons annually. Desalination plants keep pipes and machinery clear of fouling creatures by dosing circulating waters with chromic acid and chlorine, releasing the toxic effluent direct to sea. And the growing human population adds its own strains. The city of Al Khobar, a hundred kilometres to the south, slops ten million cubic metres of untreated sewage into the Gulf annually, a practice likely to be repeated here and in every city along this coast. Against this background of abuse, it feels all the more remarkable that there is still so much life underwater.

On the plane to Kuwait, my thoughts turn to the events that brought me here. It was oil that triggered war. Saddam Hussain invaded

Kuwait in August 1990, piqued by Kuwait's overproduction of oil, which he claimed was depressing global prices. He also accused the Kuwaitis of stealing Iraqi oil by drilling lateral wells beneath the border. Perhaps it was his fury over oil that made him order the destruction of the wells in Iraq's retreat from Kuwait early the following year. We can only guess.

I can see the aftermath below as we cross the border on our descent into Kuwait City: dark circles on a soot-stained desert. In the sun's glare, they shine like pools of water on the dry earth. Thousands of migrating birds fell for the same illusion, alighting on the water's surface only to find themselves mired in oil. It is hard to reconcile this peaceful if sullied landscape with the horrendous television images I watched as events unfolded. After a month of bombing, coalition troops entered Kuwait in late February 1991. Scenes of adulation and terror played out beneath a twilight pall cast across the country by its raging oil wells. Burned-out tanks and trucks were strewn across desert and highway, framed against a backdrop of fire and darkness. The gates of Hades had been flung open.

In the months that followed, the world watched in dismay as a choking shroud spread over Arabia and halfway across Asia. On the ground, summer never came, as Kuwaitis and troops suffered under a drizzle of soot and unburned oil as the thunder of over six hundred flaming wells rolled on. Progress to cap them was slow. Mines had been set around the wells, which needed clearing before firefighters could begin work. Once secure, an explosive charge had to be manoeuvred into the midst of the flames where it was exploded to snuff them out, a perilous and often unsuccessful method. But a greater danger followed for the men who fought to cap the gushing oil, as the slightest spark could reignite it. Soaked from head to foot in dark and viscous oil, they shone like bronze statues as they worked, monuments to their own bravery. To begin with it was slow and painstaking work, but soon someone had the bright idea of attaching a jet engine to the back of a truck and blowing the wells out like candles. This worked a treat and the last well was extinguished in November 1991, nine months after they had been set alight and a year before my visit.

Ironic, I thought, that the source of Arabia's improbable wealth was a gift of the sea. Long ago, the land below my plane made up the shallow floor of the Tethys Sea, a broad stretch of water that connected the Indian Ocean with what would eventually become the Atlantic. The sea that ran across Arabia and along the course of today's Mediterranean was highly productive. Throughout the mid-Jurassic, 150 million years ago, deep in the age of dinosaurs, dead plankton rained onto a seabed devoid of oxygen. For millions of years they accumulated until conditions changed and new sediments settled on top of them. This sealed their lipid-rich bodies beneath an impermeable rock cap where, over the immensity of time, the alchemy of organic chemistry turned them into oil.

My daydreaming is cut short by our plane's arrival from Saudi Arabia. Nearly two years after liberation, Kuwait is scarred by war. The charred remains of wrecked military vehicles litter the roadside. Pock marks of gunfire spatter the concrete and marble of city blocks and there are gaps where others have been destroyed. We slow to pass a road crew enveloped in a cloud of dust as they repair what looks like a bomb crater, headscarves wrapped around their faces so that only their eyes show.

At the hotel I meet Nigel Downing, who I will partner for the Kuwait surveys. Nigel is in his thirties, well spoken, vigorous, lean and good-looking. He is dressed in pale trousers and a fawn cotton shirt, every bit the Englishman abroad, like a character from a Graham Greene novel. Nigel spent many years at the Kuwait Institute for Scientific Research studying corals, so he knows the reefs here intimately. By good fortune, he left shortly before Saddam's invasion to set up on his own in England as a business consultant. This is his second visit since the war. Fearful at the plight of Kuwait's reefs, and feeling that he might be able to help, he wangled a trip with the British military five months after the end of hostilities. Although the devastation above water was shocking, the picture beneath proved more encouraging. His report concluded that the seas around the three Kuwait coral islands appeared to have emerged unscathed. But there was a caveat. The shadow cast by burning oil wells had caused sea temperatures to fall and would make it harder for the internal microbes that feed coral to produce food by photosynthesis. They might yet succumb.

In winter 1992, Nigel's prediction looked to have been fulfilled when reports of dead and dying reefs came back from an American oceanographic expedition to Kuwait. Several reefs were completely dead, they said, while corals on others were stressed and dying. In the battered but still marbled lobby of our hotel, Nigel tells me over a tall glass of iced tea that we must prepare ourselves for the worst.

The next day, we make our way to the offices of the Environmental Protection Council to meet our hosts. Dr Fahim Nasri is to be our main contact and will accompany us into the field. He is Egyptian, he tells us, and has been in Kuwait for many years. His speciality is pollution, so one would think, in a perverse way, that he would thrive in the midst of this crisis. But he seems weary and dispirited. His shabby jacket hangs off stooped shoulders and he speaks in a low monotone of thickly accented English. 'The reefs are probably dead, but we don't know because nobody has seen them since the American biologists left.' Will our trip confirm the worst? I feel like a doctor brought in to certify a death.

We meet Fahim at first light the next day. He had managed to pull strings, securing the use of a Health Ministry launch and coastguard vessel for our island survey. The ministry boat is like a barge: wide, flat-bottomed, sturdy and slow. It comes complete with resident crew whose crowded quarters have spilt grubby bed sheets, discarded pyjamas and used tea glasses into the central cabin space, which are bundled away on our arrival. The coastguard vessel is a smaller and quicker launch. Nigel and I will take the launch to Qaru where there is a coastguard post. Qaru is only a couple of hundred metres long and two hundred wide, so we should have time to swim around the entire reef before the ministry boat chugs in with several other people from various departments and ministries. While an overnight trip to the islands is no picnic, it is clear from the small crowd that many have seized the chance to come along, pleased perhaps to escape the filth and noise of the city.

Fahim travels with Nigel and me. I join him at the deck rail as Kuwait City's skyline descends into the sea. The fresh air seems to lift him and he is more forthcoming than the previous day. I ask about the war.

'It was bad,' he says. 'Saddam told us that Kuwait would become Iraq's Nineteenth Province but we knew he would not stay. They didn't care about us; they didn't care about anything. It was terrible to watch. Before the war, I thought about going back to Egypt.' He looks around to see if we are being overheard but there is nobody close. 'The Kuwaitis took me for granted. I felt like a second-class citizen here. But then Saddam arrived and I was stuck.'

'Have things got any better?' I ask.

'When the war ended, we continued to suffer from Saddam. Sometimes it was hard to tell the difference between day and night with so much smoke. It was hard to breathe. Everybody had coughs.' After the war, Kuwait deported two hundred thousand Palestinians in retribution for the Palestinian Liberation Organisation's ill-conceived support for Saddam's annexation of Kuwait. He was saddened, he said, by the expulsion of Palestinian friends. Nobody felt secure any more. 'I still want to leave, but all I have is in Kuwait.'

We reach Qaru an hour later. A low building sits in the middle of the island next to a tall communications pylon. The building has been patched but still bears visible scars from shellfire. A group of new water storage tanks stands next to it on a concrete plinth, while those they have replaced lie discarded on the beach. Ruined bunkers and half-filled foxholes mark where the Iraqis dug in.

We pull in to the jetty where we are greeted enthusiastically by the coastguards, which strikes me as odd. Arabian coastguards are usually guarded. The reason for their welcome soon becomes clear, as Fahim translates. The day before they had chased down some alcohol smugglers trying to circumvent Kuwait's alcohol ban. The smugglers are now in custody and their boat lies upturned on the beach nearby, but the whisky was ditched overboard during pursuit. The smugglers' boat has the sleek lines of a racing speedboat. It looks as if it could easily outpace the coastguard boat anchored nearby, making me wonder whether shots were fired. But there is no sign of damage.

Such a timely arrival of two marine biologists with diving gear must seem near miraculous. We are soon dispatched to the reef where I am confronted by the marvellous and completely unexpected sight of healthy corals half concealed by fish. Qaru is just a few tens of kilometres from the refineries that bled oil into the sea for months. I expected devastation. But by great good fortune the oil must have passed over these reefs just as in Saudi. Colonies have spread their branches over the reef slope like giant lily pads, some several metres across. A single chevron-striped butterflyfish holds court above each, alternately nibbling polyps and dashing at intruders. Sheltering underneath are snowflake-blotched groupers and fat sweetlips, their flanks scored with diagonal black stripes that turn to spots on glowing yellow fins. Deeper down, the bottom is covered by near-continuous grey and purple finger corals, like a scaled-down mountain range. Schools of delicate grey fish with yellow lyre-tails dance above them, while dottybacks with thunderbolt blue stripes hide among their branches.

Here and there, nestled enticingly amid the corals, are bottles of golden whisky. They look for all the world like rare and glamorous reef creatures. In a few minutes I have an armful and head back to the beach, emerging from the water to the delighted whoops of coastguards and Fahim. Just behind me, Nigel is wading out with another half-dozen bottles. The captain gestures for us to return and get some more. It is difficult to juggle note-taking with whisky collection, but again and again we are sent back until we find no more. Seventy bottles lie on the beach in neat rows. The captain slaps our backs and pumps our hands, showing a gratitude more apt for the US Navy Seals who retook his island, than for liberators of whisky. I begin to suspect that the coastguards' motives are not entirely pure. Fahim also seems animated, scarcely suppressing his excitement as we survey the contraband.

The next day we have more time for fish and coral. Qaru's reefs are not entirely unscathed, but the damage is not from oil. There is a small bomb crater close to the reef edge, although there are already signs of recovery with new corals settled on the dead. Here and there, incongruous amid the living fabric, are sections of pipe and heaps of builders' rubble. The sea has been a convenient dump for the debris of war.

Our work done, the coastguards whisk Nigel and me to the neighbouring island of Umm Al Maradem, 'Mother of Boulders', twenty kilometres away. There we will camp on the beach alone. With a wink, the captain presses a bottle of whisky into our hands as a parting gift, an illicit treat. Umm al Maradem is twenty times bigger than Qaru and was a military outpost before the war. Its beach is backed by a rim of low bushes, the sand bright and pale where it is washed by the sea, in sharp contrast to the surface above high water, soot-blackened from months of oil fires. This place was bombed savagely and the twisted wreckage of military hardware and wasted lives is everywhere. At the south end there are chaotic remains of buildings fronted by a harbour that holds the carcasses of what look like two Iraqi gunboats. 'Be careful,' Nigel warns as we leave the beach to explore. 'The Americans bombed several caches of munitions when they retook the island. There are unexploded bombs all over the place.'

Heaped sandbags and grooved trenches interrupt the natural lines of the island. The Iraqis burrowed a makeshift air-raid shelter under the concrete helicopter pad. I wonder how much good it had done them. Umm al Maradem is famous for its nesting terns, Nigel tells me. I imagine them lifting in screaming clouds above the sand.

What did the soldiers make of them? The terns are somewhere else now as we are out of the breeding season, and the island is quiet. A breeze lifts a rustle of sand around my feet. In the distance, a loose wire taps out a mournful 'ting-ting' against a flagless pole, tolling for the dead.

I point out to Nigel a four-finned plastic tail, half buried in sand, attached to something that resembles a plum. It looks like a child's toy. 'Oh shit! It's a cluster bomblet.' he says. The Americans used a cluster bomb before they stormed the island. It contained 250 of these, which go off like fireworks after the main bomb explodes. The army ordnance guys who I was here with last year told me that about a third of them don't go off in places with soft sand.' Now having a search image, we soon spot another, then another, swiftly followed by the thought of what we might not see beneath the veil of windblown sand. After that we don't stray from the beach.

That evening we watch the sun set over the sea, a blaze of carmine and purple that suffuses the water almost to my feet. Sipping my whisky, I think of the contrasting fortunes of the worlds above and below water, so close and yet so far apart. As planes hammered overhead, bombs erupted and bullets strafed the strandline, the fish, coral and other sea creatures pursued their daily lives untroubled. How odd, too, the separation of time. Where I bask in the glory of this sunset, others had recently sat tense and fearful in the face of looming battle.

The next morning, we discover that the reefs of Umm al Maradem, closer to the pollution epicentre than Qaru's, have also been spared. While there is much dead coral among the living here, it died several years before the oil. These reefs are at the extreme northerly limit of coral reef growth and they hang on in marginal conditions, Nigel explains. From the corals' viewpoint, these seas alternately swelter and freeze over the course of a year. The Gulf States suffer torrid summer heat, but then in mid-winter when winds blow hard from northern deserts, temperatures dive, sometimes far enough to nip mangrove buds with frost and kill coral. This is what we can see here. It also explains how the American scientists had wrongly announced the death of Kuwait's reefs. None had any experience of such high-latitude outposts of coral existence. These reefs would always look rough and scrappy compared to those in more clement regions of the Pacific or Indian oceans. But they are healthy nonetheless.

The coastguards return to collect us in the afternoon for another night on Qaru. The plan is for Nigel and me to visit Kubbar, the last island, by coastguard launch on the way back to Kuwait City the following day. Fahim and the others will go direct with the ministry boat then meet us at the dock later on. Next morning, Fahim seems to be struggling with his overnight bag as we walk down the jetty and I ask if he would like a hand. With a furtive look around, he whispers, 'The bag is full of whisky!' My eyebrows spring upward, prompting an explanation. 'The captain gave it to me. You know, it will make life tolerable back in the city.' I can't argue with the logic, but wonder at the risk he is taking.

On the way back we discover that Kuwait's other reefs have been spared serious damage. The variety of fish and coral is lower than further south, and the reefs poorly developed, reflecting the greater extremes of temperature. But they flourish nonetheless. Peering at a particularly lovely brain coral, its meandering valleys aglow with green and blue, I find it hard to believe that such a tender creature could survive so much. No more than a whisper of living tissue covers the skeleton. Its resilience is humbling. Oil is definitely bad for corals though, as experiments and spills in other parts of the world have shown. But here, with only a small tidal range, there was enough freeboard above the reef for most of the oil to have floated past without sticking.

There is something about my fish counts that I find intriguing. There are 40 per cent fewer fish species on average on Kuwaiti reefs compared to those of Saudi Arabia. The reefs here are less well developed, blending into sand at five to nine metres deep, compared to Saudi's fifteen to twenty. The water is more turbid, the tidal range greater and the temperature swings more violent. Peculiarly, though, fish abundance goes in the other direction. There are almost twice as many fish on Kuwaiti reefs as on Saudi ones, but most of the difference is made up by very high densities of a small number of dominant species. It seems as though increasing environmental stress winnows the number of species as their tolerances are exceeded. But could dominance by a few increase as their competitors drop away? Welcome food for thought.

When we dock in Kuwait City in the late afternoon, I am half-expecting Fahim not to be there, thinking he might have been arrested for his contraband stash. But there he is, although as we get closer I see that his crestfallen demeanour has returned. As we step ashore, he pulls me aside and almost wails in my ear, 'I have made a terrible mistake.' I look around, expecting to find police waiting to take him away, but there are none. He goes on 'I overheard the crew on the boat muttering about the whisky in my bag, and I began to worry that they would tell the police. So I went to the stern where nobody could see and threw the bottles over the side.' His voice chokes up, 'But there were no police here! Now I have lost the whisky.' I try to be sympathetic, but he is bereft.

We leave Kuwait two days later, in awe at the resilience of these reefs. Clinging on at the edge of existence, I had expected the stress of massive oil pollution to tip them into terminal decline. Their survival seems nothing less than wondrous.

CHAPTER ELEVEN

The aftermath of war

Iran, 1993

THERE IS SOMETHING EXCITING about receiving a fax. They carry news too important and urgent to trust to the post office[1] so reading them requires privacy and concentration. I choose a shady spot by the sea for this one, near my office at the University of the Virgin Islands on the island of St Thomas in the Caribbean Leeward Islands. Two years after leaving Egypt, and with an interlude of Caribbean research under my belt, I have landed a job. It is 1993 and I've been in St Thomas for a year. A warm breeze rattles palm fronds overhead as I unfurl the shiny scroll. It feels like reading a proclamation, although this is more of a summons: 'The Intergovernmental Oceanographic Commission of the United Nations Education Scientific and Cultural Organisation requests your participation in a mission to the Islamic Republic of Iran.' What a title! But there are few details as to what this mission might actually entail, other than going to Iran. Stuff about war and oil; there is a whiff of mystery. And what about the word 'mission'? Mission impossible perhaps? Maybe I should eat the fax after reading, I think with a chuckle. Naturally, I will accept.

---

1. There was no email in the early 1990s.

A trip to Iran has a special allure. Its seas are little known, marine science having been cut short by revolution. In fact, its seas are among the least known in the world. Charts show that the seabed shelves more steeply in the eastern Gulf than in the west, so deep water lies near the coast, which just might mean well-developed coral reefs. Old accounts from travellers and explorers say little about Persian coral, although they mention extensive mangrove forests in the south. The map shows two substantial islands, much bigger than those of Kuwait or Saudi Arabia, just north of a town called Bushehr. They surely have reefs. The prospect of discovery is tantalising.

An invitation to Iran is easier to issue than fulfil, it transpires. As mission departure approaches, 'difficulties' emerge. I fax a query letter. Nothing. Three days later a reply: 'Expect your ticket and visa imminently.' Meanwhile the mission 'plan' arrives, three faxed pages from somewhere deep in the Islamic Republic that look like the originals were thumped out on an antique typewriter. I manage to deduce that the mission is about pollution, but little more. Two days to go and UNESCO phones. In a precise BBC accent, an English lady apologises for the delay and asks if I can buy my own ticket and be at UNESCO headquarters in Paris the day after tomorrow. Julie grumbles at the expense and questions whether I should go.

Personally, I am delighted by the Paris diversion, having never visited the city of romance. But there is little to love about the cultural headquarters of the United Nations. UNESCO is housed in a squat post-war office block on the edge of a boulevard in central Paris. I arrive directly from the plane to deliver my passport for the elusive visa. My fellow team members are already here, drawn from several nations. Our leader, Mr Gaulther Soares, is a seasoned Portuguese diplomat who has adopted France as his own. His serious face is parchment yellow and deeply lined. The skin has sagged and the corners of his eyes and mouth curve downward, giving him a world-weary look. He seems aloof and a little bored when I introduce myself. Martin, a chemist, is English. Jean is tall and elegant and tells us he is a retired oil pollution engineer from Brest. Salim is a Belgian oceanographer. Met under other circumstances he would pass for an earthy peasant frolicking in a Brueghel winter canvas.

It turns out that I have already met the final member of our team, Xavier, a Parisian maritime lawyer who breezed out of the building as I walked in. I am also introduced to Adrienne Maxwell, the aristocratic and charming secretary I spoke to from the Caribbean. She tells me, while we wait for an audience with our UNESCO boss, that she spent ten years in Africa and the Middle East, followed by five in Paris. These stints overseas have done nothing to dent perfect English manners.

UNESCO is a shock. I expected this international body of the arts and science to be sophisticated, industrious and bright. Instead there is floor upon floor of dark corridors and poky offices with cheap steel desks and shelves, slowly buckling under mountains of paper. Strangely, there is hardly a computer in sight. Further acquaintance over the next day reveals that most people still use pen and paper (stylus and slate would feel as apt). They communicate via notes left on each other's usually empty chairs, this being the only way, I presume, to ensure the notes are noticed amid the accumulated strata of bureaucracy.

Our passports are passed to the Iranian delegation who inform us that they will be ready by 12 noon next day. We must be at the airport by 1.30p.m., but this causes no anxiety to Soares who reassures the rest of us. Privately, I am doubtful. Having tackled several layers of paperwork that morning to spring our expenses from the UNESCO bank, Martin, Jean and I spend a pleasant afternoon strolling the Champs-Élysées.

Next morning, back at UNESCO, 12 noon comes and goes. Jean tries to soothe our nerves, 'Don't worry, I'm sure they will be here soon and it's only three-quarters of an hour to the airport.' Just then a rather flustered Adrienne arrives. The Iranian Embassy won't accept a UNESCO cheque ('Probably wise,' Martin whispers in my ear) and she has no cash. Soares' brows knit almost imperceptibly. We pile into two taxis and race to the embassy to pay by cash. The door is locked and Adrienne pleads into a security speaker for a while before the door creaks open and she and Soares slip inside. For a long time, nothing happens. 1.30p.m. comes and goes, then 2 o'clock. Suddenly Soares reappears, looking stressed for the first time. Still no visas.

We've waited nearly an hour outside the embassy, which bristles with cameras, spiked gates and barbed wire. I am sure we will miss our plane. We pass another thirty minutes watching a shadowy figure watching us from above net curtains in a first-floor window. Martin helpfully reminds us of the policewoman shot dead by a Libyan diplomat from the window of their London embassy. Before I can reflect too long on this, Adrienne hurries out and hands our visas to the now freely perspiring Soares.

We hop into the taxis and, clearly an expert at this, Xavier the Parisian lawyer barks 'Vite vite!' at our driver. The car lurches into the traffic forcing me deep into the seat, only to be thrown forward seconds later at the first red light. Over the next half hour, Paris flies past in a terrifying blur before we squeal to a halt outside Departures. It is 3.10p.m. and the plane due to leave at 3.30p.m. The desk is closed but Xavier collars a couple of passing staff and presses them to call the gate. Surprisingly, they tell us to come directly with all our luggage. A hot dash later and we are there by 3.31.[1] Stepping into the plane, shaken, sweaty and last to board, I enter Iran while still in Paris. Black heads line the rows and hooded stewardesses stalk the aisles. This 747 is full, mostly of women, wafting French perfume from beneath their chadors.

We arrive in Tehran in the middle of the night so curiosity must wait. Morning reveals a dusty city set in a hollow against the soaring backdrop of the Elborz Mountains. Our hotel stands proud of a sea of boxy apartment blocks, none more than five or six stories high, cut through by narrow, winding streets. Here and there leafy patches suggest the presence of squares and gardens. Early morning light bathes the buildings in an amber warmth. Far below, street vendors

---

1. Airport security was almost non-existent back then.

unpack their wares from suitcases while a group of black clad figures look on, anonymous as chess pieces.

Mission begun, our team of distinguished international experts, as UNESCO likes to refer to us in correspondence, begins the rounds. At thirty-one years old, I don't feel very expert and certainly not distinguished. Charles Sheppard, Andrew Price and I have recently published a book on the marine environment of the Red Sea and Arabian Gulf, which I suppose is qualification of a sort, but I feel unprepared having no Iranian experience whatever. The first meeting is with our lead agency in the country, the Iranian Department of the Environment. We are shown into a sparsely furnished waiting room with metal chairs against one wall. Jean and Xavier sit but the rest of us have a closer look at a huge portrait of Ayatollah Khomeini that broods from one wall with an expression of dangerous benevolence. I don't know much about Iran bar the American hostage crisis and Salman Rushdie so I feel vulnerable, an outsider among revolutionaries. We talk in hushed whispers as if fearful of the Ayatollah's watchful presence.

A man arrives and announces that the director will see us. We follow him along a corridor that is dark but for intermittent pools of light cast by open office doors. The offices are scruffy and remind me of UNESCO, only this time without obvious paperwork. Our guide stops at an entrance grander than the rest. The director rises from his desk and waves us in. Soares begins our introductions but is brought to an abrupt halt. 'I know what you are here for,' the director says. He knows more than I do then, I think. 'But we need to change your terms of reference.' After much diplomatic circling, it transpires that he wants a 'project', not advice. A project would bring money, which would be better than people like us. Soares shakes his head sadly. The mission cannot be changed. At which point the director bids us goodbye.

The next day, we visit the National Centre for Oceanography. Professor Zomoruddian, the director, has a well-tended grey beard and piercing eyes that follow us over the top of wire-rimmed glasses. He welcomes us warmly but is puzzled. 'What can you achieve in a week?' the beard wags in admonition. 'And why was I only informed of your visit yesterday?' UNESCO inefficiency, we discover, reaches deep into Iran. We leave Professor Zomoruddian later on with little more than his goodwill. Curses are muttered about UNESCO as we wait for a taxi back to our hotel, which reminds Martin of a joke: 'How many people work at UNESCO? About ten per cent.' He can't resist another. 'When is the rush hour at UNESCO? Eleven o'clock, when those arriving late meet those leaving early for lunch.'

Our taxi swings across four lanes of traffic to an indignant blare of horns. The driver is garrulous and soon extracts our purpose from Jean, who is in the front. 'Saddam is a monster. Why didn't Bush destroy him when he had the chance?' he frowns. None of us can think of a good answer. Martin offers something about the United Nations not allowing it, but the driver has stopped listening to shout through the window at a truck that has swerved in front. Jolted from my seat, I decide that Iran's roads and earthquakes are the most dangerous things here. I expected suspicion, hostility and revolutionary zeal; after all, Salman Rushdie has been in hiding for the last four years. But instead there is unabashed curiosity.

Day three and with little to show, we head for the town of Bushehr on the Gulf coast. We will surely be able to find pollution there, despite not having found much written about it. I am excited about the prospect of discovering coral reefs, if not on the coast then, hopefully, around the islands I saw on the map.

The Iran Air plane looks tired and I worry about the effect of sanctions on supplies of spare parts. A vague smell of sick permeates the row. As the plane taxis into take-off position a reedy voice wails a prayer. The aisles resonate as every passenger, bar us, returns the required response. Jean leans over and says, 'Good. Now we will have a safe flight.' Shortly after take-off, a soldier with a Kalashnikov rifle comes briefly into view from behind a curtain and disappears. The plane is buffeted by violent turbulence most of the way to Bushehr and the passengers are anxious and silent. I am grateful for another impromptu prayer before landing.

the water, no serried line of breakers. One of the biologists interrupts my contemplation.

'You will not find any reefs here,' he says.

'What about coral?' I ask.

He gives a slight shrug. 'Sometimes the fishermen drag up pieces in their nets.'

'Is there a boat we can use,' I ask, 'to get offshore?'

He points to a slipway further down the beach. 'Our boat is being serviced,' he explains. It is propped on blocks and judging by the bloom of dust, hasn't been to sea for over a year.

'What about Khark and Kharku Islands?' I press, 'Surely there are reefs there?' Despite the setback with the boat, I nurture a hope that we can get to the islands some other way, perhaps with coastguards as in Kuwait.

He rolls his eyes and gives an incredulous laugh, 'Nobody can go there except the military!'

I feel a crushing disappointment. I've come halfway around the world hoping to discover something fresh and exciting but can do no more than paddle, like a child on a seaside holiday.[1]

The beach oil turns out to be less bad than in Saudi Arabia but worse than in Kuwait. We work our way south and the oil thins into patches until it disappears altogether forty kilometres beyond the town.

By late afternoon we reach Rostami, a cluster of low, flat-roofed houses, each within a walled compound. The dockside is crowded with broad-beamed dhows built to a centuries-old design. Many are connected to the shore by slender and wobbly planks across which seamen pass back and forth with nimble dexterity, landing baskets of fish and prawns and loading ice and provisions. I am brushed out of the way by a barrel-chested man in filthy, ragged trousers. Sweat glistens on his dark back as he balances a gleaming block of

---

1.   Decades later, the two offshore islands were discovered to support the richest and most intact coral reefs in the whole Arabian Gulf. They escaped damage by oil, and the military presence evidently dissuaded fishermen from anchoring.

ice on his shoulder. I thread my way through the crowd to look at the catch. The fish are small and varied, as expected from a bottom trawl net that takes indiscriminately from the seabed. But the fish are simply bycatch to the main prize of tiger prawns. Seeing my interest, a fisherman picks up a prawn the size of his hand and thrusts it towards me. The abdomen and legs are deeply patterned with brown stripes and its black eyes gleam like spheres of caviar. This coast has been spared the devastation I saw in Saudi Arabia where their shrimp fishery was driven to collapse by the toxic slicks.

Back in Tehran, we have a little more to go on than before, although if any of us understood Farsi we would have a lot more. Quite understandably, most of the reports on pollution we have been shown are written in Farsi, and none has been translated. This reminds me of a campsite conversation from my Saudi Arabian student days, and Alec Dawson Shepherd's definition of a consultant: someone who borrows your watch to tell you the time. But here we have to ask them what the time is because we can't read the watch! As we gently probe about what these studies involve, it emerges that most suffer from some fundamental scientific defect or other, such as too few samples, sub-standard analytical equipment or lack of controls (unaffected samples against which the affected ones can be compared). To raise sagging spirits, Jean suggests that the language barrier makes our work easier, as a fresh plan of work will be preferable to exhuming the bones of the old. Science, it seems, has been held in suspended animation since the revolution. First came the overthrow of institutions associated with the Shah, then eight years of war. Only since Khomeini's death in 1989 has there been a flickering of scientific rebirth, kindled by academics who studied outside Iran before the revolution. I begin to hope that our trip might encourage these fledgling efforts and thereby have some purpose after all.

The evening is mild and the streets bustle. Groups of young men chat and smoke at street corners while families stroll the tree-lined avenues. A couple kisses on a park bench. We make our way to the former Hilton hotel for dinner. This icon of western imperialism was nationalised after the revolution and renamed the Laleh. It towers above the surrounding buildings, a blank cliff of brutalist concrete. A cheerful slogan in golden circles gleams from the wall above the café: 'DOWN WITH USA.'

On our way to the airport next day, we pass a parade of goose-stepping revolutionary guardsmen with red bandanas and brandished guns. Today is the anniversary of the 'Imposed War' with Iraq, the driver tells us. A scooter pulls up alongside with a sheep riding pillion. The animal eyes us calmly as if on an everyday commute. The driver is wild and stubbled with a wrap of cloth twisted on his head. He catches my eye and grins broadly, revealing his last few teeth.

A month later, home again in the US Virgin Islands, the trip seems oddly surreal. The Islamic Republic of Iran was more relaxed and friendly than expected, belying fatwas and propaganda. UNESCO was the bigger surprise. Aside from its creaky, top-heavy bureaucracy, I had heard within its headquarters the distinct sound of money rushing down drains. I have an uneasy feeling that I contributed to this torrent, but I push the thought aside as I hammer out my report, struggling to avoid the conclusion that our shambolic expedition has found nothing that isn't instantly apparent to even a casual observer. Far away, Iran and UNESCO carry on, each a perplexing mix of ancient and modern. Iran's reefs, if it has any, remain intangible and mysterious. Outside my office, a pelican plunges into the sea then bobs to the surface as water streams in trembling droplets from its empty throat.

Missed again.

CHAPTER TWELVE

Shifting currents

Caribbean, 1990s

St Thomas is a perfect base from which to explore the Caribbean. It's the most populous of the three US Virgin Islands, with homes crawling up forested hills along its full eighteen-kilometre length. The university is set in rolling parkland that runs down to a palm-fringed beach and the marine science centre. The centre has a dive facility, dock and boats, and is training a new generation of Caribbean and American marine scientists. It is exactly what I had hoped to create in Egypt, salting the pleasure of having landed a job here with a tinge of regret.

My boss, a dynamic St Thomian called Laverne Ragster, has given me complete freedom to decide what I want to do. 'Just make sure,' she said, 'that your research will benefit the people of this region.' I already have a good idea, whose origins lie in a research trip made in 1991, two years previously, to Saba and Belize.

Saba is the verdant tip of an extinct volcano, halfway between Anguilla and St Kitts and Nevis in the Eastern Caribbean. What brought me here is the protected area that surrounds the island. Although it covers just thirteen square kilometres of sea, it is one of the best-managed marine parks in the world. Crucially, part of it is closed to all fishing, which I hope will give me a better idea of what a coral reef might look like in the absence of human interference.

Julie and I are given a warm welcome to Saba by the park manager, Susan White, a petite blonde American of about thirty. Originally a school teacher, Susan later tells us that she applied for the job on a whim, having been travelling in the Caribbean. Her optimistic and bubbly humour contrasts with the reticence of her Saban deputy, Percy. A mix of Dutch and Caribbean, he is tall with piercing blue eyes that seem to glow from within his tanned and weathered face.

Percy is a kindly if sometimes grumpy companion. He soon makes it clear to us that he should have been manager and Susan his deputy. We quickly fall into a routine whereby we count fish while Percy maintains the buoys that mark each dive site. Early on he takes us to Diamond Rock, one of the places fully protected from fishing. It looks more like Alaska than the tropics today. Clouds slip down the mountainside and flow offshore, hugging the dark water. A ghostly shark's tooth of stone frosted with guano glows through the mist. We tie up to a mooring and descend to level sand twenty metres down before heading for the vertical face of the pinnacle. Although the sea appeared smooth from above, there is a long ocean swell rolling in from the Atlantic that pulls us up and down the rock several metres at a time. We move with the water, so it feels like we are stationary and the pinnacle is in motion, making it hard to count fish. To add to our disorientation, fish surge across the rock face, some rising and falling with us, others remaining on station, flipping nose to tail, tail to nose with each passing wave. Further off the rock, shoals of barracudas hang like silvered clouds below the water surface and pack-hunting jacks shatter schools of creole wrasse into indigo shards.

It is a relief to finish the counts and we re-cross the seabed with that dizzy feeling of stepping off a treadmill. Percy helps us into the boat and asks, 'See any pufferfish down there?' I hadn't. 'A few months back, one of the local guides took some divers here. They

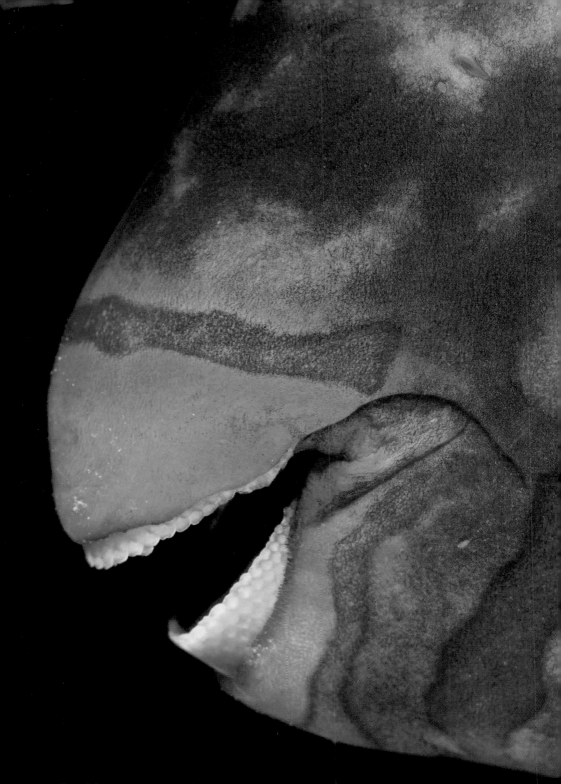

Parrotfish jaws are well adapted to scrape algae from rock, which, along with their typically flamboyant colours, give the fish a passing resemblance to their jungle namesakes. This one is a Swarthy parrotfish (*Scarus niger*), Maldives (*Ch. 2*).

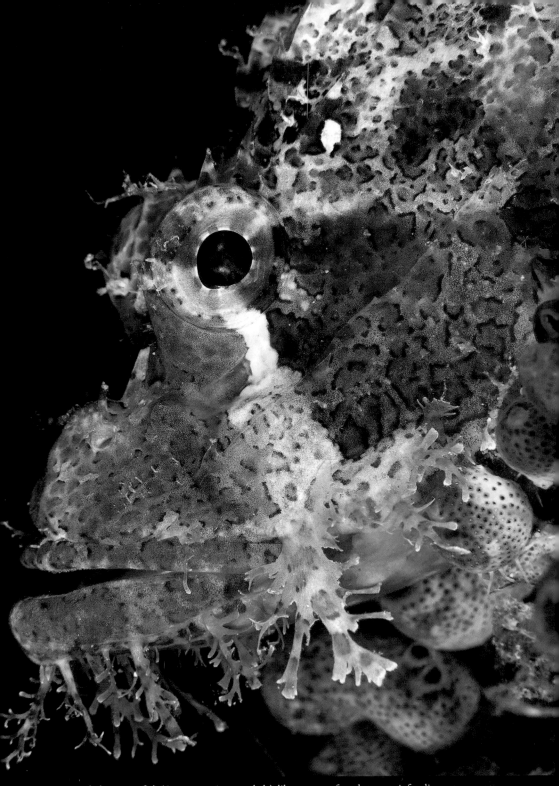

Tassled scorpionfish (*Scorpaenopsis oxycephala*), like many reef predators, wait for dinner to come to them, deploying lavish camouflage in preference to speed. Maldives (*Ch. 4*).

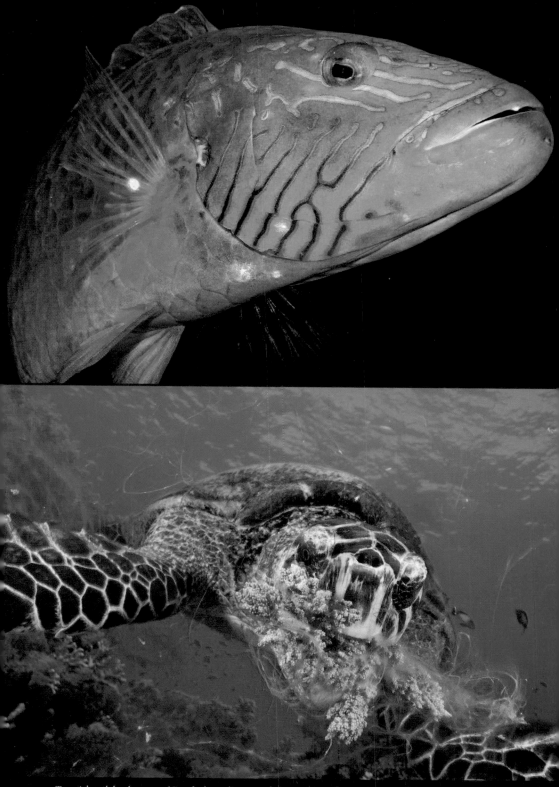

Top: A bandcheek wrasse (*Oxycheilinus digrammus*) once repeatedly attacked its reflection in my face mask, Red Sea (*Ch. 2*). Bottom: The hawksbill turtle (*Eretmochelys imbricata*) is one of the few animals not put off by distasteful chemicals in soft corals (*Ch. 5*).

Top: Coral patches like these rose as columns from the seabed in front of our Marine Research
Centre in Sharm-el-Sheikh, Egypt (*Ch. 7*). Bottom: Upward growth of coral reefs is stopped at sea
level; branching *Acropora*, Red Sea (*Ch. 8*).

Top left: A ghost goby (*Pleurosicya mossambica*) on the mantle of a giant clam (*Tridacna*), Maldives (*Ch. 14*). Top right: Squat lobster (*Galathea*) on fire coral (*Millipora dichotoma*), Red Sea (*Ch. 9*). Bottom: Batfish (*Platax orbicularis*), Red Sea (*Ch. 8*).

Life's profusion below water in the Red Sea and its scarcity above represents one of the most extreme contrasts on Earth, a difference dictated by the presence or absence of water. Sharm-el-Sheikh, Egypt (*Ch. 7*).

Raja Ampat in eastern Indonesia has the most diverse reefs in the world, a bullseye of immense reef richness in the heart of the Coral Triangle (*Ch. 9*).

get to the bottom and he sees a pufferfish, so he grabs it and makes it puff itself up with water. Then he takes his regulator out of his mouth and kisses it to impress his guests.' He gives a deep chuckle. 'Well them's not kissing fish! The puffer, he grab his lip like a vice. The guy he pulled, but the fish wouldn't let go. Then he try to put his regulator in again, but the fish is in the way.' Percy roars with laughter. 'So now he can't breathe, he inflates his jacket, bursting out of the water like a rocket with a fish stuck to his face.'[1]

Saba was an active volcano until only a few hundred years ago so the reefs are just a thin crust of corals over boulders rained into the sea by pyroclastic flows. The fish are less prolific than on better-developed reefs, making it hard to judge the effects of protection. But each count brings the answer closer. The dives are mostly uneventful and days blend one into another. Then halfway into our trip and mid-dive at fifteen metres down, a movement at the edge of vision catches my eye. It is Julie, both arms raised, jabbing the water above her head in a fair impression of John Travolta dancing in *Saturday Night Fever*. I stare back in perplexity. It is far too shallow for nitrogen narcosis. A moment later an anchor thuds to the bottom a metre to my left followed by a rumble of chain. By now Julie is beside me, eyes wide with relief. When we surface Percy says, 'We had a near miss there! The mooring line parted while I was cleaning it. I had to swim fast to catch the boat and anchor up!' He looks pleased with himself and pauses, wondering why we are slow to praise.

Near the end of the trip a pattern has emerged. Although it's only four years since protection began, fully protected reefs have nearly double the fish that fished areas have, with more of the bigger and tasty species too. Before we leave, we gain another insight diving a group of offshore pinnacles. Below us, the rope of the buoy, pulled taut by current, curves off and disappears into depth, as if held by invisible force. We kick hard and descend fast.

---

1. Luckily it was the beginning of the dive. If he had kissed the puffer later, he would probably have got the bends as dissolved nitrogen fizzed out of his blood.

There will be little time to linger when we summit the mount, thirty metres down.

As plankton clouds over the surface above, a mottling green and pink builds like a mirage in the dark water below. It solidifies into a rugged landscape scaled with plating corals. Black corals shudder in the furious current that gusts across the peak. A loose group of fish scuds across, swivelling their eyes in our direction for a close look. There are tiger groupers and black groupers that I haven't seen on reefs nearer the island, and, at the edge of visibility, a shark, its lithe body gilded by weak sunlight. These predators are still absent from the nearshore reefs despite protection. Distance from the shore and depth has spared them. With time they should recolonise the shallows as the marine park heals old wounds.

After Saba, we head for Belize, our destination Ambergris Caye at the edge of the Mesoamerican Barrier Reef. Like Saba, it has a well-defended marine park, the Hol Chan Marine Reserve, the inner part of which has been closed to fishing for four years. Rolling over the side for our first dive, I find myself above a broad seagrass plain, the sward dense and shiny. I drop the few metres to the bottom and turn towards the channel, fingertips brushing grass, scattering tiny fish. Coral outcrops rise through the canopy like Mayan temples above rainforest. A metre-long rainbow parrotfish barrels towards us, sleek as a torpedo. Its face, chest and tail are violent orange, the beak and flanks brilliant turquoise touched with royal purple.

The tide is coming in, making us work hard to get into the reef cut. Groups of fish hug the channel walls, faces to the current, tails chopping to maintain position. A group of batfish swing past, their bodies like pewter plates. Passing into the channel, fish coalesce into shoals of hammered copper, slate and sulphur, liveried with royal blue, gold and orange spots and lines. By the time we reach the seaward edge of the channel, the reef is a moving mass, corals only here and there showing through the wall of bodies. This density of fish is utterly unexpected. Only a few times have I seen anything like it, in Arabia, and only then at the far edges of the human world. We swim through living tunnels, parting snappers, grunts, groupers and jacks like Moses parted the Red Sea. These fat-bodied predators are much favoured by fishermen and are scarce in unprotected places.

Over four weeks, we count our way back and forth along a section of the barrier reef centred on the channel, both inside and outside the marine reserve. Part of Hol Chan's magnificence as a fishy Grand Central has to be because the channel concentrates food on incoming and outgoing tides. So, by way of comparison, we count in three other reef cuts that lack protection. Averaged across all our counts, protected reefs here, like those of Saba, have double the fish of unprotected sites. The channel, the pulsing heart of this reserve, has six to ten times more fish. A consequence of the strong protection, there are rarities I've never seen before, like the rainbow parrotfish. These species are so vulnerable to depletion they can only persist in places where there is little or no fishing.[1]

Hol Chan is a turning point in my understanding, revealing that reefs can support an unanticipated richness and abundance of life, and that strong protection can breathe life back into places cleared out by fishing. As important as this discovery is, Hol Chan is only a snapshot in time. I can't prove beyond doubt that it is protection rather than some quirk of exceptional habitat that is responsible for the enormous shoals of fish. I need an experiment, some place in which Julie and I can track changes before and after protection. There is something else we need too: a willing group of fishermen we can study at the same time. My findings point to a possible breakthrough that could pave the way for a rollout of marine protected areas all over the world. In benefiting fish, reserves could boost the fortunes of fishermen too.

The idea is that marine reserves are leaky. As fish populations build following protection, the animals grow older, larger and

---

1. An archaeological study of fish remains in Caribbean middens would later show that rainbow parrotfish were overfished to the point of rarity by the islands' inhabitants long before Columbus reached the New World.

more abundant. Eventually, young fish are outcompeted for the resources they need – food, space and mates – so they seek their fortunes elsewhere. Since most marine reserves are quite small, they don't have to go far to find less crowded waters, which happen to be in fishing grounds. In this way, marine reserves can spill fish into places where they will boost catches.

All those fish inside reserves play their part too. Big old fat fish produce far more young than small fish do. They are the engines of population replenishment. Eggs and larvae produced in a reserve will drift away on ocean currents, many of them ending up in fishing grounds where they will grow into animals that are later caught. In this way, reserves act as fountainheads, pouring forth young to repopulate the sea. It is a neat theory, but until now, nobody has been able to prove it works. It is this idea I plan to pursue from St Thomas.

I do not have to search long before I find the perfect place. Petit Piton is a finger of magma that soars above Soufriere Bay in St Lucia. It wears a cloak of rainforest, save for slabs of dark granite where vertical rock faces smoothed by time defeat even tropical vegetation. The sea worries at rocks tumbled from far above; below the surface, the plummeting slope is furred by corals and half-concealed under clouds of tiny fish. What makes Soufriere ideal is a new marine park that covers eleven kilometres of coast centred on this peak; this has four marine reserve zones, soon to be closed to fishing, interspersed with fishing zones. Julie and I arrive in 1994 just before the park is established, allowing us to gather critical baseline data on the abundance of fish and coral. Over two months, we sample a series of stations inside and outside protected zones, the idea being that we will return yearly to take the pulse of life here to discover how reefs respond to protection. The diving, we soon discover, can be exhilarating.

The mountain forms one side of a broad bay, accelerating spring tide currents around its flank to the strength of river rapids. There are no tide tables for Soufriere, so we use guesswork and read the signs to avoid the worst on our fish counts. When the current drags a park-zoning buoy underwater, we go somewhere else. Sometimes we misjudge and the current picks up during the dive to a ferocity that forces us to abandon the count. One such day Julie and I decide to drift off on a fast-current joyride. We whip past thickets of black coral and dislodged boulders marbled with invertebrates. Tiny damselfish hug the reef closely, struggling feverishly to maintain position. Then, rounding the point, we are suddenly dragged downwards and away from the reef in a violent eddy. The smaller bubbles from our exhaled breaths follow us down, dancing in front of our masks. Julie's eyes goggle with fear, neither of us able to fin hard enough to prevent our descent. I grab her jacket and hit the inflate button and that of my own. After a few seconds we slow to a halt and begin a stuttering ascent. By this time, the eddy has swirled us back to the reef and we creep up slope until sheltered within a maze of rocks that tames the current.

St Lucia's marine reserves are not my only interest in the Caribbean. Science is patient work. The effects of protection take time to develop and I will not get a conclusive answer to the role of protected areas in supporting fisheries until at least five years of annual monitoring have been completed. In the meantime, I return to an old interest. Saudi Arabia gave me a clear sense of the power of large-scale comparisons in answering questions about how coral reefs work. The method used by Charles Darwin and the geologist Charles Lyell to develop their understanding of the world has legs in it yet. With so many islands, the Caribbean seems an ideal place for such comparisons.

There are some jobs that you shouldn't discuss much with friends: spy, assassin, sewer cleaner perhaps. I have discovered that coral reef scientist is among them. It is a lifestyle that most people associate with exotic beach holidays, so they find it impossible to take seriously the idea that there is any work involved. Even here it is hard to persuade colleagues that there is serious research in island hopping, but several funding agencies back my plan.

Sundays in Barbados are stately affairs. A man in a black suit is walking to church with all the dignity his old bones will permit, in his hand a rolled black umbrella, on his head a bowler hat. Old ladies follow in single file on the narrow pavement, wearing elaborate dresses that appear to have come direct from the 1920s. Following a path to the beach, we leave their procession. A guy dressed only in a scruffy pair of shorts ambles towards Julie and me, dreadlocked hair to his waist. 'Have ya got evry'tin ya need, mon?' he asks. His eyes are bloodshot and watery, high on his own supply. We thank him and head for the sea.

The reef here is shallow and the scalloped limestone dotted with stunted corals. Much of the bottom is plush with algae that smooths contours and imposes a drab uniformity. Grunts shrink back at our approach, watchful and wary, no doubt expecting the glint of a speargun. We swim offshore to the seaward slope, hoping for something richer. But the corals are patchy and understated, with little of the variety or complexity of form I would expect. Rag-tag shoals of plankton-picking fish hover around chestnut outcrops of star coral. We leave the water disappointed. I'd been told these were the best reefs accessible from shore, but they remind me of the stripped-down diversity of Qatar's severely stressed reefs. Conditions here seem ideal for a much grander display, so what is holding them back?

Back in St Thomas, I search for an answer. Barbados did once have thriving reefs, it turns out, but European settlers cleared the forest to make way for sugar cane and the trees were burned to fire the rum stills. Sediment washed from the cleared soil, stifled coral growth and the reefs sickened. More recent overfishing explains the poverty of life around this collapsed habitat. I realise, with that dawning awareness that precedes discovery, that you can't properly understand Barbados's reefs without knowing their history. Until now, ecology has for me been a science of the here and now, the animals and plants living in a place that is the product of their immediate environment. But history adds deeper understanding and offers more powerful explanations for patterns in the natural world.

One thing that soon becomes apparent is that every Caribbean island has a different feel. Even islands within sight of one another can be completely different, culturally and environmentally. The contrasts are partly a legacy of long colonial histories – Spanish, Dutch, Danish, British, American – that have blended and diverged, melding with landscape and place in ways unique to every island. Slavery added its own signature, with islands populated to greater or lesser degrees from different parts of Africa.

What soon strikes Julie and me is that the contrasts continue underwater. Every island possesses reefs that look and feel different in ways that at first seem baffling. Some have blizzards of small fish, others dense shoals of predators; some have plenty of coral, others lush beds of seaweed. As the net of our travels extends, the differences begin to make sense. Each place is a piece in a jigsaw puzzle that when arranged in the correct way produce a clear picture. The key to understanding it is fishing.

Piecing together our own observations, reports by governments and international bodies, we estimate the level of fishing on each island's reefs. Reducing fishing pressure to a single metric – the number of people fishing every kilometre of reef – enables us to plot differences in reef composition on a common scale. The results are dramatic. Predatory fish, the ones most easily caught and highly desired for their succulent flesh, decline precipitously as fishing intensity rises from little to moderate, and the population remains low as intensity increases further. Jamaica, whose reefs are fished with a fearsome and destructive intensity, has only a tenth of the predators that the least fished reefs in Bonaire have. Seaweed-eating fish such as parrotfish and surgeonfish are less favoured as food, and thus decline more slowly across this gradient of fishing. Even so, by the time Jamaican rates of extraction are reached, there are just one tenth of the herbivores present that the least fished reefs have.

While fishing pressure offers a compelling explanation for the patterns, it is important to rule out other influences. Correlation does not necessarily mean causation, scientists constantly remind themselves. Disentangling the effects of multiple forces is difficult, especially when they produce similar outcomes. Fertilising pollutants in run-off and overfishing can both lead to seaweed overgrowth of corals, for example. Several islands reveal the effects of fishing in the absence of such pollution.

Dominica is an island of steep ridges and shadowed valleys, almost everywhere blanketed by dense tropical forest. Tree-covered mountains encourage clouds to disgorge copious rain, making Dominica one of the wettest places in the Caribbean. Yet the streams and rivers mostly run clear where they reach the sea, lacking the mud burden carried by rivers flowing through agricultural land. Spared the pollution meted out in less fortunate places, Dominica's reefs should astonish, but instead they have a mournful feel. The fish are undersized, vigilant and thin on the ground, being subject to intense spear-fishing and trapping, while seaweed grows in sombre drifts over patchy coral.

Further north, St John, a close neighbour to St Thomas, has been protected as a national park since 1956. Blissful trails wind among towering mahogany and kapok to an emerald sea. St John's reefs were added to the park in 1962, making this one of the longest-standing marine protected areas in the world. Preparing for my first snorkel here, my anticipation is sharpened by the fact that Lameshur Bay, where I enter the sea, was the location of the United States' first venture into undersea living, the Tektite program of the 1960s. Here, scientists, including an all-woman team led by the now celebrated conservationist Sylvia Earle, spent a week at a time in an underwater lab to become intimate with their subjects.[1] But when I snorkel across this reef that I have read so much about, the glories

---

1. But not intimate with one another. Apparently, men couldn't be trusted to behave themselves locked up underwater with women, so early groups of scientists were single sex only.

of the Tektite days are gone. The fish and corals are no better than on St Thomas's unprotected reefs.

It turns out, I discover later, that St John's marine park allows fishing by 'artisanal methods' like hook and line and trap. When the park was established, the few fishing families each set no more than a dozen traps using row boats. By the 1990s, they used powerboats to set five hundred to a thousand traps per family. The traps are bigger and stronger too, with plastic-coated steel mesh replacing sticks and woven palm fronds. There is a lesson here: so-called traditional fishing is just as capable of stripping a reef as industrial methods. For a fish, there is no distinction. Too much fishing by any means leads to few fish. And as fish decline, so do reef-building corals. In their stead, seaweeds flourish.

Returning to Barbados's long history of reef decline, I am curious to learn more of St Thomas's past. The reefs here are unimpressive, their corals spotted onto a basement of mostly bare limestone. Fish are scarce too, with few of Bonaire's chunky predators. Before long, I find an article in an old copy of *National Geographic* from the 1950s. One photograph leaps out: a grinning man in tartan shorts and rubber mask next to a rock in St Thomas bay. He has a speargun in hand and thirteen fat fish spread on the rocks beside him, six of them big predatory groupers and snappers. The bay has since been dredged and sculpted into a port and its reefs are long forgotten. But this memento speaks of a past when corals bloomed and fish crowded ledges and gullies.

I seek out people who might remember those times. Joe LaPlace is one such man. A former fisherman, now in his sixties, he is descended from French settlers who have lived on the island since the 1700s.

'I remember,' he says, gesturing at the sea from the deck of his mountainside house, 'when I could walk out across the reef at low tide and see lobster feelers waving above the water like reeds in a pond. You could pick off as many as you wanted.'

He shows me a much-thumbed black and white photograph of him and a friend. Both brandish lobsters bigger than any I have seen: the tails touch the ground while the tips of their antennae reach chest level.

'In the sixties a friend of mine found a place where Nassau groupers spawn,' he continues.

I've hardly come across any of these striking fish in over a year on the island. Their thick, pale fawn bodies are tiger striped with dark slate. They have long, smooth faces and rubbery lips that enclose bristling teeth in the carmine cavity of their mouths. They breed in a brief two-week window in January, but until then nobody knew where.

'In the early days people caught thousands of fish. There were so many fish in some of the traps that they split open as they were pulled on board and the fish got free. Soon everyone was there, but we caught less fish. Ten years on, the fisheries guys got wind of it and came to look. They found only about 2000 fish left. After that, there were none.'

Back at the university, I think about what Joe told me. To support such large catches, the spawning aggregation must have started with tens of thousands of fish. To wipe it out in ten years would mean catching two or three of every four fish arriving to spawn every year. This wasn't fishing, it was mining, and the mine was soon exhausted.

There are very few places where you can still experience mass fish spawning in the Caribbean. Most fish aggregations went the way of St Thomas: discovery, boom, bust. But Gladden Spit at the southern extremity of the Mesoamerican Barrier Reef, some forty kilometres from the coast of Belize, is a place where there are still fish enough.

To see the fish spawn at Gladden Spit you have to be there at dusk around a full moon between April and June. We camp on a sandy cay nearby, heading offshore as the sun dips low towards the horizon. The sea is dark and lumpy as we thread a channel to the outer reef, sloshing over the rail in heaving gasps. It is a relief to jump in the water and escape the lurching boat. The sun has now set leaving a ruddy glow on the western horizon.

Below us the water is grey and featureless and the bottom, twenty-five metres down, invisible in the gathering dusk. As we descend, moving patches of brightness become visible, the silvered tops of fish columns rising from the seafloor, shifting, coalescing, breaking apart, the energy building as the moment nears. As the column rises towards the surface, groups of fish split off in sprinting rushes, filling the water with the rumble of whip-crack cavitations as they accelerate. Each female, attended by several males, pours forth her eggs in a frenzied ascent, her body shaking with the release. Immediately she disappears within a white cloud as the sperm from the clustered males fogs the water. The act complete, they turn and race for the safety of the school.

More fish break from the column as the crescendo nears, like water spurting from the jet of a fountain, and the visibility falls to a few metres in the milky effervescence. Then as the passion subsides, the water ahead darkens and the clouds part as the body of a whale shark glides, submarine-like, towards me, its mouth agape, sucking in caviar. Midnight-blue flanks starred with a constellation of white spots glow in the half-light. Another mouth appears from a different direction, followed by an enormous body, two metres from top to bottom and seven long. The thunderous tumult of spawning has drawn these giants like a dinner gong. In the darkness below, the shadowed backs of bull sharks cut predatory trails through the spent shoal.

While in St Thomas I return to the question of fish dispersal on ocean currents as eggs and larvae. In the Red Sea I became convinced that selective mortality of larvae during dispersal had much influence on the make-up of fish communities on reefs. Here though I begin to wonder more about where larvae come from and where they go.

The islands of the Caribbean sit mid-stream in a great ocean river that circles the globe. When this current exits the Caribbean through the Florida Strait it becomes the Gulf Stream. Some islands, like the Windward Islands, lie upstream in the river, other places downstream, such as the Florida Keys. Could that mean that some places receive copious arrivals of larval fish from their planktonic journeys and others few? For several years I gather every study I can find on larval fish dispersal and on the power and direction of Caribbean currents. These currents, I reason, will be the highways of fish dispersal, so understanding where they travel and how quickly might be revealing.[1]

Mapping the possible oceanic journeys of larvae is a revelation. Some reefs, like those of Cuba and the Florida Keys, have ten times more upstream reef than places like Barbados, and by inference could receive a far greater influx of larvae to replenish populations. Barbados could expect to gain few larvae from reefs other than its own. Take this idea further and poor management of reefs and fisheries in places like Barbados would have severe adverse consequences because they are utterly dependent on local fish and corals for resupply. This helps explain the miserable state in which I'd found Barbadian reefs, with few fish and less coral. Reef degradation has choked off the stream of larvae. Some places are doubly blessed, however, being supplied with larvae from huge tracts of upstream reef, while also capable of supplying them to great reef complexes downstream. One such place is Dry Tortugas.

---

1. 'Only dead fish go with the flow,' said one scientist, reacting to my paper when it was published in *Science*. About this time, people were beginning to discover that fish larvae were not mere passive drifters. Late stage larvae could swim for long periods against even quite strong currents. But eggs and very young larvae probably do drift, so my basic idea remained sound for the first part of their journeys at least.

To get to Dry Tortugas you have to first reach Key West, the most westerly town in the long curve of the Florida Keys, then take a boat for the last sixty-seven miles. Dry Tortugas has been many things: fort, Civil War prison, radio station, seaplane base, national park, bird migration stopover. As the name suggests, when the Spanish discovered this remote shoal in 1513, then no more than a cluster of sandy cays with a metre or two of rise above the tide, it was the birthplace and breeding ground for thousands of turtles. After centuries of hunting, turtles are thin on the ground today.

It is 2000 and I am here at the invitation of Billy Causey, the ebullient manager of the Florida Keys National Marine Sanctuary. As Billy explains, he has unfinished business. The park covers most of the Keys and was set up in 1990, with a network of protective zones added in 1995, including zones closed to all fishing, like those I am studying in St Lucia. The biggest no fishing zone of all was to be in the Dry Tortugas, but proposals were immediately controversial and threatened to scupper the rest of the plan. Conservationists and fishermen, in opposition further up the Keys, were united here in their criticism of the planned 'replenishment reserve'. Both said it was in the wrong place, although for different reasons. Conservationists wanted more prime reef habitat, while fishermen wanted less prime fishing territory included. So a place-marker was put on the plan, to be resolved at some future time, which is now.

I have come to join a group negotiating the future of Dry Tortugas. They are an eclectic mix of fishermen, day-boat operators, park managers, conservationists, concerned citizens and others. The hook and line guys, as Billy refers to them, are critical for success. They are huge men with bodies like quarterbacks, dried and salted from endless days hauling fish. One I am introduced to, Don DeMaria, is a local celebrity, famed for his fishing exploits in the 1960s and '70s. Square-jawed and with a tousle of blond hair shot through with grey, he tells me how he used to catch upwards of ten goliath groupers a day with only a speargun. Most were more than a metre long, some more than two. And the sharks – there were days when the sharks came as fast as hooks were put in the water, thick-set bulls and hammerheads mostly.[1] But those days are long gone, which is why he is here.

I am used to fishermen fighting protected areas, fearful that giving up space means fewer fish for them. I'm here to tell them about the emerging science of marine reserves and how a protected area could help them out. In a refreshing departure from normality, I discover over days of bracing debate that everybody wants this protected area, they are just uncertain where to put it. Billy is keen to make it as large as possible because the Dry Tortugas, according to my current maps, probably supplies the rest of his park with coral and fish larvae. Eventually, a plan is reached that surprises everyone: two protected areas. Fishermen have added an extra one – Riley's Hump – a known spawning aggregation site for some of their most valuable fish. Having fished out most other aggregations, they want to save this one. Together, the two protected areas cover 50 per cent more sea than the original plan, a great result.

By this time, our research in St Lucia has proven that, given protection, overfished reefs can bounce back fast. We watched in growing wonder as, year-by-year, fish fattened up and formed ever bigger crowds. Fishermen began to benefit from the rebound, despite having given up a third of their grounds. Working closely with them, we discovered that catch rates doubled and landings grew in value as fish recovered.

There is an unexpected result too.

Close to where a river enters the bay, one of Soufriere's four marine reserve zones hugs a cliff dense with vegetation that falls over rocks blackened by damp. A few months before our first visit, this place was struck by a fierce tropical storm that dumped close on half a metre of rain in twenty-four hours. It led to landslides and washed out roads, flushing thousands of tonnes of mud into the bay. The reef here lay under the plume for days. When the water

---

1. You can see the results of his early fishing efforts at https://www.flickr.com/photos/keyslibraries/sets/72157626700168332/

cleared the corals were choked by mud. Spreading plates cupped deadly loads of clay, barrel sponges were brim full. Above the muck, coral heads rose like taller buildings in the aftermath of a mudslide.

This was no one-off calamity. For the next several years we watched this reef suffer as periods of heavy swells lifted the mud only for it to fall back again and kill more coral. Between 1994 and 2002, it lost a further half of its coral.[1] Despite the decline, the fish thrived under protection. Although less affected reefs outperformed this reserve, the fish here rebounded by two and a half times. It was an encouraging result given evidence of coral loss we'd seen in other parts of the Caribbean. Even degraded reefs are worth protecting.

---

1. St Lucia's reefs were eventually cleared of their suffocating mud by heavy swells from a hurricane that passed nearby. The storm waves resuspended the mud and it was flushed far out to sea.

CHAPTER THIRTEEN

The long goodbye

Australia, 2013

WITH HIS FLOWING WHITE HAIR and grey stubble beard, Tub looks to be in his seventies. He lives in a hut near Abbot Point on the Queensland coast, one side of which is open to the elements and the others no more than planks nailed haphazardly to uprights. The hut sits in the middle of a yard of rusting boats, abandoned cars and a decaying 1950s bus. From this modest home, Tub is a model of outback Australian hospitality. He wears Sunday best threads for our visit, shorts and a shirt less frayed than the others. A corroded freezer grumbles in a corner from which he whisks a teetering heap of white-bread sandwiches, filled with canned ham slathered in vivid yellow mustard, deep fingerprints impressed into their sides.

Lunch over, Tub takes me and my companions, Felicity and Lissa from the Australian Marine Conservation Society, to a nearby creek where he keeps his 'tinny', a flat-bottomed aluminium skiff. After a few pulls, the engine coughs into life and we are under way. He only seems to have about a pint of fuel, but there is a paddle at least.

On every corner of the creek there are dozens to hundreds of birds, roosting in trees, preening, resting on the water or messing about as waterbirds do. Whistling ducks take flight as we approach and wheel overhead, shrilling rebukes; gangly herons perch on branches or step lightly over water lilies; black and white pelicans stare from rocks, square-shouldered and broad-backed; long-necked cormorants swim half-submerged, their necks like rearing cobras. There are magpie geese, iridescent kingfishers, soaring kites, half a dozen other kinds of duck, rails, black swans and more. Their density is hypnotic, the highest I have ever seen in a wetland.

The creek opens to a wide lagoon fringed with reeds. Several swans eye us curiously from a sandbank, their plumage fresh and white as table linen. We head for open water, leaving the reeds behind. Then the engine sputters to a halt. Tub murmurs an apology as he checks it before pulling on the cord. There is a throaty cough but no spark. Wind riffles the water, drifting us slowly towards the middle of the lagoon. Loose groups of birds pepper the surface and a curl of water betrays the presence of a large fish. After more struggle, Tub manages to restart the engine, only for it to splutter out again. He apologises again, but still looks unperturbed. The engine fires up only to die before we have moved ten metres. By now breathing chestily, Tub gives another few pulls. I am beginning to paddle when he gets us going for a fourth time and we turn back.

Wild and pristine as this place seems from water level, it has a secret that I see from the air later that day. We take off from a nearby airfield in Bowen. I can hardly bear to look as the six-seater barrels towards a group of kites daydreaming in the middle of the runway. They lift off at the last moment, barely clearing the wings, then a few flaps later flop back onto the tarmac in our wake. As we level off at two thousand feet, the pilot signals to kick open the side door, then banks for a better view. Struggling to control my vertigo in the buffeting wind, I peer down. A black scar spreads over one corner of Abbot Point, encroaching on the green and silvered matrix of trees, creeks and reed beds. Coal. Vast heaps of it, endlessly renewed from a railway that follows the back of the beach. A line of covered conveyors rattles the coal to the end of a pier that extends far out to sea, spewing darkness into the open belly of a ship.

It is early 2013 and I am in Australia at the invitation of the Thomas Foundation. David and Barbara Thomas made a fortune selling mail-order wine. Now in later life they have dedicated themselves to protecting Australia's natural wonders, here teaming up with a group of Australian conservation organisations to battle proposed industrial developments all the way up the Queensland coast. If these plans are realised, most of Abbot Point's bewitching wetlands will be buried under much larger mountains of coal. But my hosts' greater concerns lie further offshore on Queensland's Great Barrier Reef, the largest reef complex in the world and one of the most varied. Australia recognised its incalculable value long ago and most of its 2,300-km length has been protected since the 1970s within one of the world's largest marine parks. But the reef is under stress and its corals are dwindling despite protection, to widespread consternation.

Unquestionably, the Great Barrier Reef is one of the wonders of the world. I first saw it in the mid-1980s – in what, in retrospect, feels like a heyday – when Julie and I spent three months studying fish on a tiny island at its southern end. One Tree Island could more accurately be described as 'One Clump Island' as the centre of this rubble cay was covered in an impenetrable tangle of screw palms. The reefs were astonishing, better even than the best of the Red Sea. I have vivid memories of one dive in which we narrowly avoided disaster. The best diving is almost always on the seaward edge of a coral reef as this is where the water is clearest and incoming planktonic food most plentiful. To get there you must cross the reef crest. Usually this means passing through a channel by boat, but One Tree is unusual in that there is no such pass. When the tide rises it floods over the reef crest all the way around to fill the enclosed lagoon, like a saucepan submerged in a sink. When it falls, it empties the same way. Timing is critical: you must swim across the reef crest with the last of the falling tide and come back with the first of the rising tide.

We got the first bit right and scudded over the reef crest as if mid-stream in a fast-flowing river, disgorging on the seaward side into a wonderland. Coral tables stepped towards the depths in overlapping terraces. Mushrooming columns thrust upward, like thunderstorms above a plain, raining fish. Surly trevally jacks with silver-plated flanks and forked tails patrolled in loose packs like gangsters, sending fish running for cover. Every ten metres or so there was a deep surge channel. Peering between the buttresses felt like surveying a claustrophobic alley from the roof of a medieval townhouse. (When storm waves break onto the reef, these cuts channel the rush of water, sparing corals on the buttresses from serious damage.) Enormous green turtles hung in the water, one above each buttress, like a figure repeated into the distance in a mirrored room. We lost all sense of time in the galleries and gardens of this coral palace, but eventually low air forced us to turn back. As we swam towards the shallow reef crest the current picked up. Contrary to expectation, it was still against us, pressing us back to sea. It took half an hour to pull ourselves, hand over hand, along the rubbled bottom until we flopped into our boat terrified but elated.

I was in Australia now because I had agreed to give a lecture, somewhat loftily named after its founders 'The Thomas Oration'. I had no idea what I was letting myself in for. Scientists live quiet lives most of the time. I stepped onto the plane in London on a chill and gusty March morning as a tired academic, relieved to have just finished a winter of intensive teaching. In Sydney, I stepped off the plane to discover myself a minor celebrity thanks to the transformative power of the press offices of several charities. For the next two weeks, I was to be the go-to expert on coral reefs and their problems. The organisers laid out a frenetic schedule of radio chat shows, TV slots, meetings and dinners with politicians, interviews with journalists, discussions with reef managers, activists, students and academics, as well as talks in five towns and cities. We would also film a TV advertisement urging Australians to unite behind reef protection, in which I would 'star'. Leafing through the five-page schedule, it didn't look like there would be much time for sleep.

I had known for some time that my talk at Sydney University was to be recorded for radio broadcast, but I am told at the last minute that it will also be filmed by ABC for its *Big Ideas* series. How, I wonder, can I simultaneously satisfy the audience in the room, the one watching on TV and another that can only hear me? I couldn't say, 'As you can see on the slide...' I'd have to paint word pictures of them without boring the TV audience or the one in front of me. It is the toughest talk of my life, like walking a tightrope across a ravine. At the end, relieved not to have messed up, a hand shoots up at the front for the first of the questions. 'What is the purpose of whales?' a well turned-out lady asks. I'd survived thus far only to be bowled a googly on the first ball.

The next day, I meet Felicity Wishart and Lissa Schindler from the Australian Marine Conservation Society at the airport in Brisbane where they join me for the connecting flight to Townsville on the central Queensland coast. Felicity, or Flic, as she introduces herself, is to lead the campaign against the wave of urbanisation and port development slated for the Great Barrier Reef coast. She is a much-admired veteran of environmental battles on land and sea. If there were medals for such things, her lapel would be hidden beneath ribbons. But she doesn't look much like a warrior, more a worrier. Her voice is soft and tentative and she is bespectacled and small, slight to the point of fragility. She greets me with a warm smile, laugh lines spreading across her face. Lissa is dark-haired, dark-eyed and twenty years younger. She is the scientific brains of the duo, with a PhD in marine park planning, a ready foil, I will come to discover, to Flic's campaigning intuition.

Townsville is an understated place, the sort of town it is easy to pass through without noticing. But for me it has been a place of pilgrimage, jumping-off point for the Great Barrier Reef, intellectual heartland of Australian reef research and base for the authority that manages the marine park. Since I was last here in 1988, new hotels and office blocks have appeared in the middle of town, attaching a disreputable look to ageing pubs and shops. We check into a scruffy hotel. The lobby is decorated in muddy shades of brown (all the better to hide the stains) and the lift smells of mould. I am glad we are only here for a couple of nights, just enough time to meet some of the key reef managers and scientists.

In the twenty-five years since my last visit, Australia has fallen in love with mining. Handsome and friendly-looking miners follow us from the airport into Townsville, beaming from huge billboards. The slogans say things like 'Digging for the benefit of all Australians'; 'Trust us, we won't bugger up your country' the unwritten subtext. The rugged faces look benign with their cosmetically applied dirt. But the industry they represent has the country in thrall. Australia was once a leading campaigner against climate change on the world stage, so much so that they introduced a pioneering tax on carbon emissions, but its environmental stance is now shot through with ambiguity and hypocrisy. We are in the last weeks before a Federal election and the right-wing opposition are confident they can oust the government.

In Townsville we lunch with Peter Doherty, one of the scientists I most admired as a student in Arabia. His thoughtful experiments set the bar high for fish research. Like me, he sought to uncover the rules, if there were any, by which reef communities were put together and I looked forward eagerly to his every new publication. Now he is a grandee at the Australian Institute of Marine Science, AIMS for short. Peter speaks slowly and deliberately between infrequent mouthfuls, enunciating his thoughts in a thick Aussie drawl. The reef is in bad enough trouble without the added stress of industrialisation, he says. For decades, scientists at AIMS have led a detailed monitoring programme, taking dozens of measurements annually at more than two hundred sites over the reef's 2,300-km length. The findings have recently been published and are deeply disquieting (its lead author, Glenn De'ath, is aptly named). The area covered by stony corals has fallen by half in the last fifteen years. The decline began in 1997--98, the year the world sweltered and corals across the planet bleached and died. Coral cover is a fairly crude measure of reef health. Another study led by De'ath added detail to the picture, revealing that coral growth rates have fallen 15 to 20 per cent since 1990. The density of their skeletons is falling too, a worrisome harbinger of ocean acidification. As he chases the last peas across his plate, Peter's message is blistering. If the corals here are in trouble, they are in trouble everywhere.

How is it, I wonder later in a quiet moment, that in a few short decades coral reefs that have flourished for millions of years could be brought so low? Watching reefs decline has been like watching a parent age. Little by little they lose strength. The changes, hardly perceptible at first, mount up to rob them of mobility, independence and even dignity. The love you feel is now touched with sadness.

Australians are the first to tell you that the Great Barrier Reef Marine Park is the best managed coral park on the planet, and they are probably right. It was established after a national outcry over plans to mine the coral for limestone and drill the reef for oil. GBRMPA – The Great Barrier Reef Marine Park Authority – is next on my visit list. Their offices sit above a public aquarium on the waterfront where I am granted an audience with half a dozen of the park's top managers.

Russ Reichelt, the park's chairman, summarises his woes. The Great Barrier Reef is subject to the same problems of global change as reefs elsewhere, mainly rising temperatures and water acidity, but the major killers are more local. While the park has admirable control over what goes on at sea, their bigger worries lie on land, where they have little influence. Queensland is a luxuriant mosaic of rainforest fragments, pasture and endless fields of sugar cane. In the rainy season, its rivers run like chocolate as tropical rains wash soil and fertilisers from the fields, carrying them far offshore. These suspended sediments block light and stress corals, while fertilisers give seaweed growth a boost at the expense of coral. But the worst impact of fertilisers comes via an unexpected route. It goes by the name crown-of-thorns. The crown-of-thorns is a wickedly spiked diadem of a starfish that grows fast, reaching a half metre armspan within a few years, nourished by coral. Starfish feed by everting their stomach over a coral like a suffocating cushion, digesting it externally and sucking up the juices. A single starfish can do a lot of damage, moving from coral to coral leaving a trail of bare and bleached skeletons. A plague of them can devastate.

For decades the Great Barrier Reef has been visited by successive outbreaking waves of tens of thousands of crown-of-thorns. Nobody knew exactly what triggered plagues. As a student, I had long discussions about it with Rupert on the shores of the Red Sea, where he'd seen more limited outbreaks. He was convinced there was a link to overfishing of their predators. Reefs with lots of emperor fish and triggerfish seemed less troubled by outbreaks. But Australian scientists remained sceptical. Compared to many places, the Great Barrier Reef was lightly fished. Chuck Birkeland, a scientist based in Hawaii, had another explanation. He noticed that reefs around high islands in the Pacific suffered outbreaks whereas low coral atolls seemed not to. The difference was nutrients. On low islands, rainfall simply disappeared into the porous coral rubble so there was no run-off. On high islands, which had deep soils and steep slopes, streams and rivers washed nutrients into the sea, which seemed to boost survival of crown-of-thorns larvae. Under these favourable conditions, legions of tiny starfish settled onto the reef.

On the Great Barrier Reef, primary outbreaks fed by nutrients in run-off led to secondary plagues when starfish reached maturity in their millions, sending waves of destruction across the reef. Rupert was vindicated too. Outbreaks, we have discovered, are more likely to start in places where predators have been depleted by fishing.

Although worried by plans for industrial development along the coast, Reichelt and his fellow managers are more anxious to staunch the flow of agrochemicals coming off the land.

I'm feeling a bit of a fraud, surrounded by such deeply knowledgeable people. Australia, and especially Townsville, is full of experts, people who have spent their lives probing the secrets of the Great Barrier Reef. But it is a human quirk to afford greater authority to an outsider. Perhaps we expect a sharper clarity of vision, untainted by local politics or past rivalries. I'm here, as Flic has told me, to be deployed as a missile directed via the media towards the heart of government. These meetings are to arm the warhead. I also feel a responsibility to the world beyond Australia. This fight may be on Australian turf, but the Great Barrier Reef belongs to all of us. In recognition of this truth, it was inscribed on the World Heritage List of places of 'outstanding universal value' to humankind in 1981, joining sites like the temples of Luxor, Notre Dame Cathedral and the Grand Canyon.

In one of those splendid ironies, the World Heritage Convention is administered from the ugly UNESCO office in Paris that I visited on my way to Iran.[1] In the car on the way to our last meeting of the day, Flic outlines a key facet of her campaign plan. 'You know there's a list of World Heritage Sites in danger?'

'Vaguely,' I reply.

'World Heritage status is a big deal. Once a place is on the list, a country is duty-bound to protect the qualities that make it special. Forever.' Her eyes twinkle as she glances across while changing gear, like a chess player who can see a win seven moves ahead. 'If it breaks that promise, UNESCO can list a site as in danger. It would be hugely embarrassing for Australia. Most of the sites in danger are in poor or war-torn countries.'

We end the day with drinks on the seafront where I am reunited with old friends. Charlie Veron, one of the world's foremost coral

---

1.   The UNESCO office has been designated a protected building as an outstanding
     example of 1950s architecture. Perhaps it's just me?

biologists, is here with his wife Mary Stafford-Smith. Mary once managed Rupert's lab and kept his life from imploding as work snowballed. We clink ice-cold stubbies and look toward Magnetic Island where the setting sun has overlaid a maroon blush on the forested slopes of Mount Cook. The island is five miles offshore and has Townsville's closest reefs, but the reefs have struggled for years in the face of dredged silt from the local port and from mud and fertiliser run-off, made worse by the odd cyclone. I snorkelled there in 1988 and came away disappointed. Wiry clumps of thick seaweed covered the bottom, half submerging foundering corals. The water was grubby and my fins raised puffs of silt when I strayed too close to the bottom.

Charlie reminds me of the last time we met. Four years previously, in 2009, he had invited me to a meeting on the future of coral reefs in a warming world. It was held in the London headquarters of Britain's Royal Society and his co-host was Sir David Attenborough. Their aim was to produce a statement on coral reef sensitivity to climate change that could feed into international negotiations on emissions reductions at Copenhagen later that year. There was already a strong sense that coral reefs were suffering more visibly than most habitats. To use a well-worn phrase, they were the canary in the coal mine, giving notice of greater tragedies to come if their warning went unheeded.

Reefs are the geological edifices of past worlds, Charlie reminded us at the outset, so by looking at geology one can read their stories. What geology can reveal, which modern experiments cannot, is how the world's reefs responded to past episodes of global warming. The picture that emerged during the day was grim and compelling. Every time that carbon dioxide levels rose markedly, as they did during four of the last five mass extinction events, reefs withered and disappeared. It wasn't just warming that did this, it was the simultaneous acidification of the world ocean. When carbon dioxide dissolves in water it increases acidity. The higher acidity attacks carbonate rock, which means it attacks coral reefs, both living and dead. The very bedrock on which coral islands sit is not safe. Already, by the time of our meeting, ocean acidity had increased by 23 per cent over pre-industrial levels, and a 109 per cent increase is expected by the end of the twenty-first century if no action is taken to curb carbon dioxide emissions.

For living corals and other creatures that make chalky structures, ocean acidification makes life tough. Acid mops up dissolved carbonate in seawater, the raw material that corals use to grow their skeletons and that coralline algae use to build the crusts that bind reefs together. With less dissolved carbonate about, it takes more energy to grow and the resulting corals have weaker skeletons. The research Peter Doherty mentioned showed that *Porites* corals on the Great Barrier Reef had produced 14 per cent less skeleton annually since 1990 than previously. Cores had been drilled into large, mound-shaped colonies, many of which were hundreds of years old. The annual growth rings visible in these skeletons showed that the slowdown in growth was unprecedented in the last four hundred years. Increased levels of carbon dioxide are giving coral reefs osteoporosis.

Reefs and carbonate sediments are a giant antacid pill for the sea. Over the span of hundreds of thousands of years, they dissolve and neutralise the extra acidity produced when the planet belches carbon dioxide and methane[1] into seas and atmosphere, making the oceans habitable again by creatures that grow chalky shells and skeletons. Once this happens, reef construction begins anew, although often with a different cast of builders. Each warming-acidification event acts like a filter, letting through a reduced company of lucky creatures. From them evolution will eventually produce diversity once again, but it is a work of millions of years.

---

1. Methane can build up as a solid in deposits known as methane hydrates, often on the seabed and in permafrost. Episodes of massive methane release are known from Earth history. It is an even more potent greenhouse gas than carbon dioxide. However, as it is a fairly reactive compound, it is soon oxidised into carbon dioxide and water.

As we gathered in London for Charlie's meeting the atmosphere was sombre despite the July sun outside. Charles Sheppard, my old friend from Arabia and Egypt, was there. Now a professor at the University of Warwick, his black humour was undimmed. Halfway through Sir David's opening address, Charles nudged me in the side and whispered, a little too loudly, 'Would you like vinegar with those coral chips?'

Throughout the day, we wrangled ideas back and forth, hopeful of relief, some glimmer of optimism from a study just out or overlooked. But we kept circling back to the same cold facts. Warming- induced mass coral bleaching episodes date back to the early 1980s. At that time the atmospheric concentration of carbon dioxide was 340 parts per million, having risen from a pre-industrial level of 280 parts per million in 1750. By the time of our meeting, the level was 387 parts per million. But, as we all knew, negotiators preparing for the Copenhagen talks were proposing limiting emissions so as not to exceed 450 parts per million, which they hoped would keep average planetary temperature rise to two degrees centigrade. Too much already.

Late that afternoon we finalised a press statement. David Attenborough and Charlie climbed onto a raised dais at one end of the room to give their closing remarks. David, stiff on his legs at eighty-three, struggled to make the step up. Summing up, Charlie listed our points of agreement one by one: 'At today's level of approximately 387 parts per million of carbon dioxide,[1] reefs are seriously declining and time-lagged effects will result in their continued demise.' Sir David shifted uncomfortably on his rickety chair. 'Proposals to limit carbon dioxide levels to 450 parts per million will not prevent the catastrophic loss of coral reefs from the combined effects of global warming and ocean acidification,' Charlie intoned. Sir David shifted position again, nudging the leg of his chair to the edge of the platform. 'To ensure the long-

---

1.   To find out how much carbon dioxide is in the atmosphere today, go to: https://www.bloomberg.com/graphics/carbon-clock/

term viability of coral reefs the atmospheric carbon dioxide level must be reduced significantly below 350 parts per million.' Our statement was hard-hitting. No scientific body had yet suggested capping carbon dioxide at levels below those in the air around us. Charlie stiffened slightly and lowered his voice for his next point: 'In addition to major reductions in carbon dioxide emissions, achieving this safe level will require the active removal of carbon dioxide from the atmosphere.' At this point there was a collective gasp, not occasioned by Charlie's statement, but by Sir David's legs sailing upwards over his head as he flew backwards off stage. We leapt to his assistance, appalled that our meeting might bring his much-decorated career to an abrupt end. But he dusted himself off quickly and carried on as if nothing had happened.

Our meeting was a watershed. Until then, statements about climate change were couched in terms of prevention rather than fix. They emphasised emissions reductions to meet some future target level of carbon dioxide still higher than the present. These predictions offered the comfort of freeboard for political negotiation. There was always still time to act. The world could party on a little longer. But now, for the first time, there was recognition that we had already gone too far. To save coral reefs we would have to find some way to suck carbon dioxide from the atmosphere and lock it back underground.

I have known Charlie over twenty years, but somehow he never ages. Perhaps it is because he has always been grilled to the colour of teak by tropical sun. I ask him now, sipping beer in this waterfront bar, what he thinks of Australia's about-face on climate change. If the plans I have seen are realised, Queensland will become one of the world's largest coal exporters, and Abbot Point the planet's biggest coal terminal. South of us and just inland, a vast layer of coal lies beneath a depression of a quarter of a million square kilometres called the Galilee Basin. Black money. He gives an embarrassed shrug. 'It's bloody awful! Look, the last thing this reef needs is half a dozen massive ports and hundreds more ships.'

I still can't get over the bombshell that the Great Barrier Reef lost half its coral between 1997 and 2012. I've shown the graph of coral decline everywhere I have spoken in Australia and the audience reaction is shock every time. The line showing coral cover bobs along on a level from 1985, when monitoring began, to 1998 when it takes a nosedive. In my presentation, I add a line to the graph that is not in the paper, albeit it with the kind of health warning that investments usually come with: 'past performance is not necessarily a guide to the future'. On the present trajectory, the Great Barrier Reef would have no coral left by 2029. When will there be too little cover to warrant the name 'coral' reef, I wonder? Already the average coral cover hovers at around 14 per cent, whereas once it ranged from 40 to 60 per cent.

What is most disturbing is that this has happened to what is supposedly the world's most strongly protected reef. The machinery of management is lavish, as I saw at park headquarters. After my meeting, I was given a tour of the monitoring centre where winking banks of computers show real-time maps of what is going on at sea, and analysts probe the data for signs of illegal activity. But it isn't enough.

Not all of the Great Barrier Reef is in trouble though. Averages are crude metrics. There must always be places with more and less. Poor old Magnetic Island and lots of other inshore reefs in the mid-section of the park have fared worst, haemorrhaging their coral. But the northernmost reefs and those in the far south, where the reef bends offshore, have been nearly unaffected. They've escaped because the northern watersheds are still intact and undeveloped, while the southern reefs are far enough from the coast not to be affected by run-off from the land. This discovery offers hope, because it means the solutions are known and still local. If Queensland's farmers and miners used methods that reduced soil and fertilisers running from their fields and quarries into rivers, and dredge material was collected for disposal rather than dumped in the sea, water quality would improve.

This has been known for a long time, so why hasn't it happened? 'It's expensive,' says Mary, 'and until recently we didn't fully appreciate the costs of pollution, so run-off wasn't taken seriously enough.' Mary studied the effects of sediment on Australian corals for her PhD, dosing captive corals with known volumes of sand to see how much they could handle. 'Too much sediment kills corals directly, but we now realise that smaller amounts make them more susceptible to other stresses, like temperature spikes.' Corals stressed by high nutrient levels die at lower temperatures than ones living in clear, unpolluted water. Alleviating the stresses we can manage, like polluted run-off, should make corals better able to cope with global warming. Well, that was the theory at least.

First thing next morning, Flic, Lissa and I drive south to Abbot Point, where we'd met Tub and contemplated the blackness of coal. Then it's on to the port town of Yeppoon to take to the water at last. There we join a local campaigner, Ginny Gerlach, the film crew making the conservation advert, and Graham Lloyd from *The Australian* newspaper.

Ginny is a pocket-sized bundle of righteous indignation. Deeply tanned with hair seared blonde by long hours outdoors, she has been propelled into environmental campaigning by proposals to build a new port in the nearby Fitzroy River delta. She wears a T-shirt with an oddly goofy dolphin on it and the slogan 'Save the Snubnose'. The plans threaten her local boat tour business as well as smiling dolphins. But, as I soon find out because Ginny is effusive and winning, her environmentalism goes deeper than mere business survival. Her face lights up and there is a faraway look in her eyes as she tells me about the Fitzroy's trackless forest, secret creeks and elusive creatures. Her love is elemental.

We make an early start, cruising fifteen kilometres offshore to Great Keppel Island where the film crew want me to explain the threats on camera. The water there is milky with silt stirred up from the bottom by strong overnight winds, denying us a look at the reef. Instead I spend the morning wading through the sea earnestly declaiming on the plight of coral. Countless takes later, my acting qualities are deemed adequate. My performance reminds me of a 1970s comedy sketch in which a cute little boy is filmed for a sweet advertisement. But he keeps fluffing his lines and when the camera is turned off the director belts him around the ear and shouts 'Get it right!'

We steam south in the afternoon, passing a conical island in a wide loop. Peak Island, Flic tells me, is one of the Great Barrier Reef's 'no entry' zones. The park has many levels of protection. Second best are its 'no-take' zones, where no fishing or extraction of anything is allowed. But its premier protection is in no-entry zones. Few parks have enough space that they can leave places for wildlife alone. The island now assumes an air of mystery, as if suddenly I were a seventeenth-century sailor approaching some pristine and alluring Eden. Occasionally, scientists are given fleeting access to find out how these places are faring. A few years ago, they made the arresting discovery that sharks were over ten times more abundant in no-entry than in no-take zones. They expected them to be the same, since there was supposed to be no fishing in either. The researchers put the difference down to better enforcement of fishing restrictions in no-entry zones. Long-lived animals that are sluggish to reproduce, like sharks, are vulnerable to even very low levels of illegal fishing. I watch the island dwindle in our wake, imagining this patch of sea teeming with reef sharks and turtles, its corals unscarred by clumsy divers.

Bringing Graham along is a calculated risk, Flic confided before we came on the boat. *The Australian* newspaper, for which he works, has enormous influence as the only nationwide daily left in the country. A strong story about the peril facing the Great

Barrier Reef would be a huge boon to the campaign. But the paper is owned by Rupert Murdoch and generally sides with business. It is also well-known for ambiguity on climate change; the paper claims to accept it as real but routinely lambasts climate scientists. Moreover, Graham is a well-known critic of renewable energy, which many readers view as incompatible with his position as environment editor. His face is sharply angular with a pointed chin and rakish goatee, giving him a permanently sceptical expression.

That scepticism is evident the moment we begin to chat. I have just published a book, *Ocean of Life*, that sets out the many ways in which the oceans are changing under human influence. Climate change looms large in it. We lock horns quickly and begin an intellectual shoving match that lasts much of the trip. But Graham clearly loves nature, talking with great enthusiasm about his annual trips to remote and little-known parts of Australia to do photo-stories for the paper. We find plenty of common ground.

We anchor at last light near the northern edge of Curtis Island. Silence settles on still water after the engines are cut. A shoal of mullet draws lazy scribbles at the surface mid-channel, their fat lips gulping kisses in the half darkness. Tomorrow we will head south to the port of Gladstone, which we are to approach through a sinuous channel between the island and mainland. For a boat our size, the narrowest section can only be passed for a short window around high tide.

We depart early on the flood, weaving through hidden shoals and the carcasses of sunken trees. Four dark cormorants sit in line on a silvery branch that juts from the water, their drying wings spread like crucifixes. Forests line both banks and crawl up the slopes, prop-rooted trees clasping the channel edges. Their foliage is dew wet, glossy and singing green. The water that laps the edge of the forest stains the tangled roots black where they break the surface. I try to follow the roots of a nearby tree by eye, to see whether I can separate them from their neighbours, but am quickly confounded. The roots knit trees one to another in an inextricable lattice of knotted stems. Anyone trying to penetrate this forest would surely give up within fifty metres of the edge, by which time, like Theseus in the Minotaur's labyrinth, they would need a trail of thread to find their way back.

Curtis Island slumbers like a green-backed whale on this shining sea. In the opposite direction on the mainland, far away in the blue distance the uninterrupted forest canopy creases into mountains. Nothing for miles but trees, water and sky. No vestige of human presence but our own intrudes upon this primordial scene. I can't imagine that it looked any different when Captain Cook passed by in 1770. I watch for the blunt blowing snout of a snubnose dolphin but only birds break the surface as they flee our clanking alien approach.

Then, ahead of us, a boxy metallic outline begins to rise above the soft billow of trees: crane towers. Around the next bend, far down the channel, I can just make out industrial shapes beneath the bristle of cranes.

'That's a new gas terminal,' says a voice from beside me. Lost in the vernal tranquillity, I hadn't noticed Ginny come up the steps to the upper deck. 'There are three liquid natural gas plants being built on the island, all of them inside the World Heritage Area.' Until now, Curtis Island has been a glorious, unbroken expanse of pristine forest passing our port side. But as we close in on the cranes, a spreading industrial scar bruises its southern end. 'This is what the north end of the island and the Fitzroy River will look like if the government has its way.'

I am speechless. This is the largest estuary I have ever visited that is still trackless and wild. Estuaries are gateways to the sea, portals for transport inland and places of safety and shelter. They have expansive fertile lowlands for crops and plenty of water to flush away our wastes. So estuaries are usually the first places developed and it is no wonder they are home to many of the world's great cities and ports. Undeveloped estuaries of this size are a great rarity in the modern world. 'This is the Sistine Chapel of estuaries,' I say. 'If it is destroyed it could no more be recovered than Michelangelo's painting. How can anyone contemplate such colossal vandalism?' Ginny doesn't have time to answer because a smaller boat has just buzzed alongside ours to shuttle us and the camera crew to a beach to meet some of the locals fighting Gladstone's port expansion.

We join half a dozen campaigners on a beach at the mouth of a nearby inlet. Through the trees, just a few dozen metres away, I can make out the glint of steel and the red wound of broken earth. They are angry and feel let down by their leaders, and who wouldn't be, were a giant industrial plant to be parachuted in next door? These terminals have made reluctant environmentalists of them. The group pass me a pair of photographs of the channel we have been cruising down, one taken before dredging, the other afterwards. Dredgers haven't just deepened the channel, they have removed a string of sandbanks and shallow wetlands. 'And you know what they did with the spoil?' a man asks me pointedly. 'They dumped it in a deep fishing hole. People round here used to catch giant groupers there. Now the hole has gone and so have the fish.' After a chat on camera, we jump back in the boat to cross the channel to an ore-loading terminal, pulling up alongside a towering cliff of rusty steel and flaking paint. Seen from water level, the boat's hull is improbably long. In the offices of the marine park, vessels like this were abstractions, tiny creeping dots on the radar as they threaded their way along dotted shipping lanes. But here it is a reminder of the mountains of raw materials our modern lifestyles consume. This time the director wants me to deliver a couple of lines while driving our boat past this giant ship. It all looks so effortless when seasoned television presenters do it, but in take after take, I either remember the lines and nearly crash the boat, or drive the boat and mess up the speech. Finally, I achieve sufficient competence in driving and recall that we can head for Gladstone.

I was last here in 1987, newly married to Julie. We hitched a cheap ride on the night supply barge to Heron Island resort on the

Great Barrier Reef, which bucked and lurched like a fairground ride for fifty gut-heaving miles. Gladstone was an industrial port even then, its shops selling postcards with titles like 'sunset over the alumina wharf'. It is almost unrecognisable now, so much has industry carved it up. We pass miles of coast shod in concrete and steel and buried under heaps of bauxite or hills of coal destined for India and China. In between, felled mangroves and raw earth give notice of the next places to be developed. How did Australians sleepwalk their way here? Somehow, almost unnoticed, grand schemes have been conjured into being that will bring the world's merchant fleet steaming through labyrinthine reef passes to gulp their fill from this moonscape coast of stockpiles, refineries and blown dust.

Container ships and merchant vessels crowd the dock and dwarf our boat. I am met at the pontoon by three film crews simultaneously demanding my impressions of the reef, Fitzroy River, Gladstone, the environmental battle – anything at all, really. I trip climbing out of the boat and give the first interview through gritted teeth, wincing at the pain blossoming in my shin. My overwhelming impression of Gladstone is of a straggling sprawl of development. Every company appears to have its own facility, so that Gladstone is more a collection of many ports than a single entity. If the mainland coast had been used more wisely there would have been little need to violate Curtis Island's rolling green flanks. Instead the planners appeared intent on wasting space rather than consolidating developments in order to minimise impact.

In my head a little timer is counting down the minutes until our plane leaves for Brisbane, but the reporters are relentless. Is this how celebrities feel, I wonder, as I grapple for wise things to say? Eventually, Flic intervenes and bundles me into a waiting taxi.

The airport is full of thick-necked, heavy-booted men in beige mining uniforms, checking onto flights to places I've never heard of. It feels like an outport in a science fiction movie, where men are whisked away to inhospitable and dangerous planets for months at a time to mine rare and vital commodities. As the plane climbs out of Gladstone, we pass above a landscape scarred with mines and containment ponds for tailings, their waters garish with mineral residues, like blobs of colour on an artist's palette.

Soon after I returned to the UK, *The Australian* published a dramatic double-page spread by Graham on the peril facing the reef. Flic's intuition had been right. Over the coming months, I received regular email updates as the 'Fight for the Reef' campaign gathered momentum. To begin with, the stories were mostly bleak. In 2013, a new right-wing government had been elected under Tony Abbot, so big business found an even warmer welcome in Canberra. It must have felt like a very strong goliath to these pipsqueak campaigners. But this was not an ordinary campaign. There is nothing ordinary about the Great Barrier Reef or the passions it provokes.

Early on, Ginny, Flic and others flew to Paris to lobby UNESCO's World Heritage Committee, urging them to list the Great Barrier Reef as 'in danger'. In a second line of attack, the campaigners travelled the world, attending the AGMs of all the big banks that were considering funding for mining and port developments that would affect the reef. One by one the banks stepped back. Scientific reviews were commissioned, which upheld the view that disposal of millions of tonnes of dredge spoil in the World Heritage Area could tip the reef towards irreversible decline. The government began to backtrack, offering concessions. Dredge works were scaled back and port developments revisited and consolidated. Then dredge spoil disposal was banned in the Great Barrier Reef Marine Park, although the government scored a spectacular own goal by proposing to dump it instead on the wetlands by Abbot Point where I met Tub. By now its extraordinary wildlife had been documented and lovingly photographed by campaigners.

In Queensland, the political tide was turning too. In early 2015, the opposition Labor Party campaigned on a promise to protect the reef. They gained a majority, which was widely credited to the campaign, soon afterwards drafting a bill to concentrate development in a few existing ports and to increase protections. UNESCO sent a delegation to Australia and although wined, dined and wooed by Abbot's government, they demanded strong measures to protect the reef's outstanding universal value. Plans were drafted to return the reef to health and published as the *Reef 2050 Long-Term Sustainability Plan.*

Yet, just as the campaigners were on the cusp of a major win, Flic suddenly died. She passed away in her sleep being driven home to Brisbane by her partner after more meetings in Canberra. She was only forty-nine. Burning the candle at both ends. In one of the many glowing obituaries, I read that Flic was disappointed that UNESCO didn't in the end place the Great Barrier Reef on their in-danger list. But Flic and her fellow campaigners had put the reef back in the forefront of public consciousness and in doing so had put Australia's mining companies on notice. Most Australians live in cities but their hearts are in the outback. They had grown complacent, taking it for granted that their lands and seas were well protected. What, after all, were all those parks for? But, little by little, the fortunes to be had from mining overrode the Australian instinct to protect. Mining interests got into bed with politicians and the concerns of ordinary people were sidelined. Flic and her fellow activists had woken the country from sleep. Theirs was a campaign masterclass.

In late 2015, I received a 'Fight for the Reef' update email with the title 'We did it!' The pro-reef Queensland government, voted in on the campaign's coat-tails, had passed the Sustainable Ports Development Act. It's a rather boring title for such an important law. It extends the previous ban on disposal of dredge spoil in the Great Barrier Marine Park to the whole of the World Heritage Area. And it protects the Fitzroy River delta and other still special places, concentrating development in ports like Gladstone that are already industrial. Of course, the reef is still not safe from muddy run-off from the land, nor from global emissions. No reef can be safe from greenhouse gases, as time would soon tell with brutal decisiveness. But the campaigners' efforts are a heartening reminder that people care passionately about beautiful, wild places and that development and the pursuit of wealth should not jeopardise that.[1]

Australia has given the world a powerful lesson: just because a place appears to be protected does not mean that it is. Real protection comes from our love and commitment, and that must be constantly renewed, generation after generation.

---

1. In 2019, Australia went to the polls again in an election of which pundits said that "climate change was on the ballot and climate change lost". The newly-elected government moved swiftly to approve the gigantic 'reef-wrecking' coalmine.

CHAPTER FOURTEEN

Youth and beauty

Maldives, 2014

A HERON CAN WAIT A LONG TIME for breakfast, bent like a cocked spring, feet clasped to a lump of upturned rubble. For the fifteen minutes I have watched this heron, it has stood motionless, intent, gimlet beak at the ready. Then, imperceptibly at first, its legs fold to a low crouch and its head slants. There is a pause, then a strike, sudden and fierce. A tiny fish wriggles at the end of its beak, scattering droplets of sea. No more than an aperitif.

Where the tide has ebbed, the sand on this Maldivian beach is smooth and white as a fresh sheet. Far away across the lagoon, a dark thunderhead glows at the edges, concealing the newly risen sun. The storm is welded to the sea at the horizon by a solid bank of rain. But here there is no hint of the squall. The sea is mirror flat, melding the steel-grey and carmine-streaked sky with mottling reef and sand underwater. The reef crest is hidden, unmarked by the breakers that normally draw its line on the sea. A shoal of mullet shake flashes from their scales as they surge past in the shallows, their beating tails bright with early morning. Above, a faint breeze whispers in the palms, duetting distant thunder.

Two dense lines of trees bristle on the green face of the lagoon. These islands were born of the ocean and the sea dictates their dimensions. Nothing rises higher than a storm tide or wind can carry it. The Maldives has 1,190 islands, they say, all of them the work of coral; every grain of sand is the product of a life, the living matrix breathing, pulsing, condensing rock from water.

Reluctantly I drag myself away to join the students for breakfast. We start early because there is much to fit in. It is 2014 and Julie and I are on our yearly pilgrimage to Magoodhoo, a tiny island on Faafu Atoll, to teach a Masters' class on coral reefs. The Maldives has a peculiar kind of geographic schizophrenia. Of the two hundred islands that are inhabited, about half are occupied exclusively by luxury resorts where wealthy people go to be treated like royalty. On the others, simpler lives are lived.

Magoodhoo is one of the latter, home to seven hundred Maldivians and an Italian university research centre. The inhabitants lead peaceful and happy lives, it seems. There is a police station but no crime, a doctor's surgery, a school and several tiny shops, all of which sell the same limited range. The streets are made of sand and handcarts outnumber the scattering of cars and several dozen scooters. The port feels like the busiest place on the island on account of three tuna boats that offload at night, but there are only two jetties, one usually empty. There is a timeless feel, as if the world has stood still. But it hasn't. Beyond these shores, the world is changing in ways that will have profound consequences for these people. They just don't know it yet.

Magoodhoo and all of the islands in the Maldives face an existential threat. The sea that gave birth to them may soon swallow them up. We have come to think of the ocean as a constant in our lives. Many coastal towns and cities have endured for millennia. Evidence pieced together from multiple sources such as mangrove swamps, Roman fish ponds, and especially coral reefs, show that sea level has moved very little in five thousand years.[1] We like that reliability. But the ocean is rising again now, this time driven by us.

Across the world, tide gauges built into the walls of harbours and oceanographic institutes tell us that the global sea level has risen slightly over twenty centimetres since the end of the nineteenth century. Satellites bouncing radar off the Earth's surface confirm the upward trend, showing with exquisite precision that sea level rise is accelerating. In the late twentieth century, the sea rose about one centimetre every five years. Today, it rises one centimetre every three years. A quarter of this rise is due to thermal expansion as water absorbs heat trapped by greenhouse gases in the atmosphere. This is because warm water takes up a little more space than cold. The rest of the rise comes from ice melt and underground water pumped to the surface for irrigation, which ends up in the sea. The oceans have taken up 93 per cent of the heat trapped by greenhouse gases since the beginning of the Industrial Revolution, acting as a gigantic planetary air conditioner. Thank goodness they have, or it would be very uncomfortable now (although perhaps we would have taken more heed of global warming). In fact, without the cooling influence of the sea, the atmospheric temperature would have risen 36 degrees Celsius above pre-industrial temperatures, instead of the one-degree rise seen to date. Most of the world would be uninhabitable already, soaring seasonally to Death Valley temperatures and above.

Sea level rise will continue to speed up. Intergovernmental Panel on Climate Change (IPCC) predictions of expected rises have been revised upward in every report. In 2008, they predicted a rise in the range of 18 to 59 centimetres by 2100

---

1.   In many places, the land has been less constant, either subsiding gently or rising, mainly due to gravity, tectonic or seismic forces, or rebounding after the immense weight of land ice melted at the end of the last Ice Age. Remarkably, Aboriginal dreamtime stories, passed from person to person over hundreds of generations, tell of periods of rapid sea level rise after the last Ice Age ended, which forced them to abandon coastal lands.

under a business-as-usual scenario. In 2013, they revised it to a 26 to 82cm rise by 2081 to 2100. This is a wide range and at its lower end doesn't look too alarming. But in truth, figures at the high end of the range are much more likely. In fact, recent science, not taken into account by the last IPCC report, suggests that a rise of more than a metre is possible by 2100.[1] Greenland's glaciers, for instance, are disgorging ice into the sea faster and faster. Many are being melted from below by warming seawater, freeing them from the drag of seabed rocks so they flow more quickly. This alone could add tens of extra centimetres to sea level rise. Greenland has a big influence on sea levels, at least over million-year timescales. If all Greenland's ice melted it would add six metres to global sea level. While that still appears very unlikely, it looks almost inevitable that the rate of sea level rise will accelerate to above a centimetre per year before this century's end.

A centimetre of rise every year seems almost unthinkable. But it is already happening today due to a little-known property of the sea: it isn't level. Oceans and seas have hills and valleys. Admittedly, these hills are not very big, a metre or so of rise across thousands of kilometres, but it makes a difference. The other thing about oceans is that they slop about in their basins somewhat as water does in a bath. When the water slops up at one end, it goes down at the other. The Pacific is the biggest bathtub of all. Those satellite measurements show that the sea off North America's west coast has remained level or even dropped a centimetre or two in the last twenty years, while islands in the western Pacific, which sit in the middle of the up-slop,[2] have

---

1. A little-known piece of scientific research, which nonetheless has a very sound foundation, says that even if we were to stop emitting greenhouse gases today, we can still expect sea levels to rise another metre and a half to two metres over the next 300 years. This will happen as an equilibrium is reached with the present level of warming and is based on a relationship between temperature and sea level extracted from the geological record.

2. Pushed by stronger than normal east to west trade winds.

experienced rises of fifteen to twenty centimetres. They are not coping well.

Kiribati, for instance, is an island nation that sits along a roughly horizontal line along the equator from the central to the western Pacific. The capital, Tarawa, is home to 55,000 people, half the country's population, and sits in the bullseye of peak sea level rise. Three or four times a year, high spring tides known as king tides flood large parts of the islands, in places to depths of half a metre. There is no escape, so people clamber onto chairs, tables and beds to wait the floods out. The islanders' response to the crisis is understandable but misguided. They fill bags with sand from local beaches and dig lumps of coral rock from the reef to fortify their homes, but that only makes matters worse. Removing these natural defences renders their land still more vulnerable.

The president, Anote Tong, has warned his people that they may have to flee. '[We must] plan for the worst and hope for the best,' he told the journalist Ken Weiss, who reported on the Kiribatis' plight.[1] As Weiss put it, however, it won't be water that drives them from their homes first, but lack of it. Life on a coral atoll is precarious. On the larger islands, rainfall supplies a lens of fresh groundwater that floats on top of denser saltwater inside the porous limestone framework. The freshwater lens allows islanders to grow limited crops, while boreholes and wells provide drinking and irrigation water during dry spells. Yet when the sea pours over the land, it taints the freshwater and the soil. You can't drink saltwater or grow crops in it. Already, the country has purchased twenty-two square kilometres of hilly land in Fiji on which to grow food. Who knows, before long that land may become home to its people too.

The Maldives has been more fortunate than Kiribati, at least until now. Sea levels here have only risen a few centimetres in

---

1.   K.R. Weiss, 'Before we drown we may die of thirst'. Nature, 2015, Vol 526: p.624.

recent decades, not enough for most people to notice. Some islands have erosion problems, beaches washing away, buildings crumbling into the sea. But it was always thus in places where land is merely heaped up sand and rubble. The islands are mobile and shift at the behest of tide, wind and storm. But what would a yearly centimetre of sea level rise do to a place like this, I wonder, as Julie coaxes our students into the boat. A small group of children has gathered by the jetty to watch, laughing and chattering as they jostle for a closer look. They are carefree now, but what does their future hold?

We cruise for just five minutes from the jetty to our dive spot, a gently banking reef at the southern edge of the lagoon where the students will practise fish identification. The reef blends into open sand fifteen metres down. Corals blossom like drifts of flowers in some glorious English garden, all self-arranged. There is no gardener here but nature. Giant clams half a metre wide sprout from limestone ledges like gladioli. Their velvet fleshy mantles are as richly colourful as prize garden blooms: deep-dyed indigo, mauve, blue and imperial purple, flecked and curled with twists of bumblebee yellow or dragonfly blue. It feels as if this garden should be heavily scented, but there is no smell underwater with one's nose trapped inside a mask. At the surface, smears of coral slime on skin from bumps and scrapes give off a sweet, fishy bouquet, but we forgo this sense down here.

A clam hugs tighter to the reef as my shadow passes. Here and there a wilder edge to this order is visible where corals have fallen over or been knocked flat, or where bare patches are being colonised afresh. Some corals have branches knobbed and furred like the antlers of early-season stags, while on others the open points are those of a male in autumn rut. Round-faced gobies flit among the interior trunks of their coral arbours, bright orange and lemon like sucked boiled sweets.

A slender jobfish, its grey body streamlined for speed that it never seems to use, pauses in transit and flares its gills. Three finger-size fish, pencil-thin and racing-striped in blue and black, zip up and dive in. The tails of these cleaner wrasse writhe like tentacles from inside the steel-plate gills as the jobfish hovers in a stance that appears half pleasure, half discomfort. With a slight cough, the cleaners are flushed out. They pick their way along the flanks, stopping to eat a scab or parasite before the jobfish departs. A school of unicornfish cruise by, sleek and expressionless, their tails beating rhythmically. They have the naïve simplicity of a child's drawing with their pointed noses, smooth oval outlines and blue triangle tails.

Uncertainty hangs above this island like a vapour, invisible to most. But coral reef problems are symbolic of wider upheaval across the Earth. My students and kids are growing up on a planet that is no longer subject to the forces of nature alone. We live in a world that is changing faster and in more ways than in all human history; it is hard to know where we are going. Change is a slippery thing. The reefs here are so vibrant and alive. Unless you see change for yourself, you're inclined not to believe in it. This is why younger generations are often blind to changes experienced by older people. There is another problem: when change happens slowly, it often goes unnoticed. A degraded environment quietly dons the mantle of the new normal. Where are the hedgehogs of my youth, tripping their way across British roads, the murmurations of starlings that darkened sunset skies, the flapping clouds of lapwings over frosted fields, the summer blizzards of moths? They have succumbed not to sudden catastrophe, but to the corrosive drip drip of a thousand minor insults.

Views are changing as the years pass. There is a feeling now that we are beyond the point where climate change is preventable, so we must adapt instead. That perspective shift helps restore a sense of purpose. Climate change has gone from being someone else's problem to our own. If they eat lots of vegetables and take plenty of exercise, some of my students may still be here in 2100, the index year on which most predictions of climate change converge. By then, on the present trajectory, sea levels may be a metre higher, the world will be at least a couple of degrees warmer, maybe three or four, and climate change will drive ever more energetic and fickle weather. By failing to act now, governments gamble with the futures of millions of people being born today. If we don't clean up, it is they who will inherit our mess, not some distant future generations.

We have made big advances since my student days in understanding how coral reefs work and what keeps them healthy. I started out watching seaweed-eating fish in an effort to unravel how similar species coexisted. It turns out that seaweed-eaters play a pivotal role enabling others to thrive, corals especially. Seaweeds grow fast in brilliant tropical sunshine. Left unchecked, they would soon smother everything. Corals are the opposite. They grow with painstaking deliberation, layering lime millimetre upon millimetre. The fastest-growing corals are things like table-shaped or open branching *Acropora* species. They can add fifteen to twenty centimetres a year. But mound-shaped Porites, animals that live hundreds of years in the right places, manage only a half to one centimetre a year. Like seaweeds, corals need light to thrive, but they would quickly be overwhelmed by tearaway algae were it not for the intervention of vegetarian fish and urchins.

It is the high intensity of reef herbivory that keeps reefs coral-dominated. Where there are lots of grazers, as I saw in the Red Sea, seaweeds are notable for their low-key presence. This is the natural condition of most healthy reefs. The commonest way for a reef to be unhealthy is to have too much seaweed and too few grazers. The change can happen slowly or come on suddenly. Slow change occurs when the competitive balance between seaweeds and corals shifts. Add nutrients to a reef from land run-off, as on the Great Barrier Reef, and they fertilise the weeds. The accompanying suspended mud or blooming plankton blocks light too, which seems to harm corals before it affects free-living seaweeds. Fast change happens when overfishing has driven down the number of grazers. These reefs may look healthy, because they can maintain high cover of coral for years after herbivores have declined. The corals limit space for seaweed to grow. But this state is unstable and susceptible to catastrophic change, a phenomenon first witnessed in Jamaica.

Jamaica came to the world's attention in the aftermath of Hugo, a vicious Hurricane that ripped across the north shore in 1979, taking out a swathe of reef in front of the Discovery Bay research centre. In the 1950s, when these reefs were put under the lens of the new science of ecology, they were covered by dense fields of elkhorn and staghorn corals. Hurricane Hugo left the reef bare, the corals smashed to bits.

The story played out under the eye of Terry Hughes, then a PhD student and now one of the world's foremost coral reef scientists. He published his findings in 1984 in what has become a classic case of 'phase shift': an ecosystem transitioning from one stable state to another. All was not well in Jamaica before Hurricane Hugo, although nobody recognised it at the time. Yes, there was plenty of coral, but by the late 1970s the reefs were badly overfished. When the hurricane swept away coral, fast-growing seaweed flourished in the newly bare space as there were few grazers to mow it back. Sea urchin grazing held back the weeds to some degree, but when their numbers collapsed under the onslaught of the Caribbean-wide urchin plague that struck a few years later, it handed seaweeds control and corals sank towards oblivion.

Seaweed domination can be hard to reverse. Seaweed-eating fish, like people, prefer tender-leaf salads. Left ungrazed, seaweeds develop physical and chemical defences like spikes and fibrous tissue loaded with unpalatable compounds. Fish shun larger seaweeds in favour of young shoots. If seaweeds escape being eaten long enough, they can thrive even when grazers start to recover. Such reefs still possess a certain beauty. Softly undulating weed hummocks waft back and forth, their fronds like a mossy forest understory. But with fewer cracks and holes to hide in, fish are sparse and usually small, and there is less variety of habitat. The transformation is like the difference between forest and grassland.

Forests and reefs have much in common. Both are built by living creatures. The species that dominate them can outlive us by hundreds of years, sometimes thousands. And amid their great architectural complexity hundreds of other species find homes. Perhaps the most underappreciated consequence of coral mass mortality is the loss of that complexity. For a time, recently killed reefs can look okay to an unfamiliar eye. The skeletons may remain upright, albeit coated in a green seaweed fuzz. But gradually, these chalk monuments succumb to creatures that bore and dissolve carbonate rock, which then weaken until they collapse. Unless new corals settle and coralline seaweed crusts cement fragments together, the reef will crumble to rock chips and dust. As it loses its structure, it loses the ability to support life, like a bombed-out city whose inhabitants have fled.

As our students confront the global scale of damage to reefs – the most authoritative estimate says that three quarters of reefs face serious threats from us, and a third to a half are already degraded[1] – it is hard to remain upbeat. But daily dives help repulse dark thoughts. After a day of troubling lectures, Julie and I slip into the sea for a late afternoon snorkel, a chance to commune with other lives.

A group of garfishes, scarcely visible against the low sun, glide silent just beneath the surface, like floating sticks. Their long blue backs are dissipated by light into unrecognisable fragments that perfectly match the ripples, so they appear like ghosts. On the reef below, four filefish amble as a group, keeping close. Their rhombus bodies are flat as planks and scribbled and dotted

1. Burke et al., *Reefs at Risk Revisited.* World Resources Institute, Washington, DC, 2011.

with turquoise graffiti, while their faces seem old and kindly. Careful, almost elaborate movements suggest politeness and respect... 'no, after you', 'please, you go first'. As I approach they sway sideways, fixing me with four one-eyed stares. If fish had eyebrows, theirs would certainly be raised. Ripples on the near-flat surface bend the low sun into bands of light that pulse across the bottom in waves. Coral branches light up like a throbbing nightclub dancefloor, while the blue tips of bushy *Acroporas* take on a scintillating, unearthly glow. Clams gape from the pillowed surface of a coral, their mantles shimmering like peacock feathers.

Ahead there is a slightly darker band of water just below the surface that looks like a cloud on the liquid horizon, a glittering cumulus of tiny silver fish like forked lightning. We leave the water only when it is too dark to distinguish one coral from another, buoyed up once again by magic.

The following day we show the students the maps of reef diversity that we developed from Sir Peter Scott's passion for listing fish. It took fifteen years for Julie, me and a growing network of collaborators to build up maps that came to include several thousand species of fish, corals, snails and lobsters.[1] The maps confirmed in great detail what we already knew in rough outline: the Coral Triangle of South East Asia has the richest reefs, a pattern repeated with minor variations in all these groups of species. Showing these maps feels like making a journey back to my own student days as we revisit the ideas I agonised over for years as I tried to unlock the secrets of that richness.

Ideas come and go, but most of the explanations for high species diversity that circulated in my youth are still around today. Perhaps that is because we have more difficulty ruling ideas out conclusively than we have coming up with them in the first place.

1.   C. M. Roberts, C. J. McClean, J. E. N. Veron, J. P. Hawkins, G. R. Allen, D. E. McAllister, C. G. Mittermeier, F. W. Schueler, M. Spalding, F. Wells, C. Vynne and T. B. Werner, *Marine biodiversity hotspots and conservation priorities for tropical reefs. Science* vol. 295 (2002): pp.1280–1284.

On one thing we were wrong though, or at least not exactly right. The tropics have been stable over long evolutionary timescales, so one explanation for high diversity is that coral reefs have accumulated more species than places with big environmental swings, like temperate coasts. In the minds of ecologists of the 1960s and '70s, high diversity became twinned with stability; diverse ecosystems like coral reefs and rainforests were viewed as more stable than simpler ones like kelp forests or deserts. But there was precious little real evidence.

The recent history of coral reef transformation and collapse seems to knock the idea dead. But perhaps only in a relative sense. Reefs that support fewer species, like those in the Caribbean and eastern Pacific, do seem worse affected by human pressures than more diverse ones, like those of the Coral Triangle, at least so far. Experiments show greater stability of ecological processes in diverse compared to simple ecosystems. With more species, many of which fulfil similar roles, loss of a species or two might not be disastrous. Reef building ground to a halt in the low diversity Caribbean in the 1980s and '90s when elkhorn and staghorn corals were wiped out by disease and star corals began to sicken. But in the western Pacific, there are dozens, possibly hundreds of species that contribute meaningfully to reef construction. That surely makes them more resilient, which is a stability of sorts.

We combined our maps of the number of species living on reefs with a map of human threats to those reefs created by the World Resources Institute in New York. The result was disquieting. The Coral Triangle, which has the most diverse reefs in the world, also has the most threatened. Virtually the whole of the Triangle is coloured blood red on the map, signifying that they are at high risk of degradation or destruction. This is a region of sprawling island archipelagos and interlacing seas, where hundreds of millions of people depend on fishing for a living. Over many decades, reefs have been fished, then overfished, then ransacked, as people trapped in poverty's spiral squeezed a living from dwindling supplies, all of which gave birth to a new term: Malthusian overfishing. Thomas Malthus was an eighteenth-century English thinker who was the first to see that human population growth could eventually outstrip the availability of food. Instead of the nets and traps of old, today many people in The Coral Triangle bomb and poison the reef to obtain fish. Such a grand scale of human impact portends not only local losses of species, but outright global extinctions.

Towards the end of the week, we look at our options. Can reefs be saved? For some students, the litany of impacts, degradation and decline leave them feeling hopeless. A hand goes up soon after I start the lecture: 'If coral reefs are doomed,' says one student, 'why bother to control overfishing or pollution? Isn't it a pointless waste of money?'

'Would we refuse treatment to somebody who is ill just because there is little chance they will recover?' I counter. It is one of the higher qualities of being human that most of us would not. And if we don't try, we will never know if they could have been saved. I throw the question back to the rest of the class, asking how many people think there is no point protecting reefs. None do, I'm glad to see.

Even if it is impossible to maintain or recover a reef to its pristine condition, well-protected reefs will always be more valuable to us than trashed ones. Julie and I saw first-hand evidence of the value of even highly compromised reefs from Noonu Atoll, in the northern Maldives, so I tell them the story now. We were at the seaward side of a channel that cut through the rim of the atoll and planned a drift dive into the lagoon with the incoming tide. Waiting in the boat with our young teenage daughters, I was nervous for them because Maldivian reefs are often flushed by powerful currents. It was clear we were in for a fast ride as the water was agitating at the surface in stiff-peaked thrumming splashes as it poured into the atoll. Dropping over the side, we were whisked off, like stepping onto a fast-moving conveyor. The water was crystalline and only half a dozen metres deep. Looking down it was immediately clear that this place had once been extraordinary but suffered horribly during the 1997-98 bleaching. Trunks of coral were heaped across the bottom, like bones in an elephant's graveyard. In my mind's eye, I tried to conjure them back to life, imagining a crowded stand of corals taller than people, their arms reaching for the surface. The limbs would have intertwined so tightly that none but fish and scuttling invertebrates could penetrate.

Seen closer as we whooshed above the bottom, the strewn bones sprouted fist- and cabbage-sized knobs of living coral. A hesitant recovery was underway, but the living coral only covered five or ten per cent of the seabed. Moments later we were washed through a living wall of humpbacked red snappers, their burgundy fins waving as the smooth grey bodies parted to let us through. Behind them a loose group of two-spot red snappers[1] frowned through their fangs as we wafted by. Deep bodied and menacing, their pupils are dark pits within orange eyes. As the current pushed us deeper and further into the atoll, the fish increased in size and numbers. Several spotted coral groupers over a metre long ambled away slowly, their round bellies swaying like diners in an all-you-can-eat restaurant. A hump-headed wrasse as big as my daughters approached for a look. Its beady swivel eyes shone like jewels in the broad emerald face, following us as we passed. Oriental sweetlips hung in lazy groups, yellow and black like fat wasps. Grey nurse shark tails poked from underneath ledges like smart leather shoes.

The current slowed as the channel opened into the lagoon, finally disgorging us onto a broad plateau colonnaded with coral

---

1. Snapper names are often unhelpfully misleading. Many turn red when they die, so there is an excess of 'red' snappers about. In life, their colours are very different. To add to the confusion, red snapper, that stalwart of restaurant menus, has often been proven by clandestine DNA testing to be anything but, substituted by a host of different fish.

to create huge floating resorts anchored within the lagoons of Maldivian atolls. Some of the plans foresee resorts big enough to have their own golf courses with submarine tunnels connecting the course with floating hotels. If reefs go belly up, Maldivians might eventually relocate to floating islands too.

It is a bleak prospect, but it chimes with what my students increasingly see as the only way out: technology. Can we, for example, rid the atmosphere of carbon dioxide that has already been released? Carbon capture and storage is already practical at the point of release, although expensive, so some oil rigs capture carbon dioxide and pump it back underground. Power stations may follow suit, using 'clean coal' technology. But sucking diffuse carbon dioxide out of the atmosphere is a much greater challenge (plants do it very well, but much of it is recycled back to the atmosphere on death so the greenhouse gas is not taken out of circulation for long).[1] Increasingly, however, carbon dioxide recapture is seen as essential if coral reefs are to survive. As our London meeting of 2009 concluded, we are already far past the 350 parts per million of carbon dioxide that reefs were comfortable with.

None of the scientists I know expect world leaders to tackle climate change decisively enough to prevent things getting much worse than they are now. For one thing, due to time lags between emissions and their effects, even if we stop releasing greenhouse gases today there is already more warming (perhaps another half-degree centigrade), more sea level rise and more ocean acidification to come. We can't, of course, reduce emissions to zero overnight, and we won't reduce emissions sufficiently until the consequences of our inaction are abundantly clear and dangerous. The root causes of climate change – human population growth and rising material aspirations – are put in a

---

1. A global programme of forest restoration could, however, help draw down carbon dioxide levels for more than a century.

box marked 'Too Difficult', so only a bold or foolhardy politician would go there.

Sadly, most politicians do not understand the gravity of our predicament. Donald Trump is the most egregious manifestation of this ignorance, putting comfort and convenience today (at least for the wealthy) ahead of the needs of countless future generations.[1] But he is not alone. When the world financial crisis struck in 2008, environmental protection budgets were among the first to be slashed by governments who considered them a soft target, luxury rather than necessity. Such a view is woefully short-sighted but few politicians these days have much in the way of science training. Science is too often viewed as just another opinion around the table rather than the foundation for rational decision-making in the public interest.

So things will get worse before they get better, possibly much worse. Is there anything we can do? If life feels overwhelming and you can no longer cope with all the demands and stress, a good doctor would recommend that you reduce the sources of stress, eat healthily to boost your immune system, and take more exercise to build energy and strength. This advice translates well into a prescription for the environment: reduce human-generated stresses, boost animal and plant population sizes and protect habitat integrity. Or, in a clamshell, fish less, using less destructive methods, waste less, pollute less, destroy less and protect more. We should rebuild depleted fish populations to keep reefs healthy, protect and restore coastal wetlands like the mangroves of Australia's Fitzroy delta, and direct industrial

1. President Trump's reaction to a 2018 Intergovernmental Panel on Climate Change report which stressed the absolute urgency of reducing net greenhouse gas emissions to zero was to suggest that climate change had already gone too far to bother doing anything about it. The same report said that if we hold greenhouse gas emissions to the Paris aspiration of only a 1.5°C rise in global average temperature, we might save between 10 and 30 per cent of coral reefs in something resembling their present condition. If average temperature rises more than 2°C, we would lose nearly all coral reefs (<1 per cent left). See https://www.ipcc.ch/news_and_events/pr_181008_P48_spm.shtml

developments away from reefs to more resilient places. We must up the coverage of highly protected marine parks to at least a third of oceans and seas, according to the best available science. These are steps that can be taken right away that could improve the prognosis for reefs. I am a positive thinker, some might say over-optimistic. But I am still troubled by a nagging question: will it be enough?

CHAPTER FIFTEEN

Déjà vu

New York City, Maldives, 2015–16

'HAVE YOU MET THE PRESIDENT OF PALAU?' Ellen asks. It is early March 2015 and Ellen Pikitch, an old friend based at New York's Stony Brook University, has invited me to speak at the United Nations on behalf of a new initiative to increase protection for the world's oceans.

For the last few years, diplomats and experts have been negotiating a set of new goals to guide humanity toward a safer, more prosperous future. The development goals agreed by the world community at the turn of the millennium, bold efforts to do things like end hunger and poverty, improve education, achieve gender equality and look after the environment, expire this year. A new set of goals, the Sustainable Development Goals, is being finalised. This time round there is a goal for 'life below water'. A key target is to increase the coverage of marine protected areas to 10 per cent of the sea by 2020. But there is no guarantee that the goal will be agreed as some nations are trying to can the idea. Tommy Remengesau, the president of Palau, is spearheading an alliance of mainly oceanic nations to ensure the goal's safe passage.

We are in a restaurant a few blocks from the United Nations in New York City. Remengesau's party includes his Environment

Minister, several senators, and Stuart Beck, the country's ambassador to the UN. There is a polite understated dignity about the group, but they are amiable and open, especially after I tell them how I fell in love with their island country on a visit years before.

The next morning, snow is falling in fat flakes, swirling in the gusts between tower blocks and muffling the city hum. The worst of this storm has yet to arrive and there is talk that the UN may have to close. Ellen seems unruffled. A lifelong New Yorker, she tells us not to worry in a voice as mellow as coffee. But she checks her phone periodically, declaring at last that the meeting is on, just thirty minutes before the scheduled start.

The blizzard has arrived and outside the air is thick with blowing snow. There is a sign telling visitors that the UN is closed, but we are shown through security to a cavernous and largely empty atrium. The auditorium beyond is familiar from television, its somewhat dilapidated interior redolent of the 1970s. The rows are sparsely populated today, but after a quick look around, Ellen says that the key nations are here, their diplomats mostly living within walking distance.

Stuart Beck starts proceedings. He is in his late sixties and was the legal architect of Palau's independence from the USA in 1994, which explains how a New Yorker became their UN ambassador. With his bald head and black-rimmed glasses, he looks like one of the founding fathers of the UN, whose black and white photographs line the halls. 'We all remember a time when the ocean was better than it is now,' he says in a commanding voice. 'Scientists have known what to do for a long time, but the political will has not been there.' This is refreshing; a high-level diplomat who doesn't water his words.

President Remengesau is next to speak. He looks about the room with firm resolve, takes a deep breath and begins. His eyes are half-closed as he talks, as if conjuring the warm breeze and island-bejewelled sea of home. 'We are already living what science is telling us about our changing world,' he says, describing Palau's deep concerns at the fragility of their coral reefs. He speaks with eloquence and passion, ending with a call to action. 'I implore member states to pass the Sustainable Development Goal for the oceans and get to work.'

Several other countries speak in support, then it's our turn. We have rehearsed these themes many times – the scale of the challenge facing humanity, the litany of examples, the outline of what we can do. There is a huge amount of energy and goodwill in the room, which gives me hope. Stuart[1] tells me at a reception that evening that the UN is filled with idealistic people, characteristics, he insists, that even the representatives of totalitarian states share.

The year 2015 is key for international action on the environment for another reason: France is hosting the 21st global climate change conference, approaching it with fresh conviction. There are high hopes for a global agreement in Paris to limit greenhouse gas emissions because countries have, for the first time, been obliged to make their plans public ahead of the meeting.

One day in early summer 2015, Rupert calls me. 'Have you seen the documents for the Paris climate change conference?' he asks. I confess that I haven't. 'There's hardly a mention of coral reefs in any of them.' He sounds peeved. The Copenhagen conference of six years ago was widely regarded as a flop. With time running out, there is an urgency about the Paris meeting, as well as much anxiety.

Coral reefs are so clearly an early victim of climate change that I'm staggered they have been overlooked. 'Coral should be all over these reports given everything we've done to raise the alarm,' I say. I'm thinking again of the Royal Society of London meeting in

---

1. Stuart Beck's diplomatic skill and deft handling of the meeting impressed me greatly that day. It is all the more remarkable in hindsight. I found out later that he had learned from his doctor that morning that his cancer had returned and was now untreatable. He died in February the following year, just before a follow-up meeting was held in Rome. He is sadly missed, but his legacy will endure. The UN Sustainable Development Goal for the oceans was successfully adopted in 2015.

2009 on the future of coral. Our conclusion could not have been clearer that greenhouse gas emissions had already overshot the point at which coral reefs became endangered. But there have been many other meetings, reports and studies in the last few years, which makes it almost criminally negligent not to feature reefs as a centrepiece of the Paris conference. Most importantly, the 2014 Assessment Report of the Intergovernmental Panel on Climate Change showed a high risk of harm to coral reefs from even modest future emissions. These reports are an accounting of the science of climate change by the world's foremost scientists, issued every six or seven years. However, in the 2014 report, coral reefs were lumped with other 'sensitive and vulnerable' ecosystems. I felt uncomfortable with their framing of the problem. Although they didn't say it outright, the conclusion that politicians would probably draw is that these systems are outliers and that most other habitats could tough it out, carrying on much as before. The 'sensitive and vulnerable' tag suggests we might just let coral reefs and all the other delicate flowers go, a satisfyingly Darwinian view that would find a ready audience among all the industry and political leaders keen to pursue business as usual.

'A few of us from The International Society for Reef Studies are organising a statement urging for deeper cuts in emissions to save reefs,' Rupert says. 'We want the world to know that limiting temperature rise to 2°C is too much. We're recommending a 1.5°C target. Will you and Julie sign it?' Of course we do.

By the time the Paris conference begins in November 2015, the statement has been endorsed by more than two thousand scientists. I'm not at the meeting. It's going to be a massive bunfest with hundreds of environmental organisations lobbying thousands of delegates, so the chances of influence are slender. I'm not optimistic. But Rupert and his fellow committee members have a trick up their sleeve. Many of the places most reliant on coral reefs are small island nations in the Pacific and Caribbean. Nations like Kiribati or Tuvalu stand to lose a great deal, perhaps

Top: Some fish, like these Bohar snappers (*Lutjanus bohar*) in Palau, gather in huge aggregations to spawn, turning the water milky at dusk with eggs and sperm (*Ch. 12*). Bottom: A Caribbean Nassau grouper (*Epinephelus striatus*) deep cleaned by tiny gobies (*Ch. 12*).

Coral growth is most vigorous at the reef face where it meets the open sea. There, the sharp water clarity allows plentiful sunlight to reach photosynthesising zooxanthellae embedded in the coral tissue that feed the polyps (*Ch. 4*).

Top: A wall of mouths surrounds the reef, plucking plankton from incoming water and capturing crucial nutrients, Maldives (*Ch. 4*). Bottom: Predators (*Caranx ignobilis*) hunt in packs along the reef front, ever watchful for fish off their guard (*Ch. 16*).

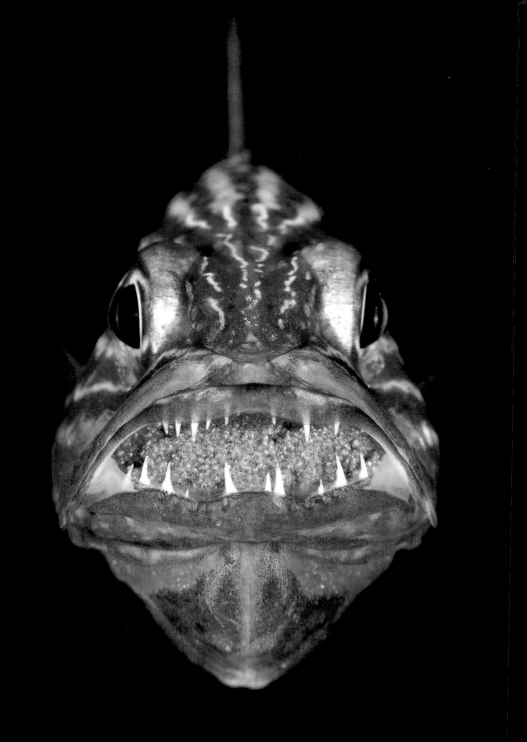

Unguarded eggs are swiftly eaten, so this male tiger cardinalfish (*Cheilodipterus macrodon*) protects his inside his mouth until they hatch into larvae and drift off into the open sea, Red Sea (*Ch. 4*).

Top: Reefs protected from fishing can support huge abundances of fish, like these blue-striped snappers (*Lutjanus kasmira*) in the Maldives (*Ch. 15*). Bottom: A humphead wrasse (*Cheilinus undulatus*) alarmed me on my first Red Sea dive, Red Sea (*Ch. 1*).

Top: It is still worth protecting reefs that have suffered mass coral death. They can support wonderful life, Maldives (*Ch. 14*). Bottom: Elkhorn corals (*Acropora palmata*) dominated shallow Caribbean reefs but were wiped out by disease in the 1980s (*Ch. 6*).

Top: Branching staghorn (*Acropora cervicornis*), the Caribbean companion of elkhorn, was also devasted by disease in the 1980s (*Ch. 6*). Bottom: The diminutive longnose filefish (*Oxymonacanthus longirostris*) all but disappeared after mass bleaching of Maldivian reefs in 2016 (*Ch. 17*).

Top: The beauty and mystery of reefs continues within (Red Sea, *Ch. 2*). Bottom left: A brain coral, *Platygyra daedalea*, Red Sea (*Ch. 1*). Bottom right: A Red Sea surgeonfish charged me on my first ever coral reef snorkel (*Ch. 1*).

everything, to climate change. People in the reef studies society, like President-Elect Yimnang Golbuu, who is from Palau, have the ear of their leaders. Within a couple of days of the conference opening, small island states, many of them members of the Ocean Sanctuary Alliance whose inaugural meeting I attended at the UN, have formed a powerful political alliance to push for a 1.5°C target.

There is never a good time for a disaster, but by the time the Paris conference is underway the world is on notice for another massive El Niño event. In October 2015, the US National Oceanic and Atmospheric Administration issues a global alert, predicting that this could become one of the biggest El Niños on record. These disruptions of ocean and atmospheric circulation above the Pacific release vast quantities of heat and cause ripple effects that propagate around the world. According to the alert, the coming El Niño might equal the 1997–98 event that devastated coral in the Indian Ocean, or the 1982–83 one that destroyed Galápagos reefs. They are forecasting another worldwide coral bleaching pulse. The alert brings coral to the centre of discussions in Paris, which is exactly what Rupert and his fellow scientists had hoped, although not for this reason.

Like many others hunched over their computers at home watching proceedings unfold, I hope for much but expect little. But the newsfeeds buzz with cautious optimism. There is an energy in Paris that was missing from Copenhagen and the big players, like the US, China, India and EU, have come to the table with serious proposals this time. The meeting closes to much fanfare in mid-December. A legally binding agreement on emissions cuts has finally been achieved. Arguments made by coral reef nations didn't quite win the day, but the final agreement owes much to them: a long-term goal of limiting the global average temperature rise to well below 2°C, and an aspiration to limit the increase to 1.5°C.

Although there are loose ends, and emissions cuts promised to date aren't enough to hit even the 2°C target, it's a good Christmas present for the world. But is it too late for coral reefs? While negotiators wrangled, El Niño has been building in the Pacific, implacable, inexorable, unstoppable. In a statement to the press, one Australian politician at the Paris Conference predicts a 'white' Christmas for the Great Barrier Reef as summer arrives. It doesn't happen quite that quickly, but by the beginning of March 2016 corals in the northern section of the reef are turning white. By the end of March, a disaster is underway. Early reports suggest that 95 per cent of the northern reefs are severely bleached, and corals to the south are ailing. Mass bleaching is also seen in American Samoa, Indonesia and Thailand.

In late March, Julie and I arrive in the Maldives with another group of students for our annual coral reef course. Right from the beginning, things seem out of kilter, a feeling of premonition. Where normally the three-hour speedboat ride to Magoodhoo is lumpy, here, in the middle of an ocean, the sea is smooth as plate glass, reflecting puffy wisps of cloud and a deep blue arc of sky. We settle into the week's teaching with heavy hearts, knowing that this place could soon suffer in the same way as Australia's reefs, remembering the devastation wrought by the last big El Niño nearly twenty years ago.

The day is breathless and the sea perfectly still for our first dive. As we roll in, the first thing to strike me is how unusually warm the water is, hot almost. I check my gauge: 31.5°C. Normally it would be the high 20s. Calm weather and hot sun have pushed temperatures into the bleaching danger zone already. It's terrible news. There is something else that Julie and I notice as the week progresses: the reefs have never looked more gorgeous. Perhaps beauty is sharpened by looming peril. Corals have mounted a vigorous comeback since the devastation of 1997–98 and have spread like a living tapestry over the bottom, attaining levels of cover last seen in the mid-1990s. In most places, half the seabed is living coral, and in a few choice spots, nearly all of it.

The Maldives has been issued a 'Level II' bleaching alert based on satellite measures of ocean warmth, meaning that mass bleaching is imminent. But what is the point of a warning when nothing can be done to avert disaster? When a hurricane looms, there are strange days of anticipation, living on borrowed time, watching as others in the path of the storm are eaten up. At least you have time to hunker down. When a coral bleaching warning is issued, it may be months before temperatures creep upward enough to overwhelm the corals, leaving vast areas dead and dying. Nothing can be done but weep: no safe-haven, no protective measures, no cure. The return of global coral bleaching comes as a severe blow to me, like a cancer patient long in remission on hearing that the disease has returned. The hopes fostered by last year's glorious dives were an illusion.

Magoodhoo's reefs are waiting. The heartbreak is yet to come. Their only hope is that the monsoon will soon turn and south-westerly winds will drag cool water to the surface and save the day. But it doesn't look likely.

It is easy to lose yourself in the joy of this place, so we set aside doubt and live for the moment. Fish have such different characters, a combination of movement, shape and whatever expression evolution has given them (fish expressions don't change; there is no furrowing of brows or withering scowl). Titan triggerfish are burly and belligerent, with teeth as crooked as Dickensian scallywags. *Pseudocheilinus* wrasses are timid, delicate and quizzical; moray eels are serpentine, suspicious and defensive; parrotfish are bumbling innocents (although males can be fractious). It is these characters that make a reef so instantly appealing and so welcoming after an absence, and there is always something new. On this visit, one of our Italian hosts points out to me, with the nail of his little finger, some almost invisible hair-like threads protruding from the warty corallites on the staghorn branches of an *Acropora* coral. How many thousands of times I have passed them by unnoticed. So too did everyone else until, a few years ago, someone looked closer and discovered that they belonged to microscopic hydroids living inside the polyps. Hydroids, or sea nettles, are usually a few centimetres tall with glassy stems and a gossamer fur of stinging cells. Such discoveries feel like finding unread pages in a book you thought you knew well. Occasionally, discoveries are so fundamental that they rewrite entire chapters.

The reef here is a steep wall, in places shadowed and mysterious, in others flood-lit. Sponges, patches of coralline algae, hydroids, corals and a hundred other crusting forms, spatter the wall like flung paint. It is as if some marine Jackson Pollock has used the cliff as a canvas. But this painting has been made without any creative hand. Life grows atop other life in a continuously reworked mural. Finger-slight gobies hover by a sea fan, their inner organs on view through transparent bodies, delicate as crystal. A shoal of fusilier fish surrounds me momentarily as they pass, their torpedo bodies, each the size of a banana, rendered in broad brushstrokes of lemon, ice blue and silver. When I enter a cave, night-black snappers scrawled with yellow hieroglyphs rush back and forth like anxious dogs. Further on, parrotfish poop is dusted on the slopes of a large hill of *Porites* coral, gleaming like coralline snow in the blue valleys.

In the shallows I come across a chequerboard wrasse nosing for morsels, an old friend from the Red Sea. I feel a surge of nostalgia for the days when my only concerns were to figure out why a fish had one mate or many, lived where it was and how it made peace with its enemies. I didn't fear for the firmament of their world as I do now. A flying fish can leap clear of danger and, with deft flicks of its tail, glide to a safer piece of ocean. If only we could escape so easily.

Magoodhoo is getting a new all-weather harbour. Diggers have scooped a large hole in the reef beside the bay and used the rubble to create new land. The harbourside is less than half a metre above high water. The engineers haven't thought very hard about sea level rise. Last night the tide rose to the top of the beach; there is little freeboard. Like the Venice of Shelley's poem, this place was born of the sea but soon may be consumed by it.[1]

---

1. 'Sun-girt city, thou hast been, Ocean's child, and then his queen; Now is come a darker day, And thou soon must be his prey.' From 'Lines Written Among the Euganean Hills' (1819).

We find it hard to tear ourselves away at the end of the final dive, hanging in the water as the students get in the boat, peering to the last at the fading outline of reef as the current drifts us away. There is some comfort perhaps, in that Maldivian reefs have all the qualities needed for great resilience: high cover of corals, crystalline water clarity, lots of coralline algae to keep it cemented together, plenty of parrotfish to mow down fleshy algae and a still light touch from people. The patient is fit enough to recover from this illness. But what of those yet to come? Resilience becomes a hollow concept when the blows fall faster than you can stand up from the last.

Soon after getting back to the UK, I receive an unusual invitation. Prince Edward, third son of Queen Elizabeth, kindly requests my participation in a conference to 'Rethink the Future of Coral Reefs'. The meeting is to be held at St James's Palace in London in early June. There is an impressive line-up of experts, including Terry Hughes, the scientist who in the 1980s reported the decline into misery of Jamaica's reefs. He has been at the centre of the Great Barrier Reef's unfolding crisis, undertaking the aerial surveys that shocked the world.

I arrive at the palace half an hour early and am checked in by a policeman. Inside I am shown up a broad staircase lined with paintings. Charles I gazes rakishly from one. He spent his last night here before execution. At the top of the stairs there is a dark panelled room whose walls bristle with the implements of imperial subjugation: shields surrounded by scimitars, their blades glinting like sunrays, and hatchets, halberds, pikes and swords all arrayed in elaborate patterns. A table runs the length of the room, reflecting the weaponry in burnished walnut. A huge silver cup forms a centrepiece. I can't resist a peek to see what great occasion this was bestowed upon: 'Best Sheep at Sandringham Show'.

The Prince arrives and mingles briefly before calling on everyone to follow him into an adjoining meeting room. There he delivers a brief, extempore introduction from his chair among the audience, explaining that his interest in coral is a result of being patron of the Cayman Islands research centre that has organised the meeting. Then Terry Hughes takes the stage. He is a softly spoken Irishman, but decades spent in America and Australia have rubbed some of the brogue from his accent. Still there is something of the leprechaun about him, with his twinkling eyes and slight frame. 'Can the world's reefs be saved?' he begins. 'What we are doing now for coral reefs isn't working.' Well, it is, I think. It's working spectacularly well as a recipe to destroy them, although I don't think this is quite what Terry means! 'Let me answer my own question, before I get into the detail,' he continues, 'Yes, if we try harder. But we are running out of time. There is no quick fix or magic bullet.'

He then updates us on the situation in Australia, now at the tail end of this horrific El Niño heatwave. 'I've spent hundreds of hours flying up and down the Great Barrier Reef in the last few months. The latest survey shows that 80 per cent of the northern section has bleached severely,[1] as has 33 per cent of the middle section and 1 per cent of the southern section. Diving surveys confirm the picture from the air. Things are looking terrible. Big, old corals like *Porites* are usually tough, but in the north, even they have bleached.'

I've always loved coming across a giant on the reef, some much-storied coral the size of a bull elephant. What extraordinary endurance to stick around for hundreds of years, like breathing rocks, weathering repeated typhoons and El Niños. With slopes

---

1.   Some reefs were worse affected than others, but early reports of 95 per cent severe bleaching in the north turned out to be too high. However, by the end of 2016, more thorough surveys showed that bleaching caused the death of two thirds of corals in the northern section of the GBR, although offshore the figure was a quarter. The central section of the reef lost 6 per cent of coral and the south 1 per cent.

wormed and pitted by clam and sponge, they've really seen life. For these corals to be toppled by this El Niño is insight enough into its preternatural intensity.

What's really distressing is that the northern section of the Great Barrier Reef was the area least affected by human activity, spared by inaccessibility. Few people lived there and the forested watershed was intact and undeveloped so there was little polluted run-off, no industry, hardly any tourists and, the cherry on the cake, it's fully protected from fishing. This is the place where coral cover held up as most of the rest of the GBR declined. We looked upon it as a refuge, a place where reefs might still thrive even if the rest succumbed.

Terry continues, as if reading my thoughts. 'We've got a network of fifty coral monitoring sites across the southern hemisphere. We've studied the data to see if there could be any climate refuges, places that seem more resistant to bleaching. But over fifteen years, almost everywhere has been hit at least once. If there are any refuges, they're very small.'

Prince Edward leads the questions from the front row. He speaks in the familiar hesitant, clipped English of royalty. 'From what you have said, this year has been dreadful for reefs. Is there any way we can use our knowledge to assist more rapid recovery after the disaster?'

'Restoration won't save reefs, I'm afraid,' Terry says. 'My team has just reviewed the evidence on reef restoration efforts worldwide. We looked at 250 studies that collectively cost $250 million. Do you know what the total area restored was? One hectare! And the outcomes were highly variable. Some places did alright but restored reefs still died when storms hit or temperatures spiked. Restoration is a very costly distraction.' The Prince looks crestfallen.

Someone else says: 'Deep water is cooler than the surface. Is there a deep-water refuge from which corals might mount a comeback?' Terry looks mournful and shakes his head. He's good at mournful looks. 'I don't think so. We've found bleaching all the way down to forty metres, almost the lower limit of reef growth.'

Later in the morning, Gareth Williams from Bangor University in Wales describes his research on remote reefs of the Pacific. He is tall and wiry with a mop of orange hair and a matching goatee. In over a decade he has visited some of the most isolated reefs on the planet. 'Comparing populated and uninhabited reefs,' he says, 'the key drivers of how a reef looks and functions are fishing and nutrient pollution. They dictate the balance between seaweed and coral.' It isn't a surprise to anyone in the room, given the long list of places where loss of herbivores or addition of nutrients has swung the balance in favour of seaweeds. But we're impressed by the clarity of his case, his careful unpicking of the roles of natural and human influences.

The next bit is less convincing. Gareth says he wants to use his understanding to determine which places across the Pacific might be more resilient to the creeping threat of climate change. 'A map of climate vulnerability,' he argues, 'would enable us to focus protection on the places most likely to survive.' And abandon those which we don't believe will make it, I think. What if we're wrong? The risk is surely too great. As if to underline that point, he then tells us about Jarvis Island. This uninhabited scrap of land and reef lies almost dead centre in the Pacific and is fully protected from fishing in a US marine park. A recent assessment ranked Jarvis as one of the healthiest pieces of sea on the planet. 'I was there a couple of years ago,' he says, 'It's one of the most beautiful places in the world. But a survey team just back brought terrible news: 80 per cent of Jarvis's corals were dead, slain by El Niño's passing heatwave'. There is a collective gasp.

After this bombshell, I don't follow much more of Gareth's presentation. It undermines one of my last untarnished hopes: the idea of protecting remote places as some kind of final bastion in the fight against planetary change. I recall a comment made by the American conservationist, Sylvia Earle, in a film about her life. She was taken to a far-flung reef in Australia's Coral Sea, once visited in youth and fondly remembered as one of the most remarkable places she'd ever dived. Underwater the reef was surprisingly drab and many of its corals dead. Surfacing from the dive in shock, she struggled for an explanation. How could it happen? 'This reef is in the middle of nowhere!' she said, followed quickly by 'but it's in the middle of everywhere.' Jarvis is also in the middle of everywhere. There is no escape from global change.

As the El Niño phenomenon spread around the planet, Terry became the go-to spokesman on the crisis. His 'coral reefs can be saved, but time is running out' line sounds like a mantra repeated hundreds of times in the last few months. But as the day progresses, it seems increasingly at odds with the rest of what he and the other scientists are saying. I keep my own counsel for the moment. I will have an opportunity to articulate these worries the following day in a panel discussion. Before then, there is a treat in store. Prince Edward has invited some of us for dinner at Buckingham Palace.

We are shown up a Persian-carpeted staircase that spirals around an ancient, caged-in lift shaft. Halfway down a long corridor, we are ushered into a room, one wall of which is occupied by three curtained windows. Peeking through a crack, I'm delighted to find this is antechamber to the royal waving balcony that overlooks the Mall, backdrop to some of the great state occasions in British history: weddings, funerals, days of celebration and victory in war.

Prince Edward is generous and attentive with his guests, laughing at their jokes. Our glasses are kept constantly full by discreet waiters. The day's proceedings have left me troubled though, proving barren of new solutions. Amid this opulence, I feel as ambassadors gathered to negotiate some peace treaty might do: entertained and banqueted while war rages on somewhere else.

As predicted, corals in the Maldives started to bleach soon after we left, three months ago. As Terry put it earlier in the day, a bleached coral is a very sick animal. By the end of May there were reports of mass mortality from all over the country. Before this El

Niño, lulled by years of strong recovery in the Maldives, I had been growing more optimistic about the prospects for coral reefs. But this is a sucker punch to hope.

I shouldn't be surprised. All the climate models predict it. Trace-element records extracted from ancient corals in the eastern Pacific said that the 1982–83 El Niño, which destroyed the Galápagos reefs, was the worst for hundreds of years. But then that was matched in 1997–98, and 2015–16 appears to be as bad again. Terry's network of monitoring sites bears this out: the temperature spikes on his underwater data loggers are getting hotter and more prolonged. Perhaps for the first time, the 2015–16 El Niño is forecast to continue into a third year. And the gaps between repeated mass coral bleaching events are decreasing. Many regional bleaching episodes have punctuated the intervals between the global El Niño-driven disasters. In fact, there have only been five years in the last fifteen when severe bleaching has not happened somewhere.

I'm pleased to see Prince Edward back the next morning, calling the proceedings to order. Princes usually flit in and out for the beginning and end of their events. Chatting with him over yesterday's dinner, I found him to be well informed and deeply concerned about the direction our world is headed. I'm on a panel this morning whose charge is to reflect on what was said the day before. Terry Hughes kicks off with his 'reefs can be saved' refrain. I've become more agitated about it over a rather sleepless night, perhaps suffering the after-effects of palace hospitality. Best estimates indicate that emissions reduction commitments made at the Paris climate change meeting will buy us only ten years more before the point where corals bleach every year.[1] 'I hate to start on a downer,' I say, starting on a downer, 'but I feel like I'm

---

1.   These commitments will not count for much if the experience of the UK is replicated elsewhere. On return from the Paris Summit the UK government trumpeted its progressive role, but then swiftly cut subsidies for renewable energy and bolstered its highly unpopular support for shale-gas fracking by removing options for local veto. Then in 2016 they axed the Department for Energy and Climate Change. Bare naked hypocrisy. Politicians are failing the world badly with their short-termism.

suffering cognitive dissonance.' A few eyebrows rise. 'What I heard yesterday seems at odds with Terry's statement that it isn't too late. I agree with the intent of the message. We must absolutely avoid giving the impression that reefs can be written off, that they are zombie ecosystems. If we withdraw management support now, we guarantee this is what they will become. But according to any reasonable climate change model, even factoring in Paris cuts, reefs will be rocked to their foundations. And that's before we even start to factor in ocean acidification.[1] So what can we do? I think we've spent too much time agonising about keeping reefs in the condition they were in thirty years ago, rather than finding out what we can do to soften the impacts. Reefs are changing fast. We can no longer prevent change, but we can improve the outlook for the creatures that live on reefs and the people who depend on them.

'Gareth's priority area selection approach is risky, not least because we might be misled into protecting the wrong places. And Terry says climate refuges, if they exist, are likely to be tiny, so there is a huge practical challenge to identifying them. Directing protection to areas that are uninhabited at the expense of populated sites could mean we ignore the very places where people most need good management to provide for their needs.

'I'd like us to do two things. First, we need to study what we can do to maintain the viability of reef life as corals decline.' I'm thinking here of the positive benefits of protecting Maldivian fish where coral has failed to come back: that extraordinary dive with my daughters through a coral mausoleum, jostled and obstructed by ten thousand scaly bodies. 'And second, despite all that's been said, I think it is worth searching for and protecting possible climate refuges. They could buy us insurance while we bring emissions down, places from which recolonisation can begin when

---

1.   Terry Hughes tells me later that he doesn't think that ocean acidification will radically affect corals, because the amount of greenhouse gas emissions needed for it to spread to tropical latitudes is very high. Those emissions will cause such disruption to the climate that we will be forced to reduce them well before we reach that point. I hope he is right.

conditions recover. Given the imprecision of pinpointing refugia and their likely small sizes, wrapping up big areas with high levels of protection seems a good strategy. That portfolio must include remote and uninhabited places, but not at the expense of failing to protect places where people live. We need both.'

Later in the day, someone at the back of the room voices what many of us probably feel: 'If we can't come up with solutions from this group of experts, then there seems to be little hope.' The comment brings us back once again to emissions. Terry somehow manages to pluck another positive from a negative: 'Scientists are not remotely interested in writing the obituaries for coral reefs. People become aware of climate change when it affects them personally. As the grip of climate change tightens, more and more will be affected, so more will care. I'm still optimistic.'

Our conclusion is as stark as it is succinct: reefs cannot be climate-proofed and they can't hide from climate change. No sophisticated management trickery or technical fixes can save them. Protection is essential, of course, as is reduction of stresses like agricultural run-off and fishing. Good initial health could make all the difference to the eventual outcome. Prevention is better than cure. It is better to keep reefs intact than try to rebuild them after degradation. But in the end, this magnificent ecosystem will only be spared destruction if we avoid extreme climate change. It all comes back to emissions. If we fail to cut them, reefs are doomed.

Back in York I feel deflated but relieved that I'm not the only scientist disconcerted by our fast-changing planet. After crystal-ball-gazing with some of the world's foremost experts, we have drawn the only reasonable conclusion. The best way to help a friend under pressure is to alleviate the pressure.

After all the strife of the last twelve months, I need some pressure relief myself. For the last few years, I have been helping with two ambitious projects to protect some of the most pristine and isolated places in the world: the Global Ocean Legacy Project of the US-based Pew Charitable Trusts, and efforts to establish a 'blue belt' of protection in UK overseas territories by Blue Marine Foundation. Their campaigns have been highly successful, supporting the creation of nine vast protected areas that collectively safeguard 6.3 million square kilometres of the Pacific and Indian oceans. It's time I saw some of it for myself.

CHAPTER SIXTEEN

Paradise on Earth

Palmyra, Pacific Ocean, 2016

SEEN FROM SPACE, one side of Earth is almost entirely ocean. A rim of land, just visible, skirts the edge of the enormous blue expanse of the Pacific. If you draw one line from the southern tip of South America to Russia's far-eastern Kamchatka Peninsula and another from New Zealand's North Island to California, beneath the 'X' of this cross lies Palmyra Atoll. For 180 years after Magellan's first circumnavigation, this flake of reef lay undiscovered and unsuspected. Just a low line of trees on the horizon, Palmyra was invisible to any ship passing farther than twenty-five kilometres away.

The first I heard of Palmyra was in 2006. Scientists from California's Scripps Institute of Oceanography returned from a research trip brim-full with excitement. Palmyra's waters teemed with predatory sharks, jacks and groupers that swam through broad panoramas of luxuriant coral. Jeremy Jackson, the expedition leader, declared he had never seen anything like it, so great was the abundance of big fish. It was as close to a coral Eden as any place on the planet. Diving Palmyra's waters was, he said, like turning back time.

Soon afterwards they published a study that quickly became famous: Palmyra's 'pyramid of biomass' was upside down. Ever since we were hunter-gatherers we have known that predators are rarer than their prey. Lions, leopards and hyenas are outnumbered on African savannahs by vast herds of gazelle and antelope; doves and songbirds outnumber hawks. At each step up the food chain, from the plants at the bottom, to herbivores to carnivores, life dwindles by numbers and weight. Big, fierce creatures lick their lips at the apex of this pyramid, having nothing to fear but hunger. But Palmyra's predators challenge this time-old wisdom, outweighing their prey, which in turn outweigh the plants at the bottom of the food chain.

How can this be? In the early twentieth century, some of the first scientists to call themselves ecologists, people who study how ecosystems are put together, recognised that the energy entering food webs – the plants – is finite. At each step upward, energy diminishes because it is diverted to growth and reproduction and is burned off to sustain life. A useful rule of thumb, which has weathered repeated scrutiny, is that only about 10 per cent of the energy consumed at one level of the chain is passed up to the next. Palmyra's food web is a paradox that demands explanation.

There is nothing supernatural about this upset of life's natural order, however. Although we often think of them as linked, the most abundant creatures here, at least by weight, are not the most productive. Patience is a virtue shared by cold-blooded crocodiles, pythons and sharks. They can wait a long time between meals, sustaining life on a miserly trickle charge of stored energy until the next prey animal, momentarily inattentive, comes their way. At the bottom of this web, the thin fuzz of seaweeds that characterises a healthy coral reef turns over at a frenetic rate, constantly cropped short by the clopping blades of the herbivore lawnmower. So in this world, appearances are deceptive: the fuel for this food web is conspicuous by its near invisibility.

I have been engulfed within fish storms on other reefs, a disorientating, blinding cumulonimbus of bodies, in which you are unable to tell up from down. Flashing flanks fork their lightning in tight, coiling, patterned vortices before you are cast forth, senses reeling, as the storm moves on. Palmyra's fish storms must be bigger and more impressive, I thought, tempests to the gales of other reefs. From the moment I hear of this incredible predator abundance, I want to dive there.

I finished writing my first book, *The Unnatural History of the Sea*, in 2006, the same year that I learned about Palmyra. In it I followed the fate of ocean life across a thousand years of human fishing and hunting. When people and ocean life met, I discovered, the same outcome replayed again and again. People are the ultimate hunters, even those using the primitive means available centuries ago. Throughout the age of discovery, every time wildlife and people came together for the first time, whether whales, seals or big fish, numbers fell rapidly under a gruesome and profitable clash of blades, nets and hooks. While the prey differed from place to place, and the declines sometimes came swiftly, other times slow, the result was the same. Today's oceans have far fewer big fish, birds, reptiles and mammals than they did before us. At the end of my five-year writing marathon I was struggling for an opener, something that would guide a reader gently into that dark night. I found it one afternoon in the tale of Palmyra's discovery. Where better than to start the book in a place that opens a window to what the oceans might have been like before us.

Today's writers are lucky to have the internet.[1] Within a few clicks it is possible to pursue a thought to conclusion that a couple of decades ago might have taken weeks and a journey to some library full of ancient books. A few giant strides took me from imagining Palmyra, to the name of its discoverer, Edmund Fanning, to the book he wrote describing how a near-death experience led to a new point for map-makers to argue over. His boat bloodied and full with the skins of thousands of fur seals

---

1.   Like many gifts, it is also a curse, an endless source of distraction.

slaughtered on the island of Juan Fernandez off the coast of today's Chile, Fanning was headed for Canton. There, Chinese noblemen would pay lavish sums for furs so fine they ranked among the world's great luxuries.

Fanning nearly didn't make it. One night, mid-crossing, he was roused from sleep by an urgent commotion overhead as his crew fought to drop the sails. From the darkness ahead there came a dread sound from this sleeping sea, the furious roar of breakers venting on a submerged reef. Vigilance and skill saved them, and probably luck too. Sunrise brought Palmyra into being before them, fresh and green as paradise.

Having tapped out Palmyra's tale and sent the manuscript to my publishers, I packed the place away into that corner of the mind we reserve for things we'd love to do in life but know we probably never will. But it didn't go away for long.

I next heard of Palmyra in 2009 when, in one of the happier legacies of George W. Bush's presidency, he made it part of the Pacific Remote Islands Marine National Monument. How Palmyra and the other islands in this far-flung protected area came to be American is a surprising tale of cotton growing, gunpowder and bird shit. By the early nineteenth century, cotton, one of the great sources of wealth for the southern US, was faltering. Cotton is a hungry crop that quickly drains soil fertility. To begin with, growers broke new ground to keep up yields, but with much of the available land occupied they desperately needed new ways to boost fertility. Their saviour came in the unlikely form of seabird poop, or guano. Vast deposits had recently been discovered on bird islands off the coast of Peru. The value of guano to crop growth was discovered by the Incas hundreds of years before the Spanish conquest. When those properties were rediscovered, a guano gold rush began. Guano also happens to be rich in the nitrogenous precursors of gunpowder, making it a powerful geopolitical commodity.

Things went well enough for several decades until Peru took control of the trade and hiked the price. By the mid-nineteenth century, guano was prohibitively expensive. In 1856, the US Congress passed the Guano Islands Act, making it a citizen's lawful duty to claim any island and its guano for the United States, provided it was not under another nation's control. By the time that means had been found to manufacture chemical fertilisers and the ingredients of explosives, fifty-six islands had been claimed, most of them in the Pacific.

The US has since rescinded many of these islands to nations having greater geographic claims, but it has kept ten Pacific territories, most extremely remote. Their unlikely destiny has been to become a beacon of wildlife conservation for the world. One of the quirks of international law is that nations can claim as their own the seas within two hundred nautical miles of any habitable land. So a tiny speck like Palmyra becomes the anchor for sovereignty over a vast area of ocean: 411,600 square kilometres, to be precise, when combined with nearby Kingman Reef, another Guano Act claim.

Few of these islands provided much in the way of guano. Many lie amid seas that are the oceanic equivalent of desert, far less productive than Peru. Off South America's coast, powerful upwelling of nutrient-rich waters creates a cauldron of life that sustains millions upon millions of birds. Their guano deposits are tens of metres thick compared to the metres of these Pacific islands. Some places, like Palmyra, would go on to prove their worth in World War II when they became refuelling depots, airports and harbours. But after the war most of the islands were abandoned to the birds or left to coconut growers to eke out a living.

These islands' fortunes changed again in the late twentieth century. In our rapidly industrialising and increasingly crowded planet, places that are still remote and wild have taken on a new value. Encouraged by prominent conservationists,[1] President Clinton used his executive power to create a 'coral reef ecosystem reserve' in the Northwest Hawaiian Islands. Clinton's powers had ebbed by the end of his time in office, embroiled as he was in personal scandal and subject to an impeachment attempt. But one thing he could still do, without recourse to Senate or Congress, was to protect places by presidential decree.

Since then, it seems to have become a habit for American presidents to protect the sea, regardless of political persuasion.[2] Perhaps time at the top leaves much to atone for. A swelling band of conservationists and, notably, his wife Laura, persuaded George W. Bush to dream big in the Pacific. He built Clinton's northwest Hawaiian Islands protected area seawards to make it one of the biggest in the world, calling it Papahānaumokuākea in honour of the deities of Hawaiian lore that gave birth to the islands. On his last day in office, Bush signed into law the Pacific Remote Islands Marine National Monument, which includes Palmyra and five other far-flung guano acquisitions: Kingman Reef, Jarvis, Howland, Baker and Wake islands. He also protected American Samoa's Rose Atoll and the Marianas Trench.

By happy coincidence, an old friend of mine, Susan White, was put in charge of the new protected area. I first met Susan in 1991 when she was manager of the tiny Saba Marine Park in the eastern Caribbean where I formed my ideas about using marine protection to benefit fish and fisheries.

I send Susan a letter of congratulation, mentioning at the end that I'd love to visit one day. She is enthusiastic. But I should have known that Palmyra could not easily be reached, that the sublime is never attained without hardship or pitfall. Palmyra's treasures lay intact and undiscovered for so long because the island lies at the heart of the greatest water wilderness on the planet. At first, it

---

1. Notable among whom are Elliott Norse, Sylvia Earle and Jean-Michel Cousteau.

2. Trump has done the opposite, seeking to shrink ocean protection in a move that is as depressing as it is inevitable.

wasn't the isolation that thwarted me, but something much more mundane. For several months in 2015, I had been 'on tour' for the Royal Geographical Society, giving a talk on how our oceans are changing today. At the end of my fourth outing, at the Brecon Theatre in Wales, I fell off stage into the orchestra pit at the end of the lecture and broke a leg. I'm not sure what was worse, the pain or the embarrassment! It scuppered plans to visit Palmyra that year. But neither Susan nor I give up on the idea.

The following summer, in 2016, I receive an invitation to take part in a working group that will consider the value of the Pacific Remote Islands protected area for the world beyond the USA. The meeting will be on Palmyra. Susan is keen to broaden the range of people who know about her park and care about what happens to it. Apart from visiting scientists and a tiny staff at the Nature Conservancy station on Palmyra, nobody lives there. So local people, usually the most passionate advocates for a protected area, simply don't exist. This place is really held in trust for the world, and Susan wants the world to know that.

It's late August and my visit is two weeks away; I'm excited. But fate intervenes again. To get to the island you must travel via Hawaii. Several scientists have recently been stopped by immigration on return from Palmyra and told that they couldn't re-enter Hawaii because they didn't have US visas. Palmyra, apparently, could be a backdoor into the US for terrorists. I need a visa.

The waiting time for a visa at the US embassy is four weeks. I'm done for. Then I have a brilliant idea. German efficiency! Sure enough, the Munich embassy has a mere two-day wait but they only return passports to German addresses. I arrange a forwarding service, book an interview and a hotel. Only when I search for a flight does it strike this genius that he won't be able to leave Germany without his passport. I beg the London embassy for a chance, more in hope than expectation, and am interviewed the following week. But it is touch and go. My visa arrives the day before I travel.

After all the tension, the warm Pacific breeze feels like a kiss as I step out of the plane in Honolulu. Next morning, I am up at first light. My balcony looks out to sea from the tenth floor of one of the high-rise hotels that crowd Waikiki Beach. Gentle waves roll shoreward in graceful curves. Within half an hour, there are hundreds of surfers in the water and a huge Hawaiian paddle canoe has charged through the breakers and now bobs a kilometre offshore, waiting for the perfect wave.

It's over ten years since I last saw Susan. We meet for brunch at a nearby waterfront restaurant. She is slim, tanned and brims with the energy of someone half her age. It is this exuberance and her passion for wild places that propelled her up the ranks of the US Fish and Wildlife Service, from marine resource specialist for Florida's refuges two decades ago, to 'monuments supervisor' of Pacific marine refuges today. She now oversees wildlife protection across three million square kilometres of the Pacific. It's a remarkable career trajectory from Saba's diminutive park to the third-biggest protected expanse on the planet.[1]

We rendezvous early next day at a private corner of Honolulu Airport. Gleaming on the tarmac is a private jet. Susan tells me that their previous charter company, which used prop-planes, had become too dangerous. In one case, they patched a hole in the fuselage with a beer can, in another landed at the exceedingly remote Midway Atoll with five minutes of fuel left having misjudged headwinds. The jet also has the advantage, she says, of cutting a five-hour flight in half. Inside, there are leather seats and walnut trim. I didn't expect to reach Palmyra in the style afforded to film stars and tycoons.

Susan and Matt Brown, the superintendent of Papahānaumokuākea, are just back from Midway Atoll where

---

1.   The biggest marine protected areas in the world are Antarctica's Ross Sea, at 1.55 million square kilometres, Papahanaumokuakea, at 1.51 million, and the Pacific Remote Islands Marine National Monument, at 1.27 million. The biggest marine protected areas eclipse, by far, the biggest parks on land; the Ahaggar National Park in Algeria is the largest of them at 450,000 square kilometres.

they hosted a visit by President Obama to celebrate his recent expansion of Hawaii's marine protection. One might be forgiven for wondering whether there was anything left for Obama. As a Hawaiian president, however, he has a special interest in the Pacific. Over his term he increased the area of the Pacific Remote Islands Marine National Monument by six times and, in the last couple of weeks, has quadrupled the area of Papahānaumokuākea.

Later, on the way to Palmyra, Susan tells me that when she thanked Obama for protecting these waters for future generations, he replied 'It's one of my cool powers.' She laughs. 'When I took the president to see the reefs, he swam very fast. We'd get in the water, swim around a reef, get out, go to the next reef, repeat. I tried to get him to slow down. Mr President, I said, you'll see more if you swim slower. But he couldn't help himself. Out of the water, he spent a lot of time just looking at the sea and thinking.'

After two and a quarter hours of uninterrupted ocean, the jet tilts into descent towards a scale of green and turquoise on the dark sea. It looks like a shark egg, two lines of reef enclosing a living heart of lagoon and islands. But most striking is what a slender foothold it has on the deep ocean. 'The islands cover only one square mile,' Susan says, reading my thoughts. One square mile out of 62 million in the Pacific. Taken together, submerged reefs and islands cover 23 square kilometres, less than half the size of Manhattan. The 28 islands alone would cover just three quarters the size of Central Park.

The landing strip is short and rough. I've had to follow a rigorous 'biosecurity protocol' to prevent the introduction of non-native plants or animals. The instructions were stern and uncompromising. 'Launder all clothing, ensure there are no seeds or plant debris, place in a Ziploc bag and freeze for forty-eight hours. Do not open until you reach Palmyra.' I had to freeze the clothes I am in too.

I'm barely off the plane when the first fish I see is a shark, a weaving dorsal fin trailing ripples about the dock. Susan sees it too and says 'There aren't as many sharks here as there were when I first visited in 2001. They were all around the boats then; it made me nervous to get in the water.'

'Why have they declined? I ask.

'We're not sure. Maybe the long-liners are getting too close.'

The Pacific bristles with long-line fishing boats. They can fish as close as fifty nautical miles from Palmyra, although it's quite likely some come nearer. This place is a long way from any coastguard. The boats set lines tens of kilometres long with thousands of hooks. Nominally, they're after tuna and billfish, but they are notoriously indiscriminate.

After a brief lunch, we're on the water at the west end of the atoll. I jump into a swift current that whisks away the bubble cloud to reveal a coralscape of hills and valleys in the crystalline transparency of water newly replenished from the open ocean. The narrow prospect between hilltops and water surface looks like pure aquamarine sky. The bottom consists of overlapping coral plates, thickets of strangely contorted branches that bend and twist in all directions, smooth folded brains, and plush lobes of chestnut and fawn flesh. They might be the seven hills of ancient Rome, their slopes built over with temples, mansions, winding streets, crowded neighbourhoods and elegant piazzas. The hills crest just below the surface, channelling fast currents through valleys. I kick hard to make headway, following channels that are sometimes steep and narrow, sometimes broad meanders. Below in the winding valleys there are scattered heaps of *Turbo* shells along with tell-tale signs of octopus's gardens and triggerfish anvils. Their coiling spirals are mottled with pink and grey corallines while pearly fragments catch sun flashes. The door to a *Turbo* shell is a button-sized disk that is flat on one side, where it attaches to the snail's muscular foot, and curved on the other. When threatened, the snail pulls the gate shut like the door of a bank vault, making predators work hard for a meal. Triggerfish have favourite rocks where they smash, lever and bite open the shell, whereas octopuses bring snails back to the den where they fiddle for ages, as if puzzling over a Rubik's cube, before finding a way in.

The streets of this city are busy. Loose groups of slender goatfish feel their way with probing barbels among shell pieces and rubble. Golden butterflyfish pick and point with tweezer jaws, slurping polyps from their calices. A round-bellied parrotfish with flanks of turquoise and jade pauses to rasp a tuft of weed. Then the familiar chevron of a reef shark skims towards me, audacious and inquisitive, and veers away, its beating tail counting out the seconds until it is lost in the shimmer of distance.

Rounding the corner of a hill, I surprise a hawksbill turtle probing for sponge. Its rounded beak and bronzed scales give its face the look of a helmeted warrior from ancient Greece. It looks at me blankly, as if in disbelief, before half clambering, half taking flight with dragon-scaled flippers, to bend its body into the current and soar away.

Back on the island, we spend the rest of the afternoon in the yacht club. Yacht club is too grand a name for this place, a ramshackle shed to one side of the research centre. Inside, the walls and roof are daubed with hundreds of drawn and painted tags from past visitors: Daydream, Vagabundo, Mystique, Eclipse… all those cheesy yacht names are here. We're an eclectic group, with Susan, Matt and their co-managers from the National Marine Fisheries Service and National Oceanic and Atmospheric Administration, Samantha and Heidi. My fellow guests include Hoku, a native Hawaiian who helped with community liaison for the Papahānaumokuākea protected area, Sean, a youthful expert on engaging kids in marine conservation via social media, and Leanne, a social scientist and former manager of the Great Barrier Reef Marine Park. Leanne now works for the World Conservation Union from a base in Fiji. Deanna, a professional facilitator from Hawaii, is in the chair. If there are any rules to protected area management, one would surely be that community engagement is central to success. But the community for this place is as remote from the islands as the islands are to civilisation. We'll spend the next few days figuring out how to find and build global support.

Next morning, I creep out of bed and dress in pitch darkness, hoping not to wake my cabin-mate who is here to study ants. There is an eleven-hour difference between the UK and Palmyra. With only a few days, I need to make jet-lag work for me. There is barely a breath of wind and the damp air smells of leaf mould. I find a spot by the edge of the lagoon and switch off my head torch. The sky is ablaze with stars, except where blanks indicate the presence of clouds. A distant roar of breakers contrasts with the liquid gurgle at the lagoon edge. To sit here is to inhale the primordial tang of sea and vegetation, at one with the world.

The sun is nearing the horizon, close enough to begin the changeover. A wader shrills low across the water and alights further along the beach, ready for a new day. The mosquitoes too seem energised, homing in on my ears with guided missile accuracy. Palms bend their dark curves over the lagoon, fronds fingertip-touching the still water.

A dry crackling gives away a crab the size of a dinner plate picking its way through dead leaves, shuffling sideways like a latecomer to a play. Its carapace is nut-brown and smooth and it has one hefty pugilistic claw. Yet it tiptoes in perfect silence once it reaches the sand, stopping at the entrance to a burrow to watch me with stalked, alien eyes. The sun has crested the horizon now, burnishing a green line of far-off trees with reddish gold.

When Fanning discovered Palmyra, the ground was covered in a metre-thick layer of fallen coconuts, with 'no signs nor vestige of habitation'. The birds were, he said, 'fearless and gentle' and 'easily taken by the hand'. The islands were deserted. He does mention though, that a Captain Donald MacKay spent several weeks there a few years later to gather beche-de-mer (sea cucumbers) and turtle shell to sell in China. MacKay came across some 'heaps of stones, which, to all appearance, from their order and regularity, were thus placed by the hands of men, although from the coat and crust of weather moss with which they were covered, it must have been at some very remote date'. His curiosity roused, MacKay dug underneath one to find 'a stone case, filled with ashes, fragments of human bones, stone, shell and bone tools, various ornaments, spear and arrow heads of bone and stone'.

It seems scarcely credible that such a remote spot should have been discovered and inhabited centuries before discovery by an American trader. The nearest land, another diminutive speck in the Line Islands, is over two hundred kilometres away, and the nearest significant land is Hawaii, 1,700 kilometres north. Polynesian voyagers spread across the Pacific beginning approximately 1050 CE, and reached Hawaii two hundred years later. These were no lucky, one-way trips, but the outcome of navigation and seamanship skills finely honed over millennia among the islands of the western Pacific from whence they came. The voyages are well known in the Pacific today, but more widely are one of the little sung wonders of the ancient world, as remarkable as any Homeric Odyssey or Babylonian temple building.

But Palmyra was never of much significance to Polynesian navigators. It was not on their main routes and may have been found only to be lost again. There was certainly little to suggest long habitation. It could have been as fleeting as a single generation, although we will never know now because military remodelling of the islands in World War II was so comprehensive. We can only speculate as to their fate.

Soon after breakfast, we're on the water, heading to the outer reef. Susan has brought Amanda Pollock to Palmyra. She was refuge manager here for five years and now oversees diving for all the Pacific refuges. Amanda is a garrulous and engaging guide, but she is serious in the pre-dive briefing. 'Things can go wrong very quickly. With no more than a few minutes' inattention, perhaps sorting out a piece of equipment, you could drift out of sight. Chances are, we wouldn't find you, it's a very big ocean. There's no search and rescue for 1,100 miles.'

Plunging in, I am confronted by the most stunning coral prospect since Australia's One Tree Island over thirty years ago. The reef veers off at forty-five degrees and is covered in pillowing mounds, shrubby bushes and tiered plates that step downward into the abyss. Vegetable colours prevail – mustard, moss and autumn bracken – but pinks, purples and Prussian blue add richness, like coloured threads in tweed. Some thickets are strewn with hundreds of disks the size of saucers, in clashing cream, plum and lime. Each is a solitary, free-living polyp, whose ridged septa radiate like closely spaced spokes from a central mouth. Giant clams pucker their painted lips from among the coral, while sea fans flex and shiver in the current. In a chromatic metamorphosis, the hues shift as the slope deepens, turning from warm to cool on the colour wheel.

Amanda tells us that some corals here bleached last year around the time that Jarvis Island was devastated. Jarvis is 730 km south, a near neighbour in this ocean wilderness. But Palmyra's bleaching was minor, a coral here, another there. There is little evidence of it now. With two thirds of the bottom covered by the living carpet the vigour is amazing. One researcher has measured fifteen centimetres of growth in a year by corals that struggle to make five in other places, putting it down to the exceptional water clarity. Palmyra's escape from bleaching was probably no more than good luck, narrowly missing the pool of overheated water that spread across the Pacific in 2015.

A jellyfish wafts past on my descent, trailing a tentacle that catches my wetsuit and recoils in shock. Tiny fish quiver on the underside of its disk like diamonds set in a ring. Purposeful shoals of jacks pass me like commuter trains. Slinking sharks glide by too, all small black-tips. Before the dive, Amanda had had apologised for not taking us to a spot renowned for big predators, but the swells are too big today. There are plenty here for this unseasoned observer, however. The small things fascinate too. In a scalloped recess among the corals, I find a group of bullet-shaped fish in semi-darkness. Each has five horizontal dark stripes along a translucent body, one of which continues through the eye, concealing it. At the base of each tail is another eye, bright lemon with a black pupil, making the fish look back to front. Some fish in schools align with one another, but these cardinalfish go to great lengths not to face the same way as their neighbours. When one changes direction, the others follow, in a jerky series of rearrangements. I wonder why?

Nearby, a lizardfish surveys his patch from the blue top of a *Porites* mound, just as a lizard would look out from its rock. The resemblance is almost perfect: reptilian face, scaly elongate body and diamond-checked flanks. Next to its vantage point, there is a yellowish patch of shrubby *Acropora* coral several metres wide. At the end of each branch, clusters of pale, duck-egg blue tips gleam in the wavering light.

As we begin the ascent, a school of black surgeonfish pass by, their flattened, oval bodies indistinct against the blue of open sea, save for brilliant white tails waving like lit-up mobile phones at a night-time rock concert. Several sharks join us as we do a safety stop in mid-water, cutting in and sheering away, like excited dogs. Further out, I'm thrilled to see the enormous black rhombus and the white insignia of an oceanic manta ray.

On the way back, we drop in for a snorkel at a murky hole in the reef. It is no more than a few metres deep, and the bottom mostly bare except for patches of velvety disks. Each is about the diameter of an orange, and they carpet the bottom with a soft cloak of pinkish green tentacles, tipped with sunshine yellow. I run the back of my hand gently across a patch of these corallimorphs, feeling the caress of soft flesh. This is what a coral might feel like without a skeleton, and indeed, corallimorphs are sandwiched between sea anemones and corals on the evolutionary tree. Like hard corals, they harbour photosynthetic zooxanthellae in their tissues, but also eat animal plankton. These animals are not welcome here though, having been introduced when a rickety tuna longline boat grounded on the reef in the 1990s. The creature had stowed away, attached to the steel hull, and soon spread to cover two square kilometres around the shipwreck, perhaps benefiting from the fertilising effect of rust on their zooxanthellae.

Susan brought us to this rather unpromising hole to showcase something few other parks have ever attempted: to remove a shipwreck to protect nature; three in fact. Where others sink ships and call them 'marine parks',[1] here they recognise how damaging wrecks can be to ecology and to wilderness. A couple of years ago, a sixteen-strong team removed steel and scrap equivalent to thirty-one city buses. Surfacing from duck-dives, Susan and Amanda are pleased with the result. 'There's far fewer corallimorphs than last time I was here,' Susan says.

'And lots of coralline algae,' says Amanda, replacing her snorkel and disappearing for another minute. She comes up several metres away with a noisy blow. 'There are young corals down there too. Cool!' Red-footed boobies soar and wheel above the islands as we make our way back. Having fed their chicks, they are cooling off, Amanda says. Some are still arriving from the open sea, gliding in no more than a couple of body widths above the water.

After another discussion about faraway islands in the Yacht Club, I walk to North Beach for a change of scene. Leaves crackle underfoot on the winding track through coconut palms to a curve of white sand. With just forty people on the island I have the place to myself. Coconuts dot the edge of the sea, their husks waterlogged and dark. Further up the beach the husks are silvered and grey where they lie jumbled on the strandline, many sprouting shoots like spring ferns. Offshore the sky is

---

1. Park managers should be wary of those bringing gifts of bulky waste!

furious, boiling with an approaching squall against which the lagoon appears luminous green, as though lit from below. I am so remote, so adrift from any of the familiar world, that it is hard to comprehend the separation. Yet that world imposes itself even here. Among the driftwood, coral and heaped shells, there are dozens of plastic and glass bottles, crumbling flip-flops, engine oil canisters, screw caps, a sun-bleached pram wheel, packing straps, tens of cigarette lighters, hundreds of shoes, toothbrushes, hairbrushes, polystyrene, painted wood and thousands of plastic fragments, shivered to pieces by the long action of sun, water and waves. This cargo does not recognise isolation, voyaging for years or decades to get here.

The next day, I'm up before dawn again. My head torch picks out pinprick reflections in the leaf litter. A close look reveals that they are not minute water droplets but the eyes of wolf spiders, out for the night-time hunt. Their bodies are thick-legged, hairy, flattened and patterned. Crouched among the crisp, browning leaves, they melt into invisibility.

The sky is paling in the east and the first shouts and whistles of birds break the nocturnal insect chorus. Shadowy silhouettes pass overhead, calling to other shadows. On the other side of the lagoon there are two oblong islands, vestiges of aircraft runways built in World War II. From here they are just lines of trees, the natural and unnatural scarcely distinguishable. Ironically, some of the newest islands, built from dredge spoil in the 1940s, have the most natural vegetation. Tall *Pisonia* trees dominate, their broad, open crowns dotted with seabirds like Christmas decorations. Leggy screw palms elbow from beneath, with only the occasional coconut palm visible. On the main islands, the skyline is a near-continuous undulating wave of coconut crowns, a legacy of copra production, and of rats.

For decades, rats did much to shape the look of this place, but only recently have we been able to appreciate just how far reaching their influence was. Like most islands, Palmyra was long-ago colonised by black rats although nobody is sure when. Rats ate the fruit of native trees, cementing dominance by tougher coconuts. Tree-nesting seabirds prefer native trees to coconut palms so they declined with the loss of favoured trees, while ground-nesting birds like shearwaters were decimated by rat predation. So were land and shore crabs. Even coconut crabs suffered. While gnarled old behemoths half a metre or more in width dragged their armoured rear ends through the leaf litter, younger generations were missing.

Yesterday on the boat, Susan told me with evident pride about their recent success in ending the rat supremacy. 'We tried in 2001 using a grid of ground-based bait stations across every island but the rats were soon back. So we got a PhD student to figure out what went wrong. They discovered that lots of the rats lived in the treetops so ground bait didn't get them. We tried again in 2011, this time using slingshots to fire bait into every third tree, as well as the ground stations. It took a month and was a huge effort, but it worked. There hasn't been a rat seen in Palmyra since.'

How wonderful that a PhD student could find the weakness of a creature we think we know so well. Within a matter of weeks there were changes. Mud crab numbers began to rise, soon reaching hundreds per square metre of beach. Two species of crab not seen before appeared and young coconut crabs are now commonly encountered at night, tearing the hearts from screw palm fruit. Their backs are the colour of tortoiseshell, their undersides striped and spotted with violet. Long antennae probe the darkness like leather horse whips, ending to either side of stalked eyes that glow like hot coals.

The lagoon is the only disappointment. Shallow lagoon waters usually teem with fish and corals, but the bottom is muddy with patches of scalloped grey limestone where there should be coral. Thousands of grazing *Strombus* snails scribble trails through the mud. Empty giant clamshells, none bigger than a hand, are strewn across the bottom. Here vagabond butterflyfish live up to their name, hanging out by holes and shell heaps like rough sleepers under city bridges. I see a handful of burrowing gobies and a few juveniles of other species, but even hardy damselfish shun the low-rent dilapidation.

You don't have to look far for a reason. The military comprehensively disrupted Palmyra during the war, dredging channels, building islands and blocking water flows with roads. Coral gardens were rendered to rubble, buried or trapped in stagnating ponds. Seen from water level, it all looks surprisingly natural today, but from the air, the islands are boxy and placed askew from where nature would have put them. The corals in this lagoon were starting to come back before being hit by the El Niño warming, which killed most of them off.

Palmyra differs from the popular conception of a desert island. Left unchecked by human interference, plants cover the islands to the edge of the tidal zone, so there is little beach. Fanning and his crew had to battle their way through a dense scramble of tree trunks and foliage to get ashore, an experience we repeat today on the uninhabited 'refuge' islands, but with a modern twist. To visit them you must don brand new clothes and shoes, all previously frozen, so as not to accidentally introduce plant seeds, ants or other stowaways. Susan issues us with Fish and Wildlife Service staff shirts. Having seen the care they are lavishing on this place, and felt their passion and commitment to its protection in our discussions, I feel honoured to wear the badge.

I have one more appointment with pre-dawn tranquillity before we leave; the stars are brilliant and the limestone path glows between dark thickets. A heavy splash in the lagoon beyond suggests that a hunting shark has struck. Sometimes a place inhabits the imagination so completely that the idea of it seems more tangible than reality. But not here. After the years of anticipation, this lone green mote in the blue wilderness has lived up to its promise.

Dawn silvers the edges of clouds, then touches water with fire. The wind is up this morning and heavy breakers draw a brilliant line between sea and sky. Not far offshore, a turtle pops its head up and exhales heavily. There is something timeless about a coral sea, the reflected billow of a cumulus sky, the mottling brown of life beneath. It is a small step for the imagination to turn back geological time, leafing through life's pages until one arrives in the Cambrian, the dawn of shell and coral. What might that dark patch signify then? What strangeness would the surface conceal? There are corals of a sort and strange jawless fish; scuttling, scratching invertebrates press their marks into the mud, perhaps to be trapped for posterity and one day put on display in a museum. That timelessness makes it all the harder to grasp the precarious delicacy of the present reef crisis. The reef here is majestic in its solidity. Its inhabitants celebrate life in all its variety. They thrum with the energy of existence. I can't help but feel energised by this visual feast.

Corals have waxed and waned in the vast span of geological time, and nature keeps reinventing what it means to be a coral reef. Yet it is hard not to see our own time as some sort of zenith. We are fortunate to live in the greatest period of coral reef growth in planetary history. Yet we might bring it all to an end within the space of a few human generations. It is an extraordinary position, and one that I still grapple daily to understand. Our discussions complete, I take this up with Susan just before leaving Palmyra.

'Are you worried?' I ask.

'Of course I worry,' she says, 'who wouldn't? But our mantra is "We're here to give coral reefs their best chance". We're taking away as many stresses as we can and hoping it will be enough.'

'What about Jarvis Island?'

Susan winces. 'We were heartbroken at the news. You know fish numbers went right down too after the coral died. But it's all about resilience. Palmyra isn't far from Jarvis, but the reefs here were largely unscathed. So taken together, I think we're doing OK.' She sounds optimistic, but her expression is more doubtful. The near complete wipe-out of a chunk of your protected area will never be cause for celebration, no matter how well the rest is doing. 'Jarvis will bounce back and quickly, we hope,' she adds.

I hope so too.

CHAPTER SEVENTEEN

Fin

Maldives, Jamaica, Alderney, 2016–19

THE REEF LOOKS LIKE ONE OF THOSE CONCRETE REPLICAS in a second-rate public aquarium. The coral shapes are accurate, and the colonies arranged with an artistic sensibility that suggests intimate familiarity with the real thing. Fish swim around the sculpted forms in loose groups, their colours a blazing contrast to the monumental grey. But this is no imitation, nor is it an aquarium. Here and there, a scrap of living coral peeks from a niche in the bedrock and sponges crawl over broken branches. Twelve months ago, richly hued corals dappled the seabed in the wave-refracted light. Ninety-nine per cent of them are dead.

Last year, this reef was the paragon in a many-wondered corner of Faafu Atoll in the Maldives. We always kept it for the final day of our coral reef field course, to save the best for last. But now we are looking at the aftermath of the 2015–16 El Niño.

There was a great poignancy about last year's visit. Two thirds of the bottom was living coral, as good as any place I'd dived in the Maldives. But with a blockbuster El Niño on the way, I knew it was doomed. Maaga is an almost perfect ring reef that rises from the shallow floor of the atoll's lagoon to just below the surface. The upper edge of its outer slope was a stepped terrace of table corals, many several metres across. Their fawn surfaces were forests of tiny branches, each covered by a puckered layer of corallites. Above almost every colony there was a solitary chevron butterflyfish. With black face and tail, and pale flanks scored with herringbone lines, they defended their patches with enthusiasm, jealously guarding the polyps they eat from others of their own species.

Above the reef edge, nebulae of tiny Green *Chromis* damselfish pulsed beneath incoming waves, their bodies shining like spring leaves wetted by a shower. At my approach they withdrew into the coral, agitating among the branches, the energy of the shoal compressed in the confined space.

Branching corals sprouted among the tables, their angular blades interlaced like giant thornbush spines. Among a latticed knot of branches, I found a favourite fish. There were four of them, two male-female pairs, each fish no longer than a line of text on this page. Their bodies were diamond-shaped, narrowing from the middle to a dainty pointed nose and a rounded tail. Vivid orange or yellow spots spangled against an electric-blue ground, each spot circled in green. On their faces the spots were drawn into stripes as if the nose had been pulled to a point from a blob of hot Venetian glass. Millefiori eyes were perfectly round, and were orange like the spots, with dark egg-shaped pupils surrounded by green spokes. The fish in each pair threaded through the colonnaded interior of their coral temple like dancers, mirroring each other's movements – forwards, backwards, pirouette, repeat – with translucent fins fluttering like fans. Every now and then, one of these harlequin filefish stopped, dipped its nose and raised and lowered a spine behind its head, as if curtseying to its partner.

I search for these fish now, peering among the dead branches of patch after patch of coral. None are left. The green clouds of *Chromis* have also disappeared. The table corals are now no more than dull concrete steps, some toppled, and their cantankerous chevron butterflyfish keepers are gone too. All these fish depended on living coral. When the coral died, they died too. There was nowhere to go.

If these conspicuous creatures have been so affected, what about the invisible, the glimpsed or half-suspected animals that hide deep inside the reef? How many of them were lost? The jewel-bright porcelain and guard crabs that conceal themselves within the matrix of living coral branches are certain victims.

Swimming on, there are slumps of rubble where dead coral is already breaking down, grey sponge overgrowing them like cancer. Here and there is a savage splash of colour, a diadem of violet arms thickly spined with maroon points so dark they are almost black. They look like fat tarantulas and their embrace is just as lethal, for they are crown-of-thorns starfish, forcing their stomachs into crevices to suck the life from the last living fragments of coral. They too are doomed, like shipwrecked sailors adrift in a boat, down to their last biscuit.

Not all the reefs around here are like this. Most have some coral left, having fewer crown-of-thorns starfish to gnaw at the carcass. One or two, close to cooling water flowing into the lagoon from the open sea, have almost escaped harm. Where corals have been spared, the dependent fish are too, like chevron butterflyfish and green *Chromis*. But even with hours of search I can't find any Harlequin filefish. There is good news though. Apart from the crown-of-thorns infested reef, all the places we dive are pocked with tiny colonies of living coral. A few clumps have reached cauliflower size in the less than a year since the mass bleaching. The comeback is already underway.

The force of shifting baseline syndrome strikes me again on this trip. This tendency renders each new generation blind to past losses, setting their personal baseline of normality by what they first find. Although the reefs have suffered terribly, our students think they are marvellous. They love it here, they tell me. And it is still attractive in so many ways. Schools of silver baitfish flicker below the surface. Bigger fusiliers surround us, mesmerising with their deep- blue bodies, yellow stripes and electric flashes as they pluck plankton from the water. Each fish moves independently of the others for a while, and then on some unseen signal they swim together as one before going back to solitary plankton picking.

Is Maaga Reef a vision of the future, or will the future be worse? How much paint can flake from a masterpiece before it is ruined? Faced with such frailty, it is hard to be optimistic. Some have already given up hope, like Roger Bradbury, a global authority on coral reefs and professor at the Australian National University.

> It's past time to tell the truth about the state of the world's coral reefs, the nurseries of tropical coastal fish stocks. They have become zombie ecosystems, neither dead nor truly alive in any functional sense, and on a trajectory to collapse within a human generation. There will be remnants here and there, but the global coral reef ecosystem — with its storehouse of biodiversity and fisheries supporting millions of the world's poor — will cease to be.
>
> Overfishing, ocean acidification and pollution are pushing coral reefs into oblivion. Each of those forces alone is fully capable of causing the global collapse of coral reefs; together, they assure it. The scientific evidence for this is compelling and unequivocal, but there seems to be a collective reluctance to accept the logical conclusion — that there is no hope of saving the global coral reef ecosystem.

This nightmarish prophecy, entitled 'A World Without Coral Reefs', was published in the *New York Times*, appropriately enough on Friday 13 July 2012. All hope is lost, Bradbury believes, and we should abandon coral reefs to their fate; further money spent to save them is money wasted. There was an immediate backlash from scientists and conservation bodies, insisting that reefs can be saved. The gist of their counterargument was that Bradbury's prediction might well become self-fulfilling. Not to do everything to save the world's reefs would be a dereliction of responsibility to the hundreds of millions of people dependent on them, as well as to future generations who would never have the chance to experience their magic.

But are coral reefs doomed? Could Bradbury be right and the rest of us delusional? Whatever their public statements, I don't know a single coral expert who is not haunted by doubt. I certainly am. The catalogue of afflictions that reefs face is long enough to give the most ardent optimist night sweats. And the closer we look, the more problems we discover.

In 2014, early in the writing of this book and before the onset of the latest catastrophic El Niño, I found myself wondering what my old friends and colleagues now felt about the future of coral. And so, in September of that year, I penned an invitation to a 'coral reef reunion', sending it to Rupert, my former PhD supervisor; Andrew, captain of our northern Red Sea sailing expedition; Alec, Rupert's chief field scientist in Arabia; Charles, companion in southern Arabia and my boss in Egypt; and Anne, coral scientist and Charles's wife – all of them active and immensely experienced scientists who have circled the planet many times over. I also invited Mauvis, Rupert's marine scientist wife, Andrew's wife Sylvia, and, of course, Julie. The idea was to meet at Fort Clonque, a cliff-top stronghold on the island of Alderney in the English Channel, where, undisturbed by anything but the sea, we could ponder the ultimate question: will coral reefs survive us?

Meeting up in December of that year, we arrived just before the airport was closed by an Atlantic storm that would rage for the duration of our meeting. Fort Clonque, built in the nineteenth century on a rocky outcrop surrounded by sea save for a slender causeway, was a fitting location. Our rendezvous was held in a dungeon-like building with metre-thick walls and a ceiling of arched bricks. For three days, gathered around an open fire, with the wind howling and the sea roaring around us, we debated the fate of the reefs.

We considered the possibility of a desolate future in which coral reefs crumble and dissolve in warming, acidifying oceans. The political leaders of this world bicker on about global warming – whether it exists, who is responsible, what can be done – but have made no meaningful progress to counter it until at least the middle of this century. At that point over nine billion people will crowd a planet very different from ours. By then it will be too late to save the reefs. The richest ocean ecosystem will have sunk into a decay from which it will not recover for tens of thousands of years, even if we find ways in the future to improve ocean health.

A more hopeful strand of thought argues that coral reefs already survive, sometimes even thrive, in extreme environments like the Arabian Gulf. There they endure temperature swings from as low as 12°C to above 36°C. Despite this background stress, they've survived decades of oil pollution and war. Temperature rises expected on reefs in other parts of the world fall well within this range. Can corals adapt fast enough for reefs to survive?

Charles was quick to point out that acidification could hammer the last nail into the reef coffin regardless of how reefs cope with warming. The Australian coral expert Charlie Veron once said to me, 'Warming will kill reefs, but acidification will keep them dead.' But just recently, on the Pacific island of Palau, corals had been found thriving in pockets of water more acidified than levels expected from greenhouse gas emissions by the end of the twenty-first century, opening a chink of hope that they might be able to adapt. Darwin would have recognised what we are going through now as an intense episode of natural selection. Recent mass bleaching events have laid waste to corals. Were those that survived the fittest, or just lucky? If they were fitter, can we hope that corals will adapt as conditions change and there will be a resurgence later?

Reefs could adapt to changing conditions in several ways. The first is not so much adaptation but acclimation. Corals might just get used to higher temperatures or acidification, perhaps by switching on genes that code for proteins that work better in the altered environment. There are plenty of examples, like the stinging water I danced through on southern Saudi Arabian reefs where fish and corals endured hot-tub temperatures. Admittedly, there weren't many of them, but if any corals survive this century, they surely will.

The second mechanism is true Darwinian natural selection. If the corals left behind after mass bleaching aren't just lucky, but survived because they possess innate advantages, they will produce offspring that should fare better the next time the sea heats up. A few years after our reunion, science proved that corals are indeed adapting to recent warming this way. In Hawaii, in 2017, a 1970 experiment on coral heat tolerance was repeated. The two species of coral that were tested resisted bleaching for longer and survived to higher temperatures this time. But the bad news was that adaptation was slower than the rate of warming.

A third kind of adaptation takes advantage of the different heat sensitivities of the photosynthesising algae that live within coral tissues. When it comes to zooxanthellae, some like it hot(ish). Corals that bleach and then recover often survive by trading up to more heat-resistant partners. The corals that swelter in Arabian Gulf summers mostly possess a highly heat-resistant zooxanthella whose name is apt: *Symbiodinium thermophilum*.

The final way reefs might 'adapt' to warming is through a process of winnowing. Those species of coral that cope better with warming will come to dominate the community that grows back after mass mortality, just as a forest in an area prone to fire will consist of fire-resistant trees. Perhaps, instead of decline into oblivion, we will see the gradual rise of tougher, more resilient elements of reef life. Wherever there is a loser, there is also a winner.

This possibility of reef adaptation by the winnowing of the most susceptible species was confirmed by the 2015–16 El Niño. At first it seemed like a direct replay of the one in 1997–98 – it was just as hot, and if anything it dragged on for longer. But in East Africa and the Maldives at least, the impacts were less devastating. In the 1990s, most of the coral was killed; this time, more survived, a pattern that seems true of other places. The Northern Great Barrier Reef was savaged because it had never bleached before. But corals in places that had come back from past mass bleaching appeared to fare better. It's a splinter of hope but the loss of diversity is troubling. People who knew Maldivian reefs before the 1998 bleaching say there isn't the richness of colour and form today that there used to be. Every time catastrophe hits, it seems like fewer survivors stagger out the other end.

If warming were the one stress that corals faced, we might be more sanguine about their future, but the collective action of many pressures will simplify reefs to their most resilient elements. I discovered this truth as a student looking for the secrets of high species diversity. The steaming, muddy reefs of the southern Red Sea were less rich than those of more clement, clear water reefs to the north. Kuwait's reefs in the far northern Arabian Gulf, periodically cooked then frozen (at least in coral terms), were much less diverse than those two hundred kilometres south.

Where will the balance of life and death sit in a hundred years? Will there be anything recognisable as a coral reef? It is already possible to glimpse the most dystopian of reef futures. At our Alderney conference, Mauvis talked about the reefs of her native Jamaica, which have become a classic case of coral collapse. As a child in the 1950s and '60s, she saw labyrinths of elkhorn and staghorn coral seething with fish. But on a recent visit the reef was smothered in algae, dark and brooding. Without coral the reef was crumbling under the onslaught of creatures that drill, bore, scrape and dissolve the dead skeletons.

Might all the world's reefs one day sink to the level of Jamaica's? What if they all turned into the bare rocky reefs of the Mediterranean, with hardly any fish? Would people be miserable? Scientists would, because they know that once there were fish everywhere, big and small. But so many people love the Med in its depleted state, not realising it was once much richer. Every scuba-diving magazine is full of adverts entreating you to visit this or that place where the reefs are said to be pristine and extraordinary. Yet hardly any can live up to the hype. Shifting baseline syndrome again.

Knowledge can be a burden. Where others find only beauty and excitement on reefs, we see the absences, scars, and the creeping evidence of an unequal struggle against the tide of human impact. People sometimes tell me after a lecture that it must be depressing being an environmentalist. All that bad news, day after day; the feeling of impotence as things get worse. How do you cope? Sometimes, on the way to a coffee shop at my university, I'll see through a window some literary scholar giving a lecture and feel envious. Wouldn't it be lovely not to have the burden of foreboding that is never far from my own subject? How, I wonder, would the English professor and her class feel if they knew that all the books and texts they love would crumble to dust in fifty years. What if all that could be saved were snatches of text, like the clay tablets of Assyria or fragments of Egyptian papyrus? But then I remember: conservation gives me purpose in life and that feeling is hard to beat.

All was not darkness at our reunion. We found successes and hope to buoy our spirits. Central and northern Red Sea corals, for example, have stubbornly resisted mass bleaching, despite temperature shocks severe enough to have brought it on in other places. Nobody is sure why, but perhaps it is because these high-latitude corals naturally experience a wide range of temperatures.

Even for devastated reefs, as Julie and I saw in the Maldives, protection can improve the outlook. Fish can still thrive. They can still attract tourists, restock surrounding fishing grounds and feed people. My friends were moved by a story of hope from the Coral Triangle of South East Asia, the global epicentre of reef diversity that has been in desperate straits for a long time. I heard it from Alan White who had spent a long career criss-crossing the region[1], first as a Peace Corps volunteer in the Philippines in the

---

1. The Coral Triangle includes the Philippines, Indonesia, Malaysia, Papua New Guinea, Solomon Islands and Timor-Leste.

1970s. During that career, the human population of countries in the Triangle leapt from under 200 million to over 400 million. Many were desperately poor and utterly dependent on the sea for food and livelihood. As human pressures escalated, reef condition nosedived in a vortex of destructive overfishing. But Alan never gave up. For decades he worked with villagers to create marine protected areas, and his insights have been fed into the Coral Triangle Program, an international, multi-million-dollar effort to give local people the expertise to turn around the condition of their own neighbourhoods. I was heartened to hear him say that better management had led to more fish, healthier corals and more sustainable livelihoods.

On Alderney, Rupert came up with an unexpected bright spot too, reminding me of the road in Jeddah that had been built on top of the reef, where I had that life-changing first coral reef experience. He and Mauvis had revisited it the previous year and found patches of excellent coral recovery. Further north, despite all the mansions seen from the helm of my Google space craft, they encountered huge aggregations of fish; the owners of the mansions don't let people fish there. I had pretty much given up on these reefs, thinking that the damage done by digging out their marinas would have left them a kind of marine breakers' yard.

Our reunion, just like the St James's Palace meeting two years before, didn't come up with any brilliant ideas to save the reefs. The solution to the coral reef crisis is not a complex scientific problem, but a political and social one. The science bit is easy: reduce greenhouse gas emissions, abuse reefs less and protect them more. The challenge is to make that happen. Environmental scientists feel like the Trojan princess Cassandra, with whom Apollo fell in love. She spurned his advances so he gave her the ability to foretell the future but with the curse that no one would believe her. We have difficulty convincing people that the natural world is in trouble when they don't see the effects in their daily lives.

There are reasons for guarded optimism though. The rapid pace of scientific innovation is one of the wonders of our modern world. In the space of a few short decades, we have developed molecular and genetic tools that enable us to play God with nature, engineering species to our own ends. Heat-proof microbes have been produced for industrial fermentation processes; plants have been created that can manufacture the health-promoting long-chain fatty acids found in fish; unnaturally productive cattle have been developed that pour forth milk as if it were water. Technologists are now searching for the means to save coral. A heat-proof coral that can manage in the more acidified water associated with higher levels of carbon dioxide must surely be within reach.

That said, the geological record is discouraging. There are long periods following intense episodes of global warming and accompanying ocean acidification where coral reefs disappear, suggesting there is a hard limit to evolutionary innovation in calcification. When the concentration of dissolved carbonate falls, it is much harder to build skeletons. You can't construct a city without bricks and cement. Technologists may find it easier, though, to engineer more heat-resistant zooxanthellae – the microbes that feed reef-building corals – like those that live in Arabian Gulf corals[1]. Another tack is to develop strains of bacteria that can mop up the damaging free-radical oxygen produced by heat-exposed zooxanthellae, so that corals don't bleach. These approaches have merit in that large tracts of coral reef might be seeded with engineered microbes. And by tinkering with microbes rather than the corals themselves, we spare ourselves the Sisyphean task of heat-proofing upwards of a thousand different coral species.

Large-scale marine parks, like that of Palmyra, also stand to benefit huge tracts of coral reef. Studies in the Caribbean suggest

---

1. Perhaps this wouldn't be such a good idea if new research proves correct. This science suggests that zooxanthellae grow faster when the water warms, turning them from providers of food to parasites. The corals have to dump them fast or die, although many will die anyway. More heat-resistant zooxanthellae might make matters worse.

that most of the coral decline there in the last couple of decades has been from manageable human stresses, like pollution, overfishing and development, rather than climate change. By good fortune, in Holland in 2018, I caught up with the lead author of the recent analysis that drew this conclusion. Jeremy Jackson is the doyen of marine historical ecology and it was he who inspired me to dive into the past to understand the present. We were there to speak at the retirement of an old friend and colleague, Han Lindeboom, who intended to devote himself in future to securing greater protection for Holland's Caribbean coral reefs.

'I've spent the last half-dozen years gathering every coral survey I could find from the Caribbean,' Jeremy tells us over breakfast. 'That's over thirty thousand surveys. But you know what I've found?' he pauses for effect. 'Climate change isn't killing Caribbean reefs, at least not yet.' He flips his laptop around and pulls up a graph. 'Look at this,' he says, stabbing at the graph with a bony finger. 'Coral cover fell from an average of about fifty per cent in the 1960s and 1970s to about twenty per cent in the 1980s. But after that, it stays at twenty per cent through all the global coral bleaching events. The mass bleaching episodes that devastated reefs in the Indian and Pacific Oceans have barely touched the Caribbean.' At seventy-six, Jeremy has had a long career as an iconoclast. Now he's doing it again. The data certainly look robust. It's the best dataset anybody has come up with, or could.

'You want to know what I think?' he asks, not waiting for an answer. 'I think Caribbean reefs are more resilient to climate change because the corals there struggled through millions of years of it. Those left today survived highly variable temperatures through repeated Ice Ages. The Ice Ages had less influence in other parts of the world because temperature fluctuations were smaller. In that respect, the Caribbean is more like the Mediterranean than the tropics.'

Averages don't tell the whole story, however. When you dig into the details, some places are losing coral and a few are gaining. It's the usual brew of pollution, overfishing and coastal development that is killing Caribbean coral today.

'What is worrying,' Jeremy concedes, 'is that fleshy seaweeds are gaining ground in many places.' To arrest their march, we need more grazing fish – parrotfish in other words. 'If you want to save Dutch Caribbean reefs,' he says to Han, 'you've got to stop the fishing on them. Reef fish are way too important to reef health to catch and eat. Yet managers seem beholden to an industry that is worth peanuts compared to tourism. And we need to pull development back from the coast to limit pollution stress.'

It's one of those simple, common sense propositions: easy to say, but hard to do. In these days of rapid change and increasing climate stress it makes perfect sense to leave reef fish in the water. They are worth far more there than on a plate. Better to catch tuna or flying fish away from the coast than put coral at risk. But curtailing land-based pollution and development will be much harder. Developers love the beach front – its siren call is impossible to resist. Changing land use to spare the soil and reduce fertiliser inputs could take a generation or two. The good news, though, is that these causes of reef decline can be ameliorated by local action. They don't require international agreement on greenhouse gas reduction. But as Australia has so clearly demonstrated, knowing what to do and actually doing it are very different things. While acknowledging the dire peril facing the Great Barrier Reef, the government there has passed a law allowing further deforestation of its watershed, promoted coal mining and repealed laws meant to address climate change. Societal responses to the greatest period of planetary upheaval since civilisation began are messy, foot-dragging and indecisive.

Efforts to change are constantly undermined by vested interests intent on self-preservation. Like most battles where new and better technology supplants old, fossil fuel companies will lose out to cheaper, cleaner renewables in the end. Analysts say that, even without government incentives to promote uptake, the tipping point will come by the 2030s. Positive change is imminent regardless of government inaction. There is reason for hope.

Local protection is still the best option we have for reefs. Highly protected parks harness the healing power of nature, increasing resilience to other stresses. And if it turns out, despite every effort, that such parks fail to safeguard coral[1], at least by establishing them now we will know that we tried. I've seen enough marine parks in places where corals are stressed to know that nature is always more prolific and diverse where it is protected than where it is heavily exploited. Wherever well-defended marine parks exist, local communities are better off too. There is no downside to protecting reefs for the long term.

The limitations of the alternative way of giving reefs a helping hand – restoration using wire frames or other structures to support transplanted corals – were painfully exposed in the Maldives. Many resorts there had built artificial reefs, at considerable expense, to compensate for damage done during hotel construction. Apart from the problem that restoration efforts are typically on a much smaller scale than the damage, the fast-growing corals they used were highly susceptible to heat stress. When the El Niño struck in 2016 they succumbed like the rest.

Another option, increasingly favoured by misguided politicians, some industries and a worryingly large body of public opinion, is to do nothing. With evidence for climate change now so compelling that the battle to deny global warming is largely lost, the new tack is to accept it as real but ignore its consequences[2]. I'm unsettled by the way that some see coral reefs as a kind of luxury, desirable but inessential. At the St James's Palace meeting in London, one scientist

---

1. A recent study questions the ability of parrotfish to promote reef recovery after damage, for example.

2. Five stages characterise climate change denial: 1. Deny it is happening; 2. Deny it is humans that cause it; 3. Deny it is a problem; 4. Deny that we can do anything about it; and 5. It's too late to fix so we shouldn't bother trying. https://www.theguardian.com/environment/climate-consensus-97-per-cent/2013/sep/16/climate-change-contrarians-5-stages-denial

told of how he was once asked at the end of a talk whether reefs were an extravagance we could no longer afford. The questioner went on to compare the world to a copy of *National Geographic*: you could rip out an article on coral reefs and the magazine would still be wonderful.

I asked my friends at Alderney: what do people want and need from coral reefs? Is keeping them in good shape just a conservationist's dream or is it a prerequisite for the survival of reef-dependent people across the world? Thirty million people depend on coral reefs completely for their livelihoods – catching fish, collecting curios or taking tourists to see them – and two hundred million are partially dependent on them. The services that reefs provide are worth billions of dollars worldwide. As Andrew reminded us, their worth at this point had gone up tenfold since they were first valued in 1997 because their coastal protection role was better understood now, but also because reefs had declined, raising their scarcity value.

Many people are uncomfortable with valuing nature for the goods and services it provides – fish, or clean water, or beautiful places to visit. I'm on the fence here. Valuing 'natural capital', as economists call it, helps flag the extraordinary importance of nature to human well-being. On the other hand, there is a risk that in assigning monetary values to the natural world, markets will assume that the loss of habitats is just a cost of doing business.

What would we lose if coral reefs were to disappear? Not much, some might argue, especially as we seem adept at forgetting what we once had and making do with degraded remnants. To those who depend on reefs for their livelihoods, or their homes, their value is immense. But what would we really lose? There is another dimension in which the value of reefs is incalculable. What price can be put on wonder? How much is a species worth? What would we lose were we to destroy thousands of species, perhaps hundreds of thousands? The culmination of tens of millions of years of evolution is priceless and irreplaceable. This is a moral dimension we should not ignore. What right do we have to rob future generations of their chance to revel as we do in the sheer joy of what is, arguably, the greatest show on Earth? Do we have a right to destroy any of the creatures with which we share our planet? Such things are, for me at least, unconscionable.

As the sixth mass extinction gathers pace under humanity's tightening grip upon the living world, some commentators point out that nature has bounced back from repeated planetary catastrophes before and will do so again. In addition to five previous mass extinctions, there have been many lesser events in geological history in which nature has taken a severe hit. Why worry about saving species now? So what if the panda, vaquita, snow leopard or African elephant disappear? New species will evolve to replace them.

Setting aside what this desolate view of nature says about such contrarians, there is a problem of timescales. A subsistence farmer whose crops have withered from long drought will draw scant comfort from the knowledge that rain will return one day. *Homo sapiens* has existed for two to three hundred thousand years; the return time for nature after mass extinction is upwards of ten million. That's a long time to wait, assuming we could survive our self-inflicted mass extinction.

Can we curtail our destructive tendencies in time to save the biosphere and ourselves? There is one sense in which coral reefs might be our saviour. Undoubtedly, they are among the most sensitive of all habitats to climate change, wilting under the warming produced by a mere whiff of carbon dioxide. Without aggressive action to reduce emissions, carbon dioxide concentrations will soon reach levels that threaten many other species and habitats, impinging on our own well-being and eventually risking our own survival. But if we heed coral's sentinel warning now to steer a low emissions course, we might spare many more species, protecting wildlife and ourselves in one.

Will coral reefs survive us? I've come to the end of my quest and have discovered half of the answer. If we fail to ditch fossil fuels and to embrace renewables with great urgency, the answer is an unequivocal 'No'. What is much harder to know is whether we have left it too late. Are we already past the point of no return? Time will give us that answer. I've been deeply lucky in life. I'm fortunate to have known and loved coral reefs at their heart-stopping best, and to have played a part in their protection. I'm still an optimist, despite all the bad news. Now is the time for action, not mourning. There is everything to play for.

Acknowledgements

I BEGAN THIS BOOK AT CHRISTMAS 2013 and thought it would be quick to write; a year, two at the most. After all, the events were already in my head and only needed transfer to paper. But events, inconveniently, overtook the project, most significantly a global episode of mass coral mortality in 2015–16. This meant continual rewrites and added chapters in the struggle to properly capture the unfolding story of coral reefs.

I owe this book to the countless people who have propelled me on my career in marine science. Some are characters in this book, but others, no less important, have helped through many kindnesses, advice and insights freely given. My companions in Arabia, set me on the path of studying coral reefs. Rupert Ormond introduced me to coral reefs and became a lifelong friend and mentor. Alec Dawson Shepherd, Andrew Price, and Charles and Anne Sheppard were wonderful people with whom to tramp the shores and dive the reefs of the Middle East, and then beyond, follow the weaving paths of science. I thank them all, together with Mauvis Gore and Sylvia Bernard, for indulging my invitation to a reunion to ponder the fate of coral reefs, for their keen observations and thoughts, for their patience waiting for the book to finally emerge, and for their good humour in letting me include them in these pages.

Peter Sale kindly let me work at One Tree Island Research Station on the Great Barrier Reef, first as a student then as a young scientist. Thanks also to Richard Hartnoll, Andy Brand and Duncan Shaw for taking me on to work in Egypt, and to Sarah Bury and Mike Best who worked with me there. My colleagues and students in Egypt taught me a great deal about the joys and frustrations of life that have buoyed me along ever since. Nick Polunin gave me my first taste of the Caribbean and the career-changing subject of marine protected areas to research. In the Caribbean, Susan White, Percy ten Holt, Kenny Buchan and Tom van't Hof welcomed Julie and me many times to Saba, as did Kalli de Meyer to Bonaire, and Kai Wulf and Sarah George to St Lucia, while Billy Causey, John Ogden and Jim Bohnsack were gracious guides and mentors in the Florida Keys. Laverne Ragster was an inspirational boss in St Thomas, giving me the freedom to explore my interests while helping me direct them in ways that had the most benefit to people and nature. Fiona Gell collected the data on fish landings in St Lucia that showed marine parks supported rather than subtracted from fisheries, and many of my students contributed over the years to our understanding of these beautiful reefs, especially Maggy Nugues, Chris Schelten and Nola Barker. Ronnie Nicholas was unerring boat captain to all our St Lucian expeditions. Rachel Graham introduced us to the spawning aggregations and whale sharks of Gladden Spit in Belize. In the Maldives, I am very grateful to the University of Milano-Bicocca and their excellent field team for hosting our annual fieldtrips to Magoodhoo, and to BLUE Marine Foundation, Six Senses Laamu and Marteyne van Well for their generous support for conservation in the country.

Thanks also to the Thomas Foundation who kindly hosted my lecture tour of Australia. Felicity 'Flic' Wishart, Lissa Schindler Michelle Grady, Imogen Zethoven, Jessica Meuwig and Darren Kindleysides looked after me wonderfully on the tour. All were great role models in science-based campaigning for reef protection, and all apart from Felicity, who died suddenly on the campaign trail, are still fighting against Australia's retrograde policies that promote climate change and undermine ocean health. It has been a bleak half decade for Australian seas.

I was enormously lucky to have met my soulmate Julie as a student; to have continued together ever since in exploration of the natural world and the search for ways to protect it is even greater good fortune. Our daughters Alicia and Sharna love coral reefs too, which is just as well considering how much reefs are talked about in our house.

Despite the problems coral reefs face, seeing them is still a vivid, exciting, intense and sublime experience. Alex Mustard MBE manages to capture their thrill and their rich beauty better than any other photographer I know, so it is a great privilege to showcase his photographs in this book. Thanks, Alex, for your generous help in adding pictures to my words.

Patrick Walsh, my agent at Pew Literary, was very patient while I learned that science and memoir writing are different arts. I greatly appreciate his advice, support, editing skills and indulgence while I learned. John Ash at Pew Literary turned my manuscript into something ready to share with the world. Finally, my thanks to Jonathan Buckley and Mark Ellingham at Profile Books for their excellent editing skills, which turned a still bulgy and misshapen story into the tale you read here; to Susanne Hillen for meticulous proofreading, Bill Johncocks for a fine index, and to Henry Iles for all his work on the photos and text design.

Some names have been changed.

Photo credits

This book owes a major debt to Alex Mustard, whose photos make up the majority of its images. Three of the four colour-plate sections are his (the first are my own personal shots), as are most of the black and white images facing the start of each chapter. Below are details of the images, their locations and photographers' credits.

BLACK AND WHITE CHAPTER IMAGES
CONTENTS: Hawksbill turtle (*Eretmochelys imbricata*) on reef wall, Ras Mohammed, Egypt (Alex Mustard, following 'AM').
CHAPTER ONE: Elphinstone reef, Egypt (AM).
CHAPTER TWO: Blue-spotted stingray (*Taeniura lymma*), St John's Reef, Egypt (AM).
CHAPTER THREE: Red Sea surgeonfish (*Acanthurus sohal*), Ras Mohammed, Egypt (AM).
CHAPTER FOUR: A living Red Sea coral (*Favia*) (Julie Hawkins).
CHAPTER FIVE: Lionfish (*Pterois volitans*), Sha'ab Mahmood, Egypt (AM).
CHAPTER SIX: Reef octopus (*Octopus cyanea*), Similan Islands, Thailand (AM).
CHAPTER SEVEN: *Cephalopholis miniata* grouper and glassfish, Sinai, Egypt (AM).

CHAPTER EIGHT: Blue-cheek butterflyfish (*Chaetodon semilarvatus*), Ras Mohammed, Egypt (AM).

CHAPTER NINE: Male and female *Cephalopholis miniata*, Strait of Tiran, Egypt (AM).

CHAPTER TEN: Giant clam (*Tridacna*), Umm Aruk, Egypt (AM).

CHAPTER ELEVEN: Gulf cormorant in hardened beach oil, Iran (Callum Roberts, FOLLOWING 'CR').

CHAPTER TWELVE: Lemon shark (*Negaprion brevirostris*) with remoras, Bahamas (AM).

CHAPTER THIRTEEN: Wire goby (*Bryaninops yongei*) and whip coral (*Cirripathes anguina*), Sha'ab Mahmood, Egypt (AM).

CHAPTER FOURTEEN: Bohar snappers (*Lutjanus bohar*), Shark Reef, Egypt (AM).

CHAPTER FIFTEEN: Giant moray, *Gymnothorax javanicus*, honeycomb, *G. favagineus*, and undulate, *G. undulatus*, North Malé Atoll, Maldives (AM).

CHAPTER SIXTEEN: Palmyra Atoll, Pacific Ocean (CR).

CHAPTER SEVENTEEN: Longnose filefish (*Oxymonacanthus halli*), Gubal Island, Egypt (AM).

CALLUM ROBERTS PLATE SECTION

PAGE 1: Top left: Yuba Island, Saudi Arabia, 1983 (CR). Bottom left: Callum at the helm of *Hattan*, northern Red Sea, Egypt, 1983 (Andrew Price). Top right: Andrew Price checks a Red Sea Osprey nest, Red Sea, Egypt, 1983 (CR). Centre right: Fossil reef cliffs, Saudi Arabia (CR). Bottom right: Rupert Ormond with a new-born green turtle, Ras Yarbu, Egypt, 1982 (CR).

PAGE 2: Top: Saudi Arabia, 1984 (CR). Centre: Charles Sheppard (left) and Rupert Ormond, southern Saudi Arabia, 1984 (CR). Bottom: Callum and Julie Hawkins, Gulf of Suez, Egypt, 1988 (Unknown photographer).

PAGE 3: Top: Dead staghorn coral (*Acropora cervicornis*) branches, Bonaire, Caribbean (CR). Bottom: *Cyphastrea sp.*, Red Sea, Egypt (Julie Hawkins).

PAGE 4: Top left: Suez Canal University Marine Research Centre, Na'ama Bay, Egypt, 1988 (CR). Bottom left: Callum, Saba, Caribbean, 1993 (Julie Hawkins). Bottom right: Callum, Saudi Arabia, 1984 (Andrew Price).

PAGE 5: Top left: UNESCO experts, Bushehr, Iran, 1993 (CR). Centre left: Oiled beach, Arabian Gulf, 1992 (CR). Bottom left: Callum and Julie, Saba, Caribbean, 1996 (Erkki Siirilä).

PAGE 6: Top: Water Island, St, Thomas harbor, U.S. Virgin Islands. Reproduced from *National Geographic Magazine*, 1956 (Photo Charles Allmon/National Geographic/Getty Images). Bottom left: 'Tub', Abbot Point, Australia, 2013 (CR). Bottom right: The late Felicity 'Flic' Wishart, Abbot Point, Australia, 2013 (CR).

PAGE 7: Top: Julie Hawkins, One Tree Reef, Great Barrier Reef, Australia, 1987 (CR). Centre left: Callum with Susan White, Palmyra Atoll (photographer unknown). Centre right: Palmyra Atoll (CR). Bottom: Coconut crab (*Birgus latro*), Palmyra Atoll (CR).

PAGE 8: Top: Maaga Reef, Faafu Atoll, Maldives, 2016 (CR). Bottom: Maaga Reef, Faafu Atoll, Maldives 2017 (CR).

ALEX MUSTARD PLATE SECTION 1

PAGE 1: Humphead wrasse face detail (*Cheilinus undulatus*), Ras Mohammed, Egypt.

PAGE 2: Top: Maldivian anemonefish (*Amphiprion nigripes*), Baa Atoll. Bottom: Lemon goby (*Gobiodon citrinus*), Gubal Island, Egypt.

PAGE 3: Red Sea reef face at Ras Mohammed, Egypt, with scalefin *Anthias* (*Pseudanthias squamipinnis*).

PAGE 4: Moray eel (*Gymnothorax javanicus*) with cleaner wrasse (*Labroides dimidiatus*), Ras Mohammed, Egypt.

PAGE 5: Elphinstone Reef, Egypt.

PAGE 6: Top: Bohar snappers (*Lutjanus bohar*), Ras Mohammed, Egypt. Bottom: Coral trout (*Plectropomus pessuliferus*) with cleaner fish (*Labroides dimidiatus*), Sinai, Egypt.

PAGE 7: *Paguritta* crab in *Porites* coral, Similan Islands, Thailand.

PAGE 8: Top: Scissortail damselfish (*Abudefduf sexfasciatus*), Sha'ab Mahmood, Egypt. Bottom: Stonefish (*Synanceia verrucosa*), Gubal Island, Egypt.

ALEX MUSTARD PLATE SECTION 2
PAGE 1: Swarthy parrotfish (*Scarus niger*), Baa Atoll, Maldives.
PAGE 2: Tassled scorpionfish (*Scorpaenopsis oxycephala*), South Malé Atoll, Maldives.
PAGE 3: Top: Bandcheek wrasse (*Oxycheilinus digrammus*), Ras Mohammed, Egypt. Bottom: Hawksbill turtle (*Eretmochelys imbricata*) eating soft coral, Ras Mohammed, Egypt.
PAGE 4: Top: Umm Aruk, Egypt. Bottom: *Acropora microclados*, Gubal Island, Egypt.
PAGE 5: Top left: Ghostgoby (*Pleurosicya mossambica*) on the mantle of a giant clam (*Tridacna*), Kuredu, Maldives. Top right: Squat lobster (*Galathea*) on fire coral (*Millipora dichotoma*), Ras Katy, Egypt. Bottom: Batfish (*Platax orbicularis*), Ras Mohammed, Egypt.
PAGES 6–7: Sharm-el-Sheikh, Egypt.
PAGE 8: Raja Ampat, eastern Indonesia.

ALEX MUSTARD PLATE SECTION 3
PAGE 1: Top: Bohar snappers (*Lutjanus bohar*) spawn in Palau, Pacific.
Bottom: Nassau grouper (*Epinephelus striatus*), with *Gobiosoma genie*, Cayman Islands.
PAGE 2: Red Sea reef, Egypt.
PAGE 3: Top: North Ari Atoll, Maldives. Bottom: Giant trevally (*Caranx ignobilis*), Red Sea, Egypt.
PAGE 4: Tiger cardinalfish (*Cheilodipterus macrodon*) protecting eggs, Gubal Island, Red Sea, Egypt.
PAGE 5: Top: Blue-striped snappers (*Lutjanus kasmira*), Vaavu Atoll, Maldives. Bottom: Humphead wrasse (*Cheilinus undulatus*), Egypt.

PAGE 6: Top: Oriental sweetlips (*Plectorhinchus vittatus*) and white-collar butterflyfish (*Chaetodon collare*), North Malé Atoll, Maldives. Bottom: Elkhorn coral (*Acropora palmata*), Cuba.

PAGE 7: Top: Staghorn coral (*Acropora cervicornis*), Cayman Islands. Bottom: Longnose filefish (*Oxymonacanthus longirostris*), Similan Islands, Thailand.

PAGE 8: Top: Yellowtail sweepers (*Pempheris schwenkii*) in cave, Sha'ab Claudia, Egypt. Bottom left: Brain coral (*Platygyra daedalea*), Sha'ab Claudia, Egypt. Bottom right: Red Sea surgeonfish (*Acanthurus sohal*), Egypt.

Index

The suffix n following a page number indicates a footnote; *italic* page numbers refer to illustrations between chapters, while relevant material within the four colour plate sections is identified with 'pl.' then the section number, followed the page within that section. Thus

giant clam (*Tridacna*), **190**, 270, 316, pl.3:5

indicates that, beside two mentions in the text, a relevant illustration appears on the page before Chapter 10 (page 190) and another on page 5 of the second colour plate section.

A

Aal, Abdul 127–8, 132
Abbot Point, Queensland 241–3, 253, 255
Abu Ali island 193–5, 198, 200
Abu Dhabi Investment Company 160–2
Abudefduf (damselfish) 59–60, 176, 197, pl.2:8
aftershave, significance of 91–2, 141
Al Lith, Saudi Arabia 80
Alderney conference, 2014 329–33, 339
Alec (on 1982 Saudi expedition) *see* Dawson-Shepherd
algae, coralline 52, 56, 113, 118, 251, 292–3, 318, pl.1:3, pl.2:7
algal lawns 52–3, 78, 81–2, 94
Alya and Safliyah islands, Qatar 104–6, 111
Andrew (Price, captain of *Hattan*)
  on 1983 Saudi expedition 50, 58–9, 62–3, 66–8, pl.1:1
  on 1984 Saudi expedition 84–5

  at Alderney reunion 329, 339
  book coauthored with 215
  mangrove studies 79, 84
  and the World Conservation Union 191–2
anemonefish (*Amphiprion nigripes*) 11, pl.1:2
angelfish 119, 151, 156, 195, 197
Anthias spp. 79, 82, pl.2:3
Anwar (engineer in Qatar) 101–4
aphrodisiacs 69
Aqaba, Gulf of 65–8, 147, 155–6, 182
Arabian Gulf
  1992 expedition 191
  compared to the Red Sea 98, 107, 195
  as a stressful environment 107, 330
aragonite in reefs 114
Ashraf (student at Sharm) 139–40, 160
Attenborough, Sir David 250, 252–3
Australia
  2013 expedition 241–7, 255–60

changing environmental stance 246, 337
   particular view of reef life 93, 248
Australian Institute of Marine Science 79–80, 246
Australian Marine Conservation Society 241, 243, 245
The Australian newspaper 255–6, 261
Aziz (of the Saudi EPA) 193, 199

B

bacteria *see* microbes
baitfish 54, 327
bannerfish, Red Sea 167–8
Barbados 114, 230, 233–4, 236
barracuda 18, 68, 82, 179, 224
barrier reefs
   formation 37
   Mesoamerican Barrier Reef 226–7, 234
   Wedj bank 37–8, 41
   see also Great Barrier Reef
batfish (*Platax orbicularis*) 226, pl.3:5
Beck, Stuart 286–7
Beebe, William 72–3
Belize 223, 226–7, 234
the bends 225n
Bernard, Sylvia 329
biodiversity *see* species diversity
birds
   oiled 193, 201, **210**, 217–18
   wetland 241–2
   see also individual families, genera and species
Birkeland, Chuck 248
blennies
   Arabian Gulf 99, 105
   coexistence with other species 94, 99
   Midas blennies 78
   Red Sea 53–5, 94
   sabretooth 79

Blue Marine Foundation 301
bombs, unexploded 207
Bonaire, Caribbean 111–12, 114, 231, 233, pl.1:3
boobies 54, 318
books
   Arabia Through the Looking Glass, by Jonathan Raban 145
   The Arcturus Adventure, by William Beebe 72–3
   Peoples of All Nations 19
   The Periplus of the Erythrean Sea 80
   Red Sea Coral Reefs, by Rupert Ormond 30
   The Silent World, by Jacques Cousteau 18
   Sinai and Palestine, by Arthur Penrhyn Stanley 185
   Travels in Arabia, by James Wellsted 59
   The Unnatural History of the Sea, by Callum Roberts 121n, 305
Bradbury, Roger 328–9
brain corals (*Platygyra daedalea*) 22, 208, pl.4:8
Brian (Mackinnon) 99–101, 103, 105, 106
Brown, Matt 310
Bush, President George W 306–8
Bushehr, Iran 212, 216–17, pl.1:5
butterflyfish
   Arabian 197
   blacktail 43
   blue-cheek (*Chaetodon semilarvatus*) 42, **148**, 167
   chevron 167, 205, 326–7
   crown 167
   fish counts and habitats 42–3, 54, 56
   hooded 156
   near Palmyra 313
   painting 141–2
   raccoon 167
   redtail 279

territoriality and coexistence
166–8
vagabond 320
white-collar (*Chaetodon collare*)
pl.4:6
see also bannerfish

C

Cambrian period 322
carbon capture and storage 281
carbon dioxide
atmospheric concentrations 252–
3, 281, 340
and coral symbiosis 22
and ocean acidification 118,
250–1, 335
carbonate levels 117–18, 250–1
cardinalfish 317, pl.4:4
The Caribbean
Barbados 114, 230, 233, 236
Bonaire 111–12, 114, 231, 233,
pl.1:3
coral plague 115, 118
mass bleaching avoided 336
1990s appointment 223
sea urchin losses 75
catamarans, advantages 50
Causey, Billy 237–8
Cephalopholis miniata (grouper) *124,
172*
changes, as unnoticed 271
Charles (Sheppard, coral expert) *see*
Sheppard, Charles
Charlie (Veron) 249–50, 252–3,
330
'Chippr'd' *see* Sheppard, Charles
CITES (Convention on International
Trade in Endangered Species)
170n
cleaner fish 56, pl.4:1
cleaner wrasse (*Labroides dimidiatus*)
79, 224, 271, pl.2:4, pl.2:6
cleanliness, obsessive 88–90
climate change

Australia and 246–7, 253, 257,
337
failure to address 281–2, 338
Intergovernmental Panel on
(IPCC) 267–8, 282n, 288
and other causes of reef decline
335–6
Paris Agreement, 2015 287, 289,
298–9
reefs as indicators 250, 253, 340
stages of denial and acceptance
271–2, 300, 338n
see also global warming
climate refuges 295–6, 299–300
Clinton, President Bill 307–8
clothing
Muslim ladies 137
risks from 321
coal mining and burning 242–3,
253, 260, 281, 337
coastal real estate, desirability 110–
11, 337
coastguards
help with transport 38, 41,
203–6, 208
permission from 24, 30–1, 57
unpleasantness with 90–2
see also military
cockroaches 55, 161
Cocos Island 73
coexistence, peaceful 30, 55, 83, 99,
180, 272
territoriality and 78, 94, 166–7
colours, underwater 28, 56, 106,
150, 226, 316, 332
conservation
marine parks 35
pessimism as self-fulfilling 299–
300, 328, 333–4
US Pacific territories 307
construction work, Qatar 101–4
consultants, defined 220
contamination risk from clothing
321
cooperation *see* mutualism

corals
CITES protection 170n
evolution 22, 330
habitat preferences 86, 122, 155, 207
ocean acidification and 247, 250–1
oil pollution and 191–5, 199–203, 205, 208–9, 219n, 279, 330
structure and growth 21, 25, pl.3:4
temperature preferences 116, 203, 330
underlying symbiosis 22–3, 75, 203
'white plague' 120
corals, ancient see fossil
coral bleaching and mortality
1997-98 warming episode 188
2015-16 warming episode 325–7, pl.1:8
Caribbean experience 75, 114–15, 276, 336
human pathogens and 115
mass bleaching and El Niño 175, 325–7
mechanism 75
possibility of recovery 276, 278, 294–8, 327, 331–2
predictions 252, 289–91
coral ecosystems
diversity 12–13, 30, 51, 120
fragility 14–15, 230, 328
whether worth saving 277
see also reefs
coral forms and colours 9, 21–2, 26, 63–4, 84, 176
Arabian Gulf 197, 199
Pocillopora variability 84
Red Sea pl.3:6–7
coral predators
crown-of-thorns starfish 14, 116, 248–9, 327, pl.1:8
defences 14
pufferfish 93, 224–5

coral species
ancient corals 112–14
brain coral (Platygyra daedalea) 22, 208, pl.4:8
diversity and structure 122
elkhorn corals (Acropora spp) 112–15, 120, 272–3, 275–6, 317, 332, pl.3:4, pl.4:6
fire coral (Millipora dichotoma) 51, 176, pl.3:5
heat tolerance 330–1, 333, 335–6
Pocillopora 84
Porites 251, 272, 292, 294, 317
Red Sea corals (Favia) 76, 333
staghorn corals (Acropora cervicornis) 112–15, 120, 273, 276, 291, 332, pl.1:3, pl.4:7
star corals 112–13, 120, 230, 276
whip coral (Cirripathes anguina) 240
The Coral Triangle 178, 275–7, 333–4, pl.2:7, pl.3:8
coral trout (Plectropomus pessuliferus) pl.2:6
corallimorphs 317–18
cormorants 193, 210, 217, 242, 257
Corniche Road, Jeddah 25–6, 74, 102, 111, 334
Cousteau, Céline 119
Cousteau, Jacques 18, 21, 29, 72, 80, 87, 123, 147
Cousteau, Jean-Michel 307n
crabs
coconut crabs (Birgus latro) 320, pl.1:7
ghost crabs 34, 85
hermit crabs 40, 85, 88, 218
on Palmyra 314, 320
porcelain and guard crabs 13, 327
Similan Islands (Paguritta sp.) pl.2:7
crocodile fish 105
crown-of-thorns starfish 14, 116, 248–9, 327, pl.1:8

Curtis Island, Queensland 257–8, 260

Cyphastrea corallites pl.1:3

D

damselfish
  algal lawns 52–3, 78, 82, 94
  Chromis damselfish 326–7
  coexistence with blennies 94, 99
  fish counts 42–3
  new species 89
  observed and described 11, 17, 46, 89, 144, 151, 199, 229
  Plectroglyphidodon leucozona and *Chrysiptera unimaculata* 53
  scissortail damselfish (*Abudefduf sexfasciatus*) 59–60, 176, 197, pl.2:8
  sulphur damselfish 61
  territoriality 52–3, 55, 94, 166
  white-barred damselfish 61
Darwin, Charles 35, 229, 330–1
Dawson-Shepherd, Alec
  1982 Saudi expedition 24–5, 30, 37, 41, 45
  1984 Saudi expedition 79, 84, 88–9
  Alderney reunion 329
  on consultants 220
  preparing for Yemen 98–9
de Meyer, Kalli 112
De'ath, Glenn 247
deep water circulation 117–18
desalination plants 192, 200
'desert islands' and reality 321
development
  desirability of coastal real estate 110–11, 337
  fishing restriction by-product 181, 334
  need to limit 337
  two views of mud 101–2
diving
  dangerous locations and depths 150–1

dive training 136
  first Red Sea dive 27
  at night 143–6
  solo 71–2, 84
Doha, Qatar
  development plans 101–2
  West Bay Lagoon 101–4, 107, 109, 111
Doherty, Peter 246–7, 251
dolphins 69
dottybacks 155, 205
Downing, Nigel 202–8
Dry Tortugas, Florida 236–8
Dubai 109

E

ear infections and damage 31, 46–7, 56
Earle, Sylvia 118–19, 232, 296, 307n
ecosystems
  ecology informed by history 231
  food webs 304
  richness and diversity of coral 12–13, 30, 51, 120
  theories of assembly 55
Edward, Prince 293, 295, 297–8
eels
  garden eels 183–4
  honeycomb moray (*Gymnothorax favagineus*) **284**
  moray eels (*Gymnothorax javanicus*) 28, **284**, 291, pl.2:4
  observed and described 81–2, 86, 105
  undulate moray (*Gymnothorax undulatus*) **284**
Egypt
  author's employment, 1987-88 125–47
  author's employment, 1988-90 149–71
  as 'broken' 145, 163–4, 186
  bureaucracy in 132, 163–4
  Elphinstone reef *16*, pl.2:5

export restrictions 169–71
as hierarchical 152, 158
Ismailia 128, 132
see also Sharm-el-Sheikh
El Niño
   1982-83 event 75, 115, 298
   1997-98 event 175, 298, 331
   2015-16 event 289–90, 294–8,
      316, 321, 325, 331, 338, pl.1:8
   forecast 289–90
El Niño-Southern Oscillation 175
Elphinstone reef, Egypt *16*, pl.2:5
emperor fish 121, 179, 248
Endangered Species List 120, 153,
   170n
environmental impact assessments
   98
environmentalism *see* conservation
evolution
   alternative to adaptation 330–1
   balance with extinction 180, 251
   and chance controlling reefs 55
   and latitude 177, 276
extinction
   balance with evolution 180, 251
   mass extinctions 22, 180, 250,
      340
   notional value of a species
      339–40
   risk, Coral Triangle 277

F

Faafu Atoll, Maldives 266, 325.
   pl.1:8
   see also Magoodhoo
faeces, eaten by other fish 93
Fahim (Nasri, Dr) 203–6, 208–9
Fanning, Edmund 305–6, 314, 321
Farghaly, Said 152, 170, 188
faxes 211–12
feeding frenzies 73, 81–2
female students, diving 136–7, 188
fertilisers *see* nutrient run-off
filefish 274, *324*, 326–7, pl.4:7

financial crisis, 2008 282
fish (generally)
   distinctiveness of juveniles 195
   'not for kissing' 225
   painting 141–2
   population replenishment 228,
      282
   spawning grounds 234–5, 238,
      pl.4:1
fish counts
   and abundance in no-fishing
      zones 225, 227
   in Arabian Gulf 107, 196, 208
   in Caribbean 224, 229
   as non-lethal 121
   in the Pacific 178–9
   in Red Sea 28, 35, 42–3, 52,
      56–7, 60, 83, 89
   as routine 87, 92, 94
   species lists and 152–3
   by time and by distance 43, 178
'fish expressions' 290
fish farming 280
fish species *see* species
fish storms 304–5. pl.2:6
Fisher's sex-ratio theory 187
fishing
   benefits of no fishing zones 228,
      238
   and coral damage 197, 199
   economic worth compared with
      tourism 337
   longline 312
   shrimp fisheries 220
   and species diversity 120–1
   see also overfishing
Fitzroy River delta 255, 258, 260,
   262, 282
flamingos 87, 99, 103, 105
flashlight fish 146
'Flic' (Felicity Wishart, of AMCS)
   241, 245, 249, 255–6, 260–2,
   pl.1:6
floods, irrational response 269
Florida Keys 236–7

fly nuisance 85, 87
flying fish 58, 292, 337
food webs 304
forests, parallels with reefs 274
Forsskål, Peter 40–1, 59
fossil fuels, predictions 337
fossil reefs / hills / cliffs 50, 112–14, 131, 178, 335, pl.1:1
fox predation of turtles 34, 36
free radicals 335
fusiliers 10, 292, 327

G

Galápagos islands 75, 115–18, 120, 289, 298
Gareth (Williams, Bangor University) 296, 299
garfishes 274
genetic engineering 335
geographic ranges 156, 177, 207–8
Gerlach, Ginny 255, 258–9, 261
Ghobashy, Professor 129, 131, 141–2
Giant clam (*Tridacna*) **190**, 270, 316, 320, pl.3:5
Ginny (Gerlach) 255, 258–9, 261
Gladstone, Queensland 257, 259–62
glassfish 62, *124*, 144–5
Global Ocean Legacy Project 301
global warming 14–15, 250, 267, 335
    see also climate change
goatfish 40, 313
gobies
    ghost goby (*Pleurosicya mossambica*) pl.3:5
    Gobiosoma genie pl.4:1
    lemon goby (*Gobiodon citrinus*) pl.2:2
    observed 44, 179, 270, 292, 321
    wire goby (*Bryaninops yongei*) **240**
Golbuu, Yimnang 289

Golding, William 163–4, 186
Google Earth™ 109, 111, 186, 334
Google Scholar 181
Gore, Mauvis 174, 176, 329, 332, 334
Graham (Lloyd, of *The Australian*) 255–7, 261
Great Barrier Reef, Australia
    2013 expedition 243–51, 254–62
    Curtis Island 257–8, 260
    damage 254, 290, 294–5, 331, 337
    Fight for the Reef campaign 261–2
    findings as possibly atypical 93–4
    Long-Term Sustainability Plan 262
    Magnetic Island 250, 254
    marine park 243, 246–9, 256, 313
    One Tree Island 243, 316, pl.1:7
    as World Heritage site 249, 261–2
Greenland 268
Grey, Zane 73
groupers
    black grouper 226
    coral hind (Cephalopholis miniata) **124, 172, 278**
    goliath grouper 237
    Nassau grouper (*Epinephelus striatus*) 234, pl.4:1
    off Kuwait 205
    peacock groupers 65
    Red Sea 42, 62
    species near Al Lith 82
    species near Gladstone 260
    tiger grouper 226
growth rings, coral 251
grunts 106, 227, 230
guano trade 306–8
Gulf Marine Sanctuary Project 192, 200
Gulf War, first 191, 201
gut bacteria, human 115

H

habitats
    preferences, corals 86, 122, 155, 207
    preferences, fish 60–1
    separation and overlap 54–5
    variations 92
    see also ecosystems
Hafez, Captain Wessam 132–7, 142–3, 158–62, 164–5
halfbeaks 105
Hameed (boatman, Qatar) 104–5
Hass, Hans 29, 72, 128
Hass, Lotte 128
hatchet fish 144
Hattan (yacht) 50, 55, 57–9, 63, 66, 68, 84, pl.1:1
Hawkins, Julie
    academic collaboration and correspondence 71–2
    author's meeting 49
    Caribbean research 111–12, pl.1:5
    on the Great Barrier reef pl.1:7
    research at Sharm 137–9, 143, 165–6
    also mentioned throughout the text
herbivorous fish 231, 272
herons 38, 265
history informing ecology 231
Hol Chan Marine Reserve 226–7
Hughes, Terry 273, 293–5, 297–300
human gut bacteria 115
hurricanes 239n, 273, 291
hydroids 79, 198, 291–2
hypotheses, nature of 156–8

I

Iain (Watt, in Jubail) 192–3, 195–6, 199
Ice Ages 98, 114, 155, 177, 267n, 336

Indonesia 178, 290, 333n, 348, pl.3:8
inflatable boats (Zodiac) 59–61, 63–4, 66
International Union for the Conservation of Nature 74
IPCC (Intergovernmental Panel on Climate Change) 267–8, 282n, 288
Iran
    1993 UNESCO mission 211–21
    Department of the Environment 215, 217
    visa difficulties 212–13
Iran-Iraq war 211, 218
islands, artificial and natural 101, 103–6, 111
Ismailia, Egypt 125, 127–8, 132–3, 162–3

J

jacks
    presence noted 28, 43, 54, 68–9, 119, 224, 227, 303, 316
    speed of predation by 82
    trevally jacks 69, 244, pl.4:3
Jackson, Jeremy 114, 303, 336
Jamaica 231, 273, 332
Jana island, Saudi Arabia 196, 198
Jarvis Island, Pacific 296–7, 308, 316, 322–3
Jaws (movie) 72
Jean (on Iran expedition) 212–13, 215–16, 220
Jeddah, Saudi Arabia
    1982 trip 23, 31, 40–1, 45–6
    1983 trip 49–51, 54–5, 74
    1984 trip 77, 92, 102, 111, 334
    Corniche Road 25–6, 74, 102, 111, 334
    history 77–8
jellyfish 34, 316
jobfish 270–1

Jubail, Saudi Arabia 192, 194, 196, 199
Julie *see* Hawkins
Jurayd island, Saudi Arabia 196–7

K

Karan island, Saudi Arabia 196, 199
Khalifa, Sheikh, Emir of Qatar 101
Khodair, President, Suez Canal
    University 125–7, 132–4, 161–4, 186
Kingman Reef 307–8
Kiribati, Pacific 269, 280, 288
Kuhn, Thomas 158
Kuwait
    expulsion of Palestinians 204
    invasion and its aftermath 191–3, 200–2, 204

L

LaPlace, Joe 233–4
larvae
    as a dispersal mechanism 12, 235–6
    possible oceanic phase 157, 181
    see also plankton
Liittschwager, David 12–13
Lindeboom, Han 336–7
lionfish (*Pterois volitans*) **96**, 187
Lissa (Schindler, of AMCS) 241, 245, 255
litter problem 106–7, 123
Liverpool University
    Julie Hawkins' Masters degree 137
    lectureship vacancy 169, 187
    marine research collaboration 127, 133, 149, 165
lizardfish 317
Lloyd, Graham 255–7, 261
lobsters 233–4, pl.3:5
Loya, Yossi 279–80

M

Mackay, Capt. Donald 314–15
Mackinnon, Brian 99–101, 103, 105, 106
Madrassat el Bea *see* Marine
    Research Centre
Magnetic Island 250, 254
Magoodhoo, Maldives 266, 290–2
the Maldives pl.3:1, pl.3:5, pl.4:3, pl.4:5
    2014 expedition 12, 265–7, 269–70
    2016 expedition 290–
    coral bleaching 175, 297, 325, 332, pl.4:6
    Faafu Atoll 266, 325. pl.1:8
    failed restoration attempts 338
    Noonu Atoll 277–9
    relocation option 280–1
mangroves
    Arabian Gulf 193–4, 207
    Australia 282, 2160
    Red Sea 30, 41, 79, 84, 87, 89–90, 92, 139
mantis shrimps 11
Marine Environmental Management
    course 71
Marine Habitat and Wildlife
    Sanctuary for the Gulf Region
    Project 192, 200
marine life, selective blindness to 185
marine parks and protected areas
    around Sinai 181–2
    benefits to fishermen 227–8, 229, 238
    Caribbean 112, 223–4, 226–8, 232–3, 237
    Galápagos 116, 119
    Great Barrier Reef 243, 246–9, 256, 313
    largest 310n
    need for more 283, 285, 335, 337–8
    need for vigilance 263

Northwest Hawaiian Islands /
    Papahānaumokuākea 308,
    310–11, 313
Pacific Remote Islands Marine
    National Monument 296, 306,
    308–11
proposed at Al Qahma 99
Ras Mohammed 174, 182–3
see also no fishing zones
Marine Research Centre, Suez Canal
    University pl.1:4
    jetty debacle 158–9
    move 162–4, 185–6
    planned, Sharm-el-Sheikh 125,
        127, 129–30, 159–61
Marsh Arabs 191
Martin (on Iran expedition) 212–14,
    215–16
Mary (Stafford-Smith) 250, 255
mass extinctions 22, 180, 250, 340
matriarchy 12
Mauvis (Gore) 174, 176, 329, 332,
    334
Maxwell, Adrienne 213
Mediterranean reefs 332
meteorites 185
methane / methane hydrates 251
Mick (on 1982 Saudi trip) 24–5, 30,
    32–8, 41, 44–6
microbes
    human to coral migration 115
    infection contracted diving 47
    luminescent bacteria 146
    oil digesting 199
    removing free radicals 335
    temperature effects on
        zooxanthellae 203, 335
military checkpoints and
    confrontations 66–7, 183
military presence as benign 219n
mining interests 246, 260–2, 337
mint tea 31, 45, 198
'Mission Blue' voyage 118
moray eels (Gymnothorax spp) 28,
    284, 291, pl.2:4

Mubarak, President Hosni 125, 131,
    142–3, 161–2, 175, 188
mudflats, ecological importance 102
Muller, Thomas 192–3, 195–6, 198
mullet 257, 265
mutualism
    corals and zooxanthellae 22–3,
        75
    in territorial defence 78, 94

N

Na'ama Bay, Saudi Arabia 129–31,
    173, pl.1:4
Nasri, Dr Fahim 203–6, 208–9
National Oceanic and Atmospheric
    Administration, US 118, 289, 313
national parks (on land) 310n
    see also marine parks
'natural capital' 339
nature reserves see marine parks
needlefish 54
New Caledonia 13
new normals / shifting baselines
    271, 327, 332
Niebuhr, Carsten 40, 44
Nigel (Downing, in Kuwait) 202–8
night diving 143–6
nitrogen narcosis 150, 225
no fishing zones
    benefits to fishermen 228, 238
    as by-product of development
        181, 334
    no entry zones and 256
    in various locations 119, 223–4,
        226–7, 237–8, 279, 296, pl.4:5
    see also marine parks
Noonu Atoll, Maldives 277–9
Norse, Elliott 307n
Northwest Hawaiian Islands /
    Papānaumokuākea marine park
    308, 310–11, 313
nutrient recycling 93, 102, pl.4:3
nutrient run-off 248, 255, 272, 280,
    296

O

Obama, President Barack 311
ocean acidification 117–18, 247, 250–2, 281, 299, 328, 330, 335
ocean currents, and fish dispersal 228, 235–6
Ocean Sanctuary Alliance 289
octopus *108*, 312–13
'off-road' vehicles 84
oil pollution and its remediation 191–201, 217–19, 279, pl.1:5
'One Man Show' aftershave brand 91–2, 141
One Tree Island 243, 316, pl.1:7
Ormond, Rupert pl.1:1, pl.1:2
    at Alderney conference, 2014 329, 334
    Arabian expedition, 1982 21, 23–31, 35, 37–45
    Arabian expedition, 1983 49–51, 56–7, 60, 64
    Arabian expedition, 1984 79, 87–90, 92
    book, *Red Sea Coral Reefs* 30
    care of tents and office 88–90, 97–9
    Egyptian expedition, 2012 174, 176
    on Paris agreement 287–9
    on sharks 74
    on starfish 248
    visit to Sir Peter Scott 153–4
ospreys 68, pl.1:1
overfishing
    Caribbean 227n, 230–2
    effect on grazers and corals 273
    exceptions allowing 233
    'Malthusian' overfishing 276–7
    Pacific 296
    potential for recovery 238, 328–9, 334–7
    prehistoric 227n
    starfish plagues and 248
    see also no fishing zones
oxygen free radicals 335

P

Pacific Ocean
    fish counts 178–9
    threats to corals 115, 117–18
    US owned islands 306–10
    see also Jarvis; Kiribati; Palau; Palmyra
Pacific Remote Islands Marine National Monument 296, 306, 308–11
painting butterflyfish 142
Palau, western Pacific 93, 178–80, 285–7, 289, 330, pl.4:1
Palmyra Atoll *302*, 303–9, 311–22, pl.1:7
Pandolfi, John 114
Papahānaumokuākea protected area 308, 310–11, 313
parrotfish
    algal lawns 52–3, 78, 94
    bubble sleeping 144
    intraspecies variation 85
    observed and described 29, 93–4, 106, 118, 179, 279, 291–3, 313
    rainbow 226–7
    and reef recovery 231, 293, 337, 338n
    roundhead 313
    rusty 60
    swarthy parrotfish (*Scarus niger*) pl.3:1
pearl oysters 103, 105
Pearson, Michael and Connie 147, 181
pelicans 87, 221, 242
Percy (on Saba) 224–5
petroleum, origins 202
    see also oil pollution
Pew Charitable Trusts 301
phosphorescence 145–6
photographs confiscated 170–1, 187
Pikitch, Ellen 285–6
pistol shrimps 57, 65

Pitts, Rich 24–5, 31, 45, 50, 57, 77, 79, 84, 89, 99
plankton
    and petroleum's origins 202
    reverie about 34
    see also larvae
plastic litter 68, 107, 319
Pollock, Amanda 315–16, 318
pollution
    chemical 200, 232
    coal 242
    oil 191, 193–9, 201, 217–18, 279, pl.1:5
    plastic and other litter 68, 106–7, 123, 319
    sewage discharges 115, 182, 200, 279–80
    see also run-off
Polynesia, French 74, 99, 151
Polynesian navigators 315
predation, speed of 82
predatory species
    ratio to prey 304
    vulnerability 231
Price, Andrew *see* Andrew
protected areas *see* marine parks; no fishing zones
pufferfish 93, 224–5

Q

Qaru 203–6, 209
Qatar
    development plans 101–2
    development reviewed 109–10
    islands, artificial and natural 101, 103–6, 109, 111
Qatar expedition, 1986 98–107

R

Raban, Jonathan 145
Rabigh, Saudi Arabia 51
Ragster, Laverne 223
Randall, Jack 151, 155

'rapture of the deep' 149–50
rare species 13, 82, 155–6, 227
    see also endangered
Ras Fartak 65–6, 67n, 130
Ras Hatiba 30
Ras Mohammed, Sinai pl.2:1, pl.2:3–4, pl.2:6
    national park 146–7, 174, 182–4
rat infestations 319–20
rays
    devil rays 46
    eagle rays 60
    manta rays 317
    stingrays 37, *48*
Red Sea
    Arabian Gulf compared 98
    author's publications following expeditions 121
    barrier reef 37
    corals of 25–6, 175, pl.3:6–7
    Eilat 279–80
    salinity gradient 155
    Saudi expedition, 1982 17–47
    Saudi expedition, 1983 49–69
    Saudi expedition, 1984 77–95, pl.1:2, pl.1:4
    winds and temperatures 57–9, 155
reefs
    changes in composition 83
    and coastal protection 339
    degradation as reversible 279, 330
    as hazards to vessels 63–4
    nutrient recycling 93
    pessimism as self-fulfilling 299, 328
    population depending on 339
    prehistoric / fossilised 50–1, 112–14, 131, 178, 335, pl.1:1
    prospects for adaptation and acclimation 330–1
    Red Sea reef wall pl.2:3
    requirements for formation 113, 118
    restoration efforts 295, 338

road building over 25
threats to 15, 74–5, 256, 274–6,
328, 340
total area 311
width, as indicative 155
reef faces 61, 179, pl.1:3, pl.4:2
reef hooks 9–10
reef recovery
from bleaching 327
from overfishing 238, 328–9,
334–7
parrotfish and 231, 293, 337,
338n
Reef Studies, International Society
for 288–9
Reefs, Rethink the Future of Coral,
Conference 293
refuge islands 310, 315, 321
Reichelt, Russ 247, 249
Remengesau, President Tommy
285–6
research, as routine 87, 92
Rich *see* Pitts
Richard (University of Liverpool)
149–50
Roberts, Callum pl.1:1, pl.1:2, pl.1:4.
pl.1:5
run-off, nutrients 232, 248–50, 272,
280, 296, 300
run-off, sediments 230, 238–9,
248–50, 254–5, 263
Rupert *see* Ormond

S

Saba, Caribbean 223–6, 308, pl.1:4,
pl.1:5
Saddam Hussein 191, 200, 204,
216, 218
Salem, Mohammed 182
saline incursion 269
Salvat, Bernard 74
satellite navigation 62
satellite telemetry 267–8, 290
Saudi Arabia

1982 expedition 17–47
1983 expedition 49–69
1984 expedition 77–95, pl.1:2,
pl.1:4
attitudes to marine life 74, 122
chemical pollution problems 200
coastal survey work 21
confrontation with the navy 66–7
Meteorology and Environmental
Protection Administration 24,
122
offshore island reefs 61, 195–8,
pl.1:1
see also Jeddah
Save our Seas Foundation 74, 123
sawfish 86
Schindler, Lissa 241, 245, 255
science
non-lethal surveys 121, 168
philosophy of 158
status in Iran 220
scorpionfish 82, pl.3:2
Scotland 18–20
Scott, Sir Peter 153–4, 275
sea fans 146, 165, 179, 292, 316
sea levels
historic 98, 114, 266, 267n
recent and projected 267–70,
272, 281, 292
sea urchins 75, 116, 273
seabirds 20, 115, 306, 319–20
see also boobies; cormorants;
pelicans; terns
seagrass
Caribbean 226
The Gulf 104–5, 192, 218
Red Sea 30, 37, 79, 84, 92, 147,
186–7
seals and sea lions 116–17, 119,
157, 305–6
sea snakes 105–6
seastars 119
seaweed
fertiliser run-off and 248
fleshy, spread of 336–7

overgrowth 232, 272–4, 280
  sargassum 81, 106
sediment / run-off, damaging reefs
  230, 238–9, 248–50, 254–5, 263
sewage discharges 115, 182, 200,
  279–80
sex change, anemonefish 12
sexual dimorphism 168
Sha'ab Claudia, Egypt pl.3:8
Sha'ab Mahmood, Egypt *96, 240,*
  pl.2:8
sharks
  black-tip shark 39, 43, 45, 316
  bull shark 86, 235, 238
  Cocos Island 73
  decline and conservation 72–4,
    147, 226, 238, 256, 312
  great white 73–4
  grey nurse shark 278
  grey reef shark 10, 39–40
  hammerhead 119–20, 147, 238
  lemon shark (*Negaprion
    brevirostris*) *222*
  Pacific Ocean 303–4, 311–13,
    316–17
  risk from and to 27–9, 34, 38–41,
    44, 56–7, 72–3
  tasselled carpet shark 79
  whale sharks 235
  white-tip shark 43
Sharm-el-Sheikh pl.3:4, pl.3:6–7
  1987-88 project 132–3, 137, 139,
    141, 147, 162–3, 165
  2012 revisit 173–4, 181–2, 185,
    188
  development 160–2, 173–4
  history and appearance 126–7,
    129, 151–2, 173–4
  jetty debacle 158–60
  species diversity 154–6, 176–7
  see also Marine Research Centre
Sheppard, Anne 128–9, 131, 529
Sheppard, Charles
  at Alderney Conference, 2014
    329–30

at 2009 Royal Society meeting
    252
  book co-authored with 215
  in Egypt, 1987-88 125–9, 131–3
  in Egypt, 1988-90 169
  in Saudi Arabia 1984 79, 83–4,
    88–92, pl.1:2
shifting baselines / new normals
  271, 327, 332
Shu'aiba, Saudi Arabia 45, 82
Similan Islands, Thailand pl.2:7,
  pl.4:7
Sinai *124*, pl.2:6
  archaeology 184–5
  Israeli occupation 126, 146–7
  national parks 146–7, 174, 181–4
  Ras Fartak 65–6, 67n, 130
  Ras Mohammed, Sinai pl.2:1,
    pl.2:3–4, pl.2:6
  tourism 147, 175
  see also Sharm-el-Sheikh
Sinai and Palestine, by Arthur
  Penrhyn Stanley 185
slavery 80, 110, 231
sleeping fish 143–4
snails 320
snappers
  blue-striped (*Lutjanus kasmira*))
    279, pl.4:5
  Bohar snappers (*Lutjanus bohar*)
    264, pl.2:6, pl.4:1
  gold-lined 279
  observed and described 82, 105,
    121, 197, 227, 233, 292
  red snappers 278
Soares, Gaulther 212–15
sooty falcons 61
Soufriere Bay, St Lucia 228, 238
sounds, underwater 57, 138n
South East Asia see Coral Triangle
Spanish Dancer flatworm 144
species diversity
  and ecological stability 23, 93–4,
    272, 276
  and fishing 120–1

in Kuwait 208–9
and latitude 177, 276
mapping 12–13, 275
in Palau 179
and reef structural complexity
122
of reefs as unrivalled 12–13, 23,
30
variations 107, 120, 179–80
species diversity riddle 77, 86, 120,
152, 178, 275–6, 332
species (of fish)
competition and coexistence 30,
54–5, 78, 83, 93, 99, 180
distribution patterns 35, 82,
154–7, 177
endangered, list 120, 153, 170n
juvenile fish 195
lists of 152–3
notional value 339–40
preferred by fishermen 231
rare species 13, 82, 155–6, 227
territoriality 78, 94, 166–7
see also coral species
Species Survival Commission 153
specimens confiscated 170–1, 187
spiders 55, 319
spoonbills 87, 99
spotted drum 195–6
squat lobster (Galathea) pl.3:5
St Catherine's Monastery 182
St James' Palace meeting 293–300,
334, 338
St Thomas, US Virgin Islands 211,
223, 228–35, pl.1:6
Stafford-Smith, Mary 250, 255
Stanley, Arthur Penrhyn 185
starfish, crown-of-thorns 14, 116,
248–9, 327, pl.1:8
stingrays 37, 48
stone tools 184–5
stonefish (Synanceia verrucosa) 64,
pl.2:8
Suez, Gulf of 129, 156, 182

Suez Canal University 125–7, 133,
161, 163, 169, 185, 188
see also Marine Research Centre
surgeonfish
algal lawns 52–3, 78–9, 82, 94
Arabian Gulf 197
Galapagos 119
Palmyra 317
Red Sea (Acanthurus sohal) 17,
29, 45, 52–3, 55, 70, 151, 231,
317, pl.3:8
territoriality 166
Susan (White, in Saba and Palmyra)
224, 308–11, 313, 315, 318,
320–2, pl.1:7
Sustainable Development Goals, UN
285, 287
sweating underwater 86
sweepers, Yellowtail (Pempheris
schwenkii) pl.4:8
sweetlips 197, 205, 278, pl.4:6
Sylvia (Bernard) 329
symbiosis in corals 22–3, 75
see also mutualism

T

taphonomy 114
Tazieff, Haroun 80, 123
Tektite Program 232–3
temperature
effect of oceans 267
effects on stressed reefs 203, 255,
338
and fragility of coral ecosystems
14–15, 75, 117, 175, 330, 333,
336
preferences of corals 116, 155,
331
terns 59, 106, 197, 206–7
territoriality 46, 52–3, 56–7, 99,
166–8
mutualistic defence 78, 94
Terry (Hughes, reef scientist) 273,
293–5, 297–300

Thomas Foundation (David and Barbara Thomas) 243–4
Thomas (Muller, in Jubail) 192–3, 195–6, 198
tides, Red Sea 51
Tim (undergraduate on 1983 expedition) 50–2, 55–7, 59, 62–3, 66
Tiran Island 66–8, 130, 156
Tony (contractor's representative) 100–4
tourism
    damage to reefs 137, 165–6, 174–5
    levy and national parks 182
    planned developments for 147, 161
trevally jacks 244
    giant trevallies (*Caranx ignobilis*) 69, pl.4:3
Trevor (undergraduate on 1983 expedition) 57, 60, 62, 67, 77, 84, 88, 94
triggerfish 28, 53, 248, 291, 312
Trump, President Donald 282, 308n
Tub (host at Abbot Point) 241–2, pl.1:6
tuna / tunny 10, 68, 266, 312, 337
Turbo shells 312
turtles
    and Dry Tortugas 237
    fox predation 34, 36
    green turtles 32, 244
    hawksbill turtle (*Eretmochelys imbricata*) 6, 106, 313, pl.3:3
    Maldives 279
    mating 36
    Mick's enthusiasm for 25, 35–6, 38
    nest building and egg laying 32–4, 35–6
    at Palmyra 322

U

UK government 298n
UK overseas territories 301
Umm al Maradem 206–7
UN Sustainable Development Goals 285, 287
UNESCO
    1993 Iran mission 211–13, 215–16, 221
    jokes about 216
    World Heritage sites 249, 258, 261–2
unicornfish 56, 271
US Pacific territories 306–10
US Virgin Islands 221, 223
Uwainidhiya Reef, Saudi Arabia 59

V

Veron, Charlie 249–50, 252–3, 330
Virgin Islands, University of 211, 221, 223
visa requirements 99, 212–14, 309
volcanoes, extinct 80, 87, 99, 223, 225

W

Wallace, Alfred 35
wars *see* Gulf; Iran-Iraq
Watt, Iain 192–3, 195–6, 199
Al Wedj 37–8, 55, 57
Weiss, Ken 269
Wellsted, James 59, 63–4, 69
Wessam (Hafez, Captain) 132–7, 142–3, 158–62, 164–5
West Bay Lagoon, Doha 101–4, 107, 109, 111
wetlands 153, 242–3, 259, 261, 282
wetsuits 27
whisky, salvaged 204–9
White, Alan 323
White, Susan 224, 308–11, 313, 315, 318, 320–2, pl.1:7

Williams, Gareth 296, 299
Wishart, Felicity 'Flic' 241, 245, 249,
   255–6, 260–2, pl.1:6
women, and Middle Eastern science
   136–7, 188
World Conservation Union 191, 313
World Heritage sites 249, 258,
   261–2
World Resources Institute 274n,
   276
World Wildlife Fund 116, 153
wrasse
   bandcheek (Oxycheilinus
      digrammus) pl.3:3
   chequerboard 292
   cleaner (Labroides dimidiatus) 79,
      271, pl.2:4, pl.2:6
   creole wrasse 224
   humphead (Cheilinus undulatus)
      29, 278, pl.2:1, pl.4:5
   noted or described 65, 81–2, 93,
      199
   Pseudocheilinus 291
wrecks and wreck dives 187, 318

X

Xavier (on Iran expedition) 213–15

Y

yacht Hattan 50, 55, 57–9, 63, 66,
   68, 84, pl.1:1
Yanbu Al Bahr 31–2, 83
Yemen 21, 40, 77, 88, 92, 99
York, University of 20, 49, 71–5,
   109, 154, 300
Yuba Island 61. pl.1:1

Z

Zodiac (inflatable boat) 59–61,
   63–4, 66
Zomoruddian, Professor 215–16
zones, no fishing 119, 181, 223–4,
   226–8, 237, 279, 296, 334. pl.4:5
zones, within reefs
   selective damage 112
   and species abundance 30
zooxanthellae 22, 75, 86, 116, 317–
   18, 331, 335, pl.4:2